Song of the Forest

D1552832

Pitt Series in Russian and East European Studies

Jonathan Harris, Editor

SONG of the FOREST

Russian Forestry and Stalinist Environmentalism, 1905–1953

Stephen Brain

UNIVERSITY OF PITTSBURGH PRESS

SD
629
.B73
2011

For Marchelle

Published by the University of Pittsburgh Press, Pittsburgh, Pa., 15260

Copyright © 2011, University of Pittsburgh Press

All rights reserved

Manufactured in the United States of America

Printed on acid-free paper

10 9 8 7 6 5 4 3 2 1

Library of Congress Cataloging-in-Publication Data

Brain, Stephen.

Song of the forest : Russian forestry and Stalinist environmentalism, 1905-1953 / Stephen Brain.

p.　　cm. — (Pitt series in Russian and East European studies)

Includes bibliographical references and index.

ISBN 978-0-8229-6165-9 (pbk. : alk. paper)

1. Forest policy—Soviet Union. 2. Forest management—Russia. 3. Forests and forestry—Soviet Union—Philosophy. 4. Forests and forestry—Russia—Philosophy. I. Title.

SD629.B73 2011

634.90947—dc23　　　　　　　　　　　　　　　　2011034166

CONTENTS

University Libraries
Carnegie Mellon University
Pittsburgh, PA 15213-3890

ACKNOWLEDGMENTS

I would like to convey my sincerest gratitude to all the people and institutions that helped me complete this book. First, I would like to thank the University of California-Berkeley Graduate Studies Office, the Doris Quinn Foundation, the U.S. Department of Education, and the University of Arizona for providing the funds without which this project could scarcely have been contemplated.

Second, I would like to thank the many archivists and librarians in Moscow who assisted me in finding the materials that inform this study. There were numerous times when the experts at the Russian State Agricultural Library, the Russian State Library, the Russian State Economic Archive, the Russian State Archive of Social-Political History, and the State Archive of the Russian Federation might have lost patience with my endless lists of requests, yet I can say that I was never denied access to any document I requested in almost two years of primary research. I would like to extend my special thanks to the personnel of the *lichnyi fond* of the State Archive of the Russian Federation, who made available a select few crucial files that I might have missed, but that clarified the internal dynamics of Soviet environmental policy in the postwar period.

Third, I cannot express the depth of my gratitude to my two primary advisors, Yuri Slezkine and Douglas Weiner. Both were, and continue to be, incredibly generous with their time, regardless of tremendously busy schedules. Yuri at every turn urged me to think of a book-length project as though it were a work of art, broadening my perspective at a time when I might otherwise have focused on merely connecting the dots. Whether this study will move its readers I cannot know, but I can say that Yuri's prompting to engage history emotionally as well as intellectually greatly deepened my own personal relationship with the past and with the individuals and events described here. Doug's role in my development as a scholar has been still more profound—when he first agreed to meet with me and discuss the possibility of graduate study under his direction, I did not yet know that such a field as environmental history existed. Nonetheless, he never stinted on encouraging words, never lacked for time to discuss even the most abstruse episodes in the history of Soviet science or environmental studies, and never gave any hint that he expected less than a successful end product. Every junior scholar should be so lucky as to have advisors such as mine.

Finally, I would like to thank my wife, Marchelle, for her steadfast and invariable support through all the ups and downs of the process that has, after so many years, produced this book. Words cannot suffice.

INTRODUCTION

The Song of the Forests, Dmitrii Shostakovich's seventh choral piece and his first oratorio, debuted in Leningrad on 15 November 1949. The Moscow debut, eleven days later, so delighted the Party's cultural arbiters that they awarded Shostakovich the Stalin Prize the next year. The oratorio's success was scarcely accidental, as the project had been designed specifically for propaganda purposes. The score, soaringly harmonious and studiously accessible, used folk themes to evoke patriotic fervor, while the libretto unself-consciously celebrated Stalin's brilliance:

> In the Kremlin, the first rays of dawn shone.
> The Great Leader, in wise contemplation, went up to a great map.
> About the glorious deeds, about the invincible homeland, about the people's
>   happiness, our beloved Leader thought.
> And with his strong hand, which had led regiments to victory, he took the
>   pennants from the map.[1]

In accordance with Stalin's conviction that the country must be reforested in order to save it, the oratorio called upon listeners to "dress the homeland in forests," thereby creating a new national guard of maples, beeches, and oaks.[2]

The obviously calculated nature of *The Song of the Forests* brought Shostakovich personal anguish—he is said to have returned home and collapsed in sobs after the first performance, having compromised himself with such blatant and unseemly propaganda—but it raises a curious question: why would eulogizing the forest represent an effective means of currying the favor of

Joseph Stalin? The most direct answer points to the Great Stalin Plan for the Transformation of Nature, a vast effort to establish millions of acres of forests in southern Russia, which had been announced the year before. Yet this explanation leads to another question: why did Stalin's government, so often described as hostile to environmentalism and wild nature, see afforestation as a worthy aim and trees as possessing the power to cure Soviet ills? A complete answer to this question reaches back to the first decade of the twentieth century, long before the Soviet era, when there emerged alternative environmental ethics linking Russian identity, forest health, and sustainable economic development. These ethics gained great popularity before Bolshevik policies, and especially the policy of rapid industrialization, made such ideas irrelevant. However, forest conservation soon reemerged as an item of active concern in Stalin's Soviet Union, precisely because proponents of conservation were able to convince the Party leadership that a healthy Russian landscape, one that would sustain intensive economic development, required the preservation of forest cover. Forest conservation returned to prominence, and the Soviet Union in the 1940s went about protecting from exploitation more forested land than any other country in history.

Accordingly, it is accurate to say that the Soviet Union developed a real and effective environmentalist program, although an unusual one. In the United States and in Europe, environmental protection evolved in the nineteenth century to promote either conservationism (the belief that natural resources are scarce and special steps need to be taken to make them last in perpetuity) or preservationism (the belief that untouched nature possesses an inherent value and thus should be set aside for human enjoyment). But environmentalism reaches beyond preservationism and conservationism; if environmentalism is defined as the political and philosophical program that seeks to impose limits on human activity so as to preserve the integrity of the environment—a definition that encompasses public health initiatives as well as conservationism and preservationism—then the Soviet Union did indeed pursue environmentalism. In the story told here, Stalin emerges as a peculiar kind of environmentalist: although not apparently driven by conservationist or preservationist concerns, his policies withdrew millions of hectares from economic exploitation on the grounds that this would improve the hydrology of the Soviet Union. These millions of hectares were left more or less untouched, in keeping with the supposition that complex, wild forests best regulated water flows, and thus one may conclude that Stalin's policies were steadfastly environmentalist—and because of the way they were carried out, preservationist as well.

Such an assertion, clearly, represents a significant revision to the existing consensus about Soviet environmental politics, which holds that Stalin's government was implacably hostile to environmentalist initiatives. This consensus emerged for good reason: by the late 1980s, scholars of Soviet environmental history had documented a number of grave environmental problems in Russia, many of which had roots, or appeared to have roots, in the Stalin era. Soviet promethean proclamations from the 1930s, typified by Gorky's famous dictum "Man, in changing nature, changes himself" and Ivan Michurin's motto "We cannot wait for kindnesses from nature; our task is to wrest them from her," strongly influenced this view, along with accounts of the mammoth engineering projects of the first Five-Year Plan.[3] The failure to adopt meaningful emissions controls like those enacted in the West in the 1960s further reinforced the impression of Stalinist enmity toward nature. Marshall Goldman, in 1972, first drew attention to the severely polluted Soviet landscape and assigned considerable blame to Stalin's rule: "For more than three decades after Lenin's death in 1924, slight attention was paid to preserving the country's natural resources. There was little enforcement of existing laws and almost no enactment of new laws. . . . Ecological interests were not important to the Soviet leaders of the day."[4] Charles Ziegler sounded a similar note, underscoring "Stalin's attempt to forcibly and rapidly industrialize the Soviet Union without regard for the environmental consequences" and concluding that during Stalin's tenure, "the value of the natural environment was totally ignored in the campaign to transform the USSR into a modern industrial society."[5]

The consensus received its last major refinement with the publication of Douglas Weiner's two tremendously influential books about Soviet environmental history, 1988's *Models of Nature* and 1999's *A Little Corner of Freedom*. In these two works, Weiner traced the origins and development of a unique network of nature preserves dedicated to scientific research, the *zapovedniki*. Weiner's discussion of the *zapovedniki* shows how remarkable the preserves were for their strict inviolability, and how they enjoyed firm governmental support in the period before Stalin's ascent to power. However, after Stalin's consolidation of power, the preserves were eviscerated.[6] Weiner's analysis of the *zapovedniki* revised the consensus about Soviet attitudes toward nature by demonstrating the potential for environmental protection inherent in the Soviet system, as well as the concern for nature expressed by a number of isolated members of the Soviet apparatus and by activist groups in society. At the same time, Weiner reinforced the consensus by suggesting that Stalinist development and environmentalism, as represented by the *zapovedniki,* were fundamentally incompatible. Murray Feshbach summarized the refined consensus well: "Initially, the ambitions of the Soviet government seemed truly human. In public health and nature conservation, for instance, the revolutionaries' programs included pioneering efforts—and for a time, notable progress—in controlling disease, ensuring public hygiene and protecting forests and parks. Within a dozen years of their seizing of power, however, Soviet Communists had changed their priorities."[7] According to this interpretation, environmentalism in the Soviet Union fell victim to Stalin's Great Turn, yet another promising avenue of NEP (New Economic Policy) culture barricaded off by a regime too illiberal to value conservationism.

Although the shortcomings of Soviet environmental policy were real and important, each with lasting consequences for the Soviet Union's successor states, they have been extrapolated into a sweeping conclusion that conservationist or preservationist awareness in the Stalin era was entirely lacking. Ronald Suny's discussion of the first Five-Year Plan provides a representative expression of this interpretation: "The rush to modernity . . . meant that attention was paid almost exclusively to output and productivity and almost no notice was taken of the impact of rapid industrialization on the natural environment. This insensitivity to the limits of nature was characteristic of capitalist industrialization as well, but in the Soviet Union general ecological ignorance was compounded by the bravado of the Communists, who looked upon nature simply as an obstacle to be overcome on the road to progress."[8] So dominant is this interpretation that countervailing evidence has been unable to shake it: William Husband's recent survey of Soviet children's literature from the Stalin era, for instance, revealed a multiplicity of encoded attitudes toward nature, with a "small but significant number" of books depicting nature in a nonadversarial way.[9] Yet for Husband, such sympathetic portrayals of nature did not suggest that official Soviet policy makers intended to recognize alternative meanings of nature, but instead indicated only the limitations of the Soviet apparatus: "Stalinist-era literature," he writes, "eluded the hegemony the dictatorship sought, and in so doing it demonstrated an important limit to political control in the USSR."[10] Although the English scholar Jonathan Oldfield recently pointed out the need for scholars to "move purposefully beyond broad understandings of the Soviet environmental legacy," the consensus remains basically unchallenged.[11]

The story told here suggests that one key to this broader understanding is the recognition that environmentalism—and forest conservationism especially—can produce benefits that redound to the collective just as much as to the individual. Preserving the integrity of the environment has often been linked with quality of life and liberal individualism, but it can also be linked, as Douglas Weiner demonstrates, with other values; in Stalin's Soviet Union, environmentalism received sanction because its advocates promised that industrial output would suffer without adequate environmental protection.[12] The perceived industrial importance of forested land, therefore, played a key role in reviving forest conservation as an active element of Soviet policy—though had it not been for the deep cultural connection between Russia and its forests, the arguments for protection might never have been articulated, let alone transformed into Soviet law.

Russia is unimaginable without its forests. The birthplace of the Russian state was not on the steppe, which Russians colonized only in the seventeenth century, but in the dark and dense forests around Moscow, Vladimir, and Novgorod. "The virgin forest was the nursery of Great Russian culture," James Billington claimed in *The Icon and the Axe*, "and in the early formative period, the forest represented a kind of evergreen curtain for the imagination, shielding it from the increasingly remote worlds of Byzantine and Western urbanity."[13] Leonid Leonov's 1955 novel *The Russian Forest* pointed to a more personal aspect of the connection: "The forest greeted the Russian at his birth and attended him through all the stages of his life—with the cradle of the infant and the first booting . . . the steam-bath switch and the balalaika, the splinter that did service for a lamp in the peasant's hut . . . the wild honey and the beaver, the mushroom and the incense . . . the coffin hollowed out of a log and lastly, the wooden cross on the grave, decorated with fir branches."[14] The most famous Russian historian of the late nineteenth century, V. O. Kliuchevskii, contended that the forest (not unlike the frontier for the American historian Frederick Jackson Turner) shaped the very way that Russians think: "Nature asked of the forest settler a difficult riddle: he had to study his place, all of its conditions, in order to find suitable land. This explains the great powers of observation in the Russian. Life in isolated villages did not teach him to work in large groups; he fought with nature by himself, in the depths of the forest, with an ax in his hand. This is why the Great Russian works better alone, and why it is dangerous to hem him in, why he is eternally unsociable, introspective and lost in his own mind."[15] The forest entered the lexicon, as well; the Russian language contains a number of folk-inspired words for specific types of forests, such as *bor,* a pine forest on poor or sandy soil; *ramen',* a mixture of spruce and fir, sometimes with pine and deciduous species; and *dubrava,* an oak forest with an admixture of other wide-leafed deciduous species on rich soil.[16] Equally emblematic were Russian proverbs featuring forest imagery, such as "When you cut down the forest, the chips will fly," "Everything that grows in the forest has a use," "The world sighs when the forest withers away," and "Where our grandfathers stacked logs, now you can't cut a stake."[17] And the observation of pre-Christian religious rites centered on the forest survived well into the nineteenth and even the twentieth century; in the springtime in southern Russia, rural people celebrated "Rusal'naia Weeks," fertility rituals focused on the veneration of one special birch in the forest, which was decorated with "bits of cloth, thread, and garlands."[18]

The proverbs, Kliuchevskii's musings about the Russian soul, Leonov's coffin draped with fir boughs—all of these demonstrate the fundamental importance of the forest in Russian culture. But more specifically, they link the forest to old Russia, either a beautiful and noble Russia to be preserved or an embarrassingly backward and weak Russia best abandoned, depending on one's point of view. Over the course of the nineteenth century, many of the most famous voices in Russian cultural life adopted the former view and fretted about the disappearing forest as though mourning the loss of Russia's premodern authenticity. Anton Chekhov's Dr. Astrov voiced the premonition that something valuable was being lost, slowly but inexorably:

Now, look here. This is a map of our district, as it was fifty years ago. The dark and light green areas indicate forests—over half the area is covered with them. . . . On this lake, here, you see great flocks of swans, geese, ducks, and, according to the old timers, birds of every kind. Enormous numbers of them, hovering like great clouds. . . . Now moving on. This is the region as it was twenty-five years ago. You can see the forests only cover one-third of the total area. The wild goats have disappeared, although the elk remain. The green and blue areas are much lighter. And so on, and so forth. Let's move on to the third map, our district as it appears today. You see the green areas here and there, but not dense sections, mere blotches. The elk are gone, as are the swans as well as the wood grouse. . . . In general, the map shows that gradually, yet undoubtedly, the whole region moves into decline which will be irreversible within ten to fifteen years. . . . [They've] destroyed almost everything and created nothing to take its place.[19]

Dr. Astrov's apprehensions had a firm basis in fact: in the years between 1696 and 1888, the forest cover of central Russia fell from 56 percent to 36 percent, and would decline further still to 30 percent by 1914.[20] At risk was more than just greenery and wildlife. When the forests died, Astrov (and, one suspects, Chekhov) worried, something in the Russian people died, too—their empathy, perhaps even their humanity:

Didn't that doctor just say, just now, that people recklessly cut down forests, and soon there won't be anything left on earth? Well, men like you recklessly destroy people the same way, and pretty soon, thanks to you, there won't be any faithfulness left on earth, or purity, or self-sacrifice. Why do men refuse to see a woman's indifference, especially when she belongs to another man? Because—and that doctor was right about this—the devil of destruction lives in every one of you. You don't have any sympathy for the forests, or for birds, or for women, or for one another.[21]

Astrov had urged some of the other characters in the play to recognize that forests "enhance the beauty of the land, that man learns what's beautiful from them, that they . . . instill in him higher thoughts and feelings"—what would become of the Russian people if the forests were to vanish?[22]

By the time that Chekhov wrote *Uncle Vanya*, the idea that Russia's forests were under threat was scarcely a new one. Literary expressions of angst about the fading forest had circulated for nearly a half century.[23] In 1858, Nikolai Nekrasov had eulogized the dying forest in his poem "Sasha," best known for the couplet "Sasha had come to know sorrow well / Sasha had wept as the forest was felled." According to Jane Costlow, "Sasha" is notable for "the violence of imagery used by Nekrasov to describe the felling [of trees]," its deployment of rhymes such as *pechali/vyrubali* (sorrow/felled) and *zhalko do slez/kudria-vykh berez* (pity-filled tears/curly-haired birches), which together with the plot of the poem creates a "powerful orchestration of sympathy for the forest and its creatures . . . [as a place] of 'intrinsic worth' as habitat and place of serene beauty."[24] Costlow contends that when Nekrasov lamented the destruction of trees, he was simultaneously condemning the devastating practices of the Russian ruling class toward its subjects and that in doing so he was drawing upon a history of analogizing men and trees in Russian letters.[25] Leo Tolstoy, too, who took interest in the forests on his ancestral estate and understood something of forest management, used forests to symbolize concepts much greater than mere standing timber. "Tolstoy's defense of the forest" in *Anna Karenina*, Costlow asserts, "is grounded not in economics or legislation, but in religious ethics and spiritual transformation"; the hero of the novel, Levin, originally intends to cut down his forests to pay off loans, but later has a change of heart.[26] Although irrational from a strictly calculating point of view, Levin's choice "not to cut down the linden is an act of faith . . . faith in the possibility of continuity," and later in the novel Levin "seeks refuge in woods and groves," running "to the forest, ly[ing] down under the aspens and [beginning] to think almost in a rapture."[27] For Tolstoy, the forest is a place of communion with larger forces—historical, social, spiritual—and to cut it down thoughtlessly is to destroy a link to the transcendent and to the past.

There was a similar recognition of the forest's deeply metaphorical value among nineteenth-century Russian landscape painters. The emphasis among painters, Christopher Ely argues, was on issues of national identity more than spirituality, but nonetheless represented a growing appreciation of the symbolic importance of the Russian forest; new approaches developed by painters such as Ilya Repin, Aleksei Savrasov, Fedor Vasil'ev, and Ivan Shishkin "constituted a founding myth of Russian national identity."[28] Over the course of the nineteenth century, Russian landscape painters moved away from mimicking aesthetic forms established by Western European artists and learned to appreciate their native landscape—a landscape offering vistas perhaps less dramatic or varied than the European ideal, but beautiful in its own humble way. The dark, homely, disordered forests, so unlike the rocky promontories, rushing seascapes, and picturesque Roman ruins that apotheosized Romantic standards of beauty, became valued specifically for their unassuming charm. Perhaps the most beloved depictions of this aesthetic were painted by Shishkin, whose paintings seemed defiantly commonplace, "as if he might have simply turned ninety degrees to the right and paint[ed] whatever he saw before him."[29] Shishkin's paintings depict an unorthodox beauty nearly omnipresent in the Russian forest; his forests "sprawl in every direction. Trees spill outside the frames of the paintings and overlap each other into the interior until it becomes impossible to differentiate one from another. . . . Dead branches, fallen trees, and decaying vegetation occupy a prominent position in almost all of these landscapes."[30] His canvases, as a contemporary critic had it, were "deeply national [*narodnyi*], healthy, serious, and severe, like northern nature itself. . . . No, he's like a true son of the wilds of the northern forest, in love with its impenetrable, severe wilderness, with its pines and firs, stretching to the sky, with the mute, untamed hinterlands of the gigantic trees. . . . He's in love with the distinctive character of each tree, each bush, and each blade of grass, and like a loving song he values each wrinkle on his mother's face."[31] Shishkin's paintings, Ely claims, are notable for conveying their nationalistic content without employing the more typical symbols of the Imperial court or the Orthodox church. His paintings "offered his audiences of city-dwellers a chance to take in appreciation of the rural values and spirit of the nation. . . . By creating numerous realistic scenes of simple Russian forests and fields that stood as symbols of Russian nationality, Shishkin invited urban Russians to imagine a profound connection between themselves and their natural surroundings."[32] Shishkin himself felt the nationalistic content of his paintings lay in the shared childhood experience of all Russians, of rambling in the dark and tangled woods—perhaps intimidating to the uninitiated, but as comforting as home for those properly acculturated.[33]

Russian scientists also sensed what Russian writers and painters were feeling. In the first decades of the twentieth century, forest specialists devised theories inspired by the idea that the forest embodied Old Russia, and in the Soviet period, these concepts did not vanish, but instead survived, evolved, and in some ways thrived. The most important figure in this drama was Georgii Fedorovich Morozov, a professional forester and professor at the St. Petersburg Forest Institute who at the turn of the century grew alarmed that the Russian forest was in danger and set out to understand why. Morozov explicitly tied the forest's plight to management practices adopted uncritically from abroad and ill-suited to the Russian setting: "Our slowly advancing science of forestry arose in Western Europe, having begun with the Germans. But our forestry, without discarding the importance of the general, the idea of the West, will make an attempt to allow for the unique properties of *our* forests and *our* country."[34] Morozov critiqued German forest practices for their tendency to abstract the forest and minimize the influence of local variation. He claimed his task was to "show that forest biology has ignored the role of the particular and has not identified different 'taxonomic' or systematic communities, whose biology we must understand first of all."[35] Morozov's goal, however, was not just to understand the forest, but to prevent it from changing. Morozov, from his position as the editor of the country's most influential forest publication (*Lesnoi zhurnal* [The Forest Journal]), urged the state to adopt forest practices that would maintain the various kinds of forest—"stand types," in his terminology—as they were. He wanted to identify the various stand types of Russia and devise specific management plans so that each forest could be harvested without hindering its regeneration. As Anna Bramwell notes, there appeared in many countries ecological movements motivated by "a sense of loss of the past, associated with, but not limited to, the passing of the old, rural world"—but Morozov's forest management differed from other movements by attempting to blend preservationism with economic exploitation and striving to maintain landscapes as they were, even if that meant that a given plot of land looked more like a Shishkin painting than a regularized, German forest.[36]

Morozov's influence was amazingly persistent. His ideas remained a feature of the political landscape, from their formulation at the beginning of the twentieth century until the conclusion of the debates about the Great Stalin Plan for the Transformation of Nature, which was shuttered after Stalin's death in March 1953, and far beyond. From the earliest days of its articulation, Morozov's theory of stand types drew stubborn opposition from advocates of maximized output, who objected to the constraints that management guided by stand types would have placed on unchecked exploitation. The enormous appeal of Morozov's system for professional practitioners, however, and its emotional and nationalist resonance, ensured its continued popularity both before and after the Bolshevik revolution of 1917. Morozov's stand types reappeared in the 1926 forest organization instructions (the document indicating how foresters should delineate and harvest timberlands) and, after a period of retrenchment during the Great Turn of 1929–31, reemerged as a central plank in the programs of Stalin's forest-protection agencies. Morozov's ideas did not fit seamlessly into Stalin's environmental initiatives; "Stalin's environmentalism," I will argue, although a real phenomenon, focused more on hydrological function than on the moral value of the forest. But when Stalin chose to set aside huge tracts of Russia's best forestland in order to safeguard its hydrological properties, largely in response to the entreaties of Morozov's surviving students, and required that the protected forests remain essentially unchanged over time, Morozov's teachings essentially became official state policy. Morozov's influence reached its zenith during the Great Stalin Plan for the Transformation of Nature, when a basically conservative project designed to restore the Russian landscape to its prehistoric ideal was twisted into a promethean endeavor dominated by Trofim Denisovich Lysenko. By the time that Morozov's supporters succeeded in wresting control away from Lysenko, Stalin's death ended state support for the venture.

A contemporaneous environmental ethic, which increased the role of the Russian peasant in state forest management, intersected with the Morozov narrative during the Great Stalin Plan. At the end of the tsarist period, the strict divide between peasant forests and state forest management and the rural population borrowed from Germany, although still strong, began to weaken. Foresters at the local level throughout the country questioned whether the policy of excluding the peasant, often deemed too irrational to participate in a scientific endeavor such as forest management, was not harmful for both the forest and the rural population and moved toward integrating them into the day-to-day work of overseeing the state's forests. After a doomed attempt during the revolutionary period to professionalize the forest completely, the democratizing approach was restored for a short time during the 1920s, and peasants were exhorted to view the forest as a dear friend to be loved and defended. Such romanticism was dispensed with after the introduction of rapid industrialization and the collectivization of agriculture in the late 1920s and 1930s, and when, in the late 1940s, collective farmers were once again urged to become an integral part of state forest policy so as to help fulfill the Great Stalin Plan, their alienation from the state apparatus and forest matters helped doom the plan.

Soviet forest policy reflected the fact that Russian forest management was not only an economic enterprise but also a product of the nation's cultural imagination. This imagination continued along its prerevolutionary trajectory during the Stalin period, despite the concerted effort of the Soviet state to dictate its development. Russian and Soviet economic policies, their considerable inefficiencies and drawbacks notwithstanding, created room for foresters to conceive of and implement forest theories that emphasized environmental or cultural considerations rather than economic expedience. As a result, a line of continuity can be drawn through the works of Morozov, written in the first decade of the twentieth century, to a December 1917 editorial in the journal *Lesnaia zhizn' i khoziaistvo* (Forest Life and Management) claiming that "the forest has always had . . . an enormous beneficial influence on the psyche and spiritual store of humans," to the speech of a delegate at a January 1949 forest conference asserting that "the forest is an enormous moral force for our country."[37] Stalin's rule did not destroy the trend of Russian forest management to reflect deeper culture streams; rather, Morozov's ideas, and forest protection in general, received more institutional support during the years from 1947 to 1953 than at any other time in Russian history. In fact, many of Stalin's environmental policies, and the Great Stalin Plan for the Transformation of Nature in particular, inadvertently brought to life the words of Chekhov's Dr. Astrov:

> Man is blessed with intellect and creative powers, so that he might enhance that which he is given. But he doesn't create, he only destroys. . . . But when I pass one of my peasant's forests that I've saved from the axe, or when I listen to the wind in the leaves of my young trees, trees that I planted with my own hands, I know that the climate is in my control, at least that tiny fraction. And if man is happy in a thousand years, then maybe I will be responsible for a little bit of that happiness. When I plant a birch, then see it grow green and move in the wind, my soul fills with pride and I . . .[38]

To be sure, the survival of environmentalist concerns is not the only noteworthy trend in Soviet forest management in the years between the October Revolution and Stalin's death: most of the Soviet Union's forests, and half of those in European Russia, were classified as "Group III" forests and exploited remorselessly. But the Stalinist political and economic system made meaningful economic and political sacrifices in the interests of environmentalism—even if explicit ideological support for the program was extremely weak—that gave the nineteenth-century linkage between Russia and the forest and Morozov's teachings a permanent place in Soviet environmental policy.

OLD GROWTH

The Origins of Russian Forest Management

In the decades before the Bolshevik revolution, Russian foresters began to suspect, to their great alarm, that their mighty red Russian forest was turning white. Ruddy-barked pine and spruce, for centuries an invaluable source of foreign currency and construction material, were disappearing across Russia, replaced after logging with pale-skinned aspen, alder, and birch. Distressingly often, though, even white forest failed to grow among the stumps, and especially in the far north and south, valuable forests were changing into worthless swamps or barrens. Although such wastelands could be reclaimed, the costs associated with draining remote swamplands made this measure too expensive for the limited resources and ambitions of the tsarist government, and private owners generally preferred to sell rather than reclaim. Many proposed expensive reafforestation via planting or sowing, but new artificial forests, offering to insect pests vast expanses of defenseless saplings, perished so frequently as to drive their overseers to despondency, as one manager reported: "And so it happens: you plant seeds or pine seedlings. Some time passes, you see them all in rows, and your heart rejoices. But then more time goes by and something changes. The seedlings turn yellow and dry out. In the first year alone as many as 50 percent die. As a result, many forest workers despair and lose hope."[1]

Russian foresters thus came face to face with the vexing problem of ecological regeneration, a process so unpredictable that the future of the forest seemed at risk. Perhaps even mystical powers oversaw the forests, a suspicion conveyed in the obituary of a forester murdered by brigands while conducting his rounds in 1912: "Wandering in this place, studying his oaken homeland, Kornakovskii tried to grasp the mind and understand the hidden secret of his oaks, its holiest of holies—regeneration. It was here that Kornakovskii, blood flowing from numerous wounds, asked the sky and his native forest with terrible anguish: 'Why, why did they kill me?!' The forest answered sadly: 'For this, you wonderful, fascinating old man—because you loved me so much that you tried so to understand and to grasp for the future all the beauty of my ancient oaks.'"[2] If this hidden secret of regeneration remained a mystery, and unsustainable felling continued, a growing and influential faction of foresters feared, the Russian forest as a whole might soon vanish. A letter to the editor of *Lesnoi zhurnal* (The Forest Journal) warned in 1905 that the forests were disappearing, that "in those places where there should be nothing but trees, in those places where the forest is the main sustenance of the people, there stand only skeletons of spruce and pine."[3] The most pessimistic analyses predicted that European Russia would be stripped of its most valuable forests in a matter of decades.

In response to this threat, Russian foresters began to examine more closely the foundations of the management system they had borrowed from Germany two centuries before—the dominant system around the world at that time. A few leading reformers began to gravitate toward the belief that Russian forests substantially differed from European woodlands and that the Russian people possessed a closer cultural, historical, and spiritual connection to the forest than the prevailing management system recognized. Accordingly, new approaches emerged that questioned the existing emphasis on industrial output and instead emphasized the personal knowledge of forest workers. On a symbolic level, the foresters were engaged in a reevaluation of how society should operate, since the poor condition of the forests, the reformers believed, reflected the fact that Russia required neither a slavish imitation nor a chauvinist repudiation of Western practices, but a synthesis of native and foreign knowledge—in this case, a new science and a new economic model to save Russia from ruin.

Russia was an early adopter of modern forest management, a set of practices that was born in France but came of age in Germany. The desultory practices common in northern Europe in the Middle Ages, which largely amounted to the protection of noble privileges in the forest,[4] were transformed by Louis XIV and his minister of finance, Jean-Baptiste Colbert, into a regularized, state-centered group of policies with biological considerations incorporated into the law. Colbert, concerned that "France [would] perish for lack of woods," instituted in 1669 a series of forest ordinances that forbade all cutting in royal forests and codified, in the words of one forest historian, "the best usage of the time."[5] The state of the art at that time consisted of *tire-et-aire* management, in which forestland was divided into a number of sections of equal area, that number being equivalent to the number of years required for regeneration. For example, if a given forest required forty years to mature, then the forest would be divided into forty equal parts, and one area would be cut each year. By 1825, however, when France founded its first forestry school at Nancy, German forestry had advanced so far beyond *tire-et-aire* that the Nancy school was frequently threatened by French government authorities with closure for assigning so few French authors, so dominant were German teachings.

In the intervening period, German scholars essentially reinvented forestry. Their attention on domestic resources focused by the exigencies of mercantilism and perhaps by a lack of foreign colonies, German foresters pioneered a series of revolutionary practices and theories aimed at maximizing the production of timber, among them *Hochwald* (the policy of lengthening crop rotations so as to produce only large trees) and *Femelschlag* (a rudimentary system of thinning, whereby all trees unsuitable for ship masts were removed). German scholars in this period also developed sophisticated mathematical models to determine the ideal size and shape of an area to be logged so as to produce a sustainable yield year to year, better methods of surveying and appraisal, and a tool to determine the height of a tree while still standing (the hypsometer), all of which maintained relevance well into the twentieth century. Meanwhile, Germans founded the world's first forestry school, the world's first journal dedicated to forestry, and published the world's first textbook about scientific forestry. Luminaries such as Heinrich Cotta and Georg Hartig (together often referred to as the fathers of modern forestry) produced works so influential that for most of the nineteenth century, "German forestry" and "modern forestry" were synonymous.

The history of German forest scholarship is too vast and diverse to allow for an easy summary, but a number of tendencies stand out as particularly characteristic. Foremost among them was the tendency to conceptualize the forest mathematically, to apply to the forest what had proven so fruitful to physics. The mercantilist and cameralist impulses of the era led German foresters to describe the forest in quantitative terms, then evaluate it from an economic perspective. Accordingly, German forestry abstracted the forest into a space filled with *Normalbäume* (idealized "normal trees," easy-to-calculate shapes based on conic equations), grouped into age classes with expected yields.[6] Over time, the model took priority over reality, and forest managers came to advocate the removal of trees that did not resemble *Normalbäume* so that real forests would more closely resemble their model. Although an important romantic backlash appeared in the late eighteenth century, making too simple any attempt to present German forestry in toto as exclusively rationalistic, the abstract approach gained undeniable supremacy throughout Germany during the eighteenth and nineteenth centuries and then rapidly spread to other countries. Indeed, the German emphasis on abstraction only intensified when exported: foreigners studying in Germany, and Russians in particular, appear to have concentrated on the more generalizable lessons offered to them, making the version of German forestry taken abroad even more analytic than the original.[7]

Another important tendency of German forestry was its penchant to seek general solutions applicable for all situations. As German forest management embraced mathematical formulas, its policies in turn became more formulaic. Although foresters such as Friedrich Pfeil held that "the one general proposition in forestry is that there are no general propositions," universal prescriptions were in fact rather characteristic of German forest scholarship, and as a result official policy tended over time to swing abruptly from one method to another, applied uniformly throughout a region. In Saxony, for instance, from 1820 to 1840, "mixed stands and natural regeneration were favored, large-scale cuts were avoided, and special preference given to pine," but from 1840 to 1860, "pine was rejected and pure spruce stands with wide clear-cuts became the fashion." The period from 1860 to 1880 "saw a struggle between proponents who favored pure spruce stands logged in broad swathes and those who preferred mixed stands logged in narrow belts," after which, from 1880 to 1915, pure spruce stands and clear wide logging belts came back into vogue.[8] Because administrative districts were relatively small and homogeneous, states such as Saxony, Prussia, and Bavaria could publish their own forest management instructions and not suffer catastrophe as a result of implementing policies devised for a different ecological region. But German forestry policy suggested a widely held belief in the existence of one optimal solution for all forests, and German forest science tended to center around the search for this optimal system. This assumption, like the inclination to abstraction, was exported along with the other components of German forest management when other countries chose to follow the German example.

A third important tendency of German forestry was the preference for low diversity, biological and otherwise. Forests comprised solely of one kind of tree, all planted at the same time, were generally favored in German forests, even when this entailed considerable expense. The vastly influential Georg Hartig, founder of the first German forest bureau, recommended that "the forester keep things simple by following a small number of general rules and reliable methods," and in practice this led to an affinity for silvicultural methods producing tree farms more than forests, where the timber-producing capacity of woodlands was emphasized to the exclusion of all other functions.[9] But German foresters also promoted a second kind of low biological diversity: nonforesters, in general, were excluded from forest spaces, and forest managers came to think of the forest as a space where people untrained in forest science could only do harm. The development and combination of these three tendencies in the late seventeenth, eighteenth, and nineteenth centuries made the German forest one of the most "modern" spaces in Europe, a place ruled by strict mathematical rules, orderly scientific prescriptions, and firm state control.[10]

The period of rapid advancement in German forest management coincided with Peter the Great's decision to consciously emulate European models, especially the way that European governments and armies functioned, and Russian forest management felt the influence of Western ideas as much as any discipline did. For essentially all of the eighteenth and nineteenth centuries, German ideas and terminology dominated Russian forestry as they did most economic disciplines, while Germans filled the country's most important teaching posts and academy positions. It cannot be said that Peter issued the first decrees about forest use in Russian history—earlier Russian rulers had introduced regulations regarding the chase resembling those of Western Europe, and Peter's father, Alexei Mikhailovich, created hunting reserves near Moscow and Murmansk.[11] However, these rules said little about forestry per se and focused more on taxation and access than methods to allow for the forest's future. Peter, "Russia's first forester" according to one recent analysis, departed from these practices by instituting conservation measures in order to provide a reliable supply of masts for his nascent navy.[12] As he did so, he essentially imported the Prussian administrative mechanism, titles included. In 1696, before creating Russia's first forest bureau, he invited two *forstmeisters* (scientific foresters) from Germany to advise him on its creation, and once his Great Northern War with Sweden had ended, he created inside the Admiralty Collegium a bureaucracy populated by *ober-val'dmeisters, val'dmeisters,* and *unter-vald'meisters.*[13] German titles were not replaced with Russian equivalents until the mid-nineteenth century.

German influence on Russian forestry persisted, and perhaps even grew, after Peter's death. In 1726, for instance, the Admiralty Collegium, befuddled as to why "His Majesty's ships rotted so dreadfully, and often wound up in such poor condition," concluded that the reason lay in poor forest practices and invited three experts from Hamburg to come to Russia for four years and oversee the forests most important to shipbuilding. These experts were charged with bringing Russian forests up to the level of German forests, but also were asked to make them "better, if possible." First among these experts was Ferdinand Gabriel Fokel, who in addition to his duties as supervising surveyor for the admiralty, prepared a manual for use throughout the empire, *On the Provision of His Imperial Excellency's Navy with Timber,* which laid out specific policies drawn directly from German practice, and authored the first book written in the Russian language about Russian forests (translated from his native German), *A Collection of Forest Scholarship,* filled with references to German and Swiss statutes. Fokel also became Russia's first forest educator, leading tours throughout Russia and instructing students in the skills of surveying and silviculture. During his tenure in Russia, eventually extended from four years to twenty-five, his students came to fill the admiralty's forest department.

Fokel's efforts notwithstanding, a decided lack of know-how plagued Russian forest management throughout the eighteenth century, a gap that Russia filled with Germans. Plans devised under Catherine II in 1782 for improvement of the shipbuilding forests had to be shelved due to a lack of knowledgeable workers, since the government considered Russians to be incapable of the tasks involved and Germans possessing the requisite language skills were too few.[14] Russians did work in the forests, of course, but always in subordinate positions. Until 12 March 1798, when a government decree created two new positions (*oberforstmeisters* and *forstmeisters*) to replace Peter's *val'dmeisters,* supervisory positions were held "exclusively by experts from Germany and their students."[15] Only after the promulgation of the March 1798 decree did Russians begin to rise to positions of prominence in the forest bureaucracy, and the process proceeded slowly.

Although Germans exerted tremendous influence from their positions in the Russian forestry ministry, their sway may have been greater still in forest education. Gabriel Fokel and Peter's seventeenth-century forest advisors began the trend of building Russian policies on German foundations imparted by German experts, a trend that was only accelerated by Catherine the Great's creation of a "forstmeister kurs" offered in the economic department in 1798 and then with the founding of Russia's first forest school in the early nineteenth century.[16] The school was established after the director of the Russian Imperial Forest Department (a German named Karl-Ludwig Hablitz) appointed a fellow countryman, Friedrich-Kasimir von Stein, to be the first organizer of the new forest institute. Once a translator was hired to help von Stein with the Russian language he spoke poorly, the school was founded and opened in 1803. For quite some time, only Germans studied there. Of the eight graduates in the class of 1807, seven were German, and in the second graduating class of 1811, Germans took every diploma.[17] The directors and instructors came from the West as well. The names of the directors of the Forest Institute from 1815 to 1853 were Meder, Breitenbach, Lamsdorf, and Schwengelmann. By the second half of the nineteenth century, native Russians began to penetrate into these posts, but until then, in the words of the noted Russian forestry professor Nikolai Shelgunov, "Russian forest management wore a German robe."[18]

Perhaps the most important source of German influence, however, was the German university system and the self-regenerating belief among Russian forest experts that a correctly trained forester had to possess a familiarity with German practices and the German landscape. Right up until the Bolshevik revolution, a year or two studying in German forests and classrooms, if not a German degree, remained obligatory for any Russian forest professional sincerely wishing to build a career. Indeed, the first forest organization instructions for Russia were composed only after their author, Fedor Karolovich Arnol'd, visited Saxony and Prussia in 1842 and absorbed the teachings of Heinrich Kotta and George Hartig.[19] A typical tour, such as the one taken by Georgii Morozov and Aleksei Sobolev from August 1896 to December 1898, included visits to seventy different forests, participation in meetings with regional foresters, lectures at the University of Munich, and an additional side trip to Austria.[20] Denmark and France also appeared on such itineraries, though much less frequently. On these trips, young Russian foresters not only learned German methodology but also developed an abiding faith in German authority. Only time and native accomplishments could reduce the resulting sense of deference to the successful, well-developed, and systematized collection of policies from the West. However, as the twentieth century approached, this faith in German superiority began to pinch and chafe, as Russian foresters came to suspect that their problems stemmed not from a deficit of German order, but from a shortage of Russian soul.

Philosophical conflicts aside, the life of the prerevolutionary forester offered an abundance of hardships and little in the way of comfort save for the fact that the grueling schedule of work brought the forester in contact with the outdoors. Foresters in training were treated with the strictness of military cadets, with a daily routine that required them to rise at seven, study all day, maintain the schoolhouse in the evening, and be in bed by ten.[21] Graduates could count on meager pay and dismal housing, with steady material discomfort in their deep-woods outposts an unavoidable fact of life, as one forester lamented: "In general one must say that life in the backwoods without companions and with the lack of medical care and without a full guarantee of safety—all of this is highly damaging for the health and happiness of the spirit of a person, all the more because over twenty-five years I have had scarcely any vacations: one time for two months and three times for two weeks. After almost half of such a lifetime, only a sad memory of the young and strong fellow that I was remains."[22] Worse still, all too often peasants assaulted foresters as they proceeded on their rounds, and incessant pleas for weapons were honored in the breach. Academic foresters living in the comfort of the capitals were spared the physical suffering, but forestry scholars were anything but revered. Foresters were often considered politically unreliable, rebels too "distinguished by their free-thinking" and worthy of the government's suspicion. Among the Petersburg officer corps, a recent forest history asserts, an especially low opinion prevailed.[23]

Furthermore, Russian forest experts lived under an odd curse: the fear of an impending catastrophe that others simply failed to see. The threat stemmed from the illusory strength of the Russian forest. Its vastness masks the fact that Russia's extreme latitude and vast patches of poor soil create conditions nonconducive to rapid regeneration. "Do not exaggerate the wealth of the Russian forest," wrote Mikhail Orlov, Russia's preeminent forest organizer of the early twentieth century, "for it is not as great as you think. . . . We must escape the preconception that our forests are many and that they grow by themselves."[24] Similar sentiments abound in the forestry literature of the era: "We have in Russia two opposing attitudes to the forest: on the one hand there is indubitable love for it, but on the other, the most predatory destruction. Such an opposition is explained by the widespread but mistaken belief in the inexhaustibility of our forests."[25] The curse was made only worse by the belief among foresters that they guarded not merely an economic resource, but also a cultural one—and yet it proved hard to marshal public opinion to defend the nation's birthright. Concerted lobbying had succeeded in pressuring the tsarist government to pass a forest-protection law on 4 April 1888, but its provisions were so vague—any forest could be clear-cut if its landowner proclaimed an intention to "reorganize his management"—that experts considered the law largely impotent.[26]

Internal social friction complicated the lives of prerevolutionary forest workers still further, since the professionalization and expansion of the field in the late nineteenth century destroyed the unanimity regarding proper management principles that had existed when forestry was overseen by a relative few. The state's growing forest holdings necessitated a tremendous increase in the labor force, and as was true in most professional fields, individuals with different social backgrounds percolated into positions of power. Nearly all of the nineteenth-century foresters deemed noteworthy by a recent survey of influential forest professionals came from noble or military families, but the list of those practicing in the year 1900 shows that by that time, half had been replaced by sons of shopkeepers, teachers, and doctors.[27] As a result, the intellectual leaders of the forestry world disagreed on the question of maintaining aristocratic privilege in the forests.

The division between the top and the bottom of the profession grew more strained over the course of the nineteenth century in part also because the responsibilities of field workers were growing mightily, as the state took an ever more active role in forest management. The academic forester's allies in the countryside, the forest rangers, were mostly peasants, and the inability of these more humbly educated workers to meet the increasing demands of twentieth-century forestry opened a divide between foresters in higher positions and those charged with carrying out their instructions.[28] Whereas a nineteenth-century forest ranger largely intercepted poachers, a twentieth-century ranger was expected to understand science and mathematics as well as enforce the law. The transition from law enforcement to mensuration was not a smooth one, and those rangers who read their trade journals would have found that many of their superiors believed that they were "unqualified for their own specialty, unable even to correctly describe a typical stand."[29]

Thus, Russian foresters found themselves in an odd position, divided among themselves socially yet trained to prefer unanimity, fiercely patriotic yet suspected of sedition—and these contradictions do not represent the most ambiguous aspect of their political position. Forest management, neither fully rural nor fully urban, does not fit easily into any one category. Foresters resemble farmers, miners, and scientists in their economic function, but differ from all three in important ways. Foresters work on the land with plants and therefore are agriculturalists of a sort, but they produce primarily industrial goods rather than fiber or food and have historically (at least until very recently) had to struggle against farmers, peasants, trappers, and hunters in order to implement practices they considered more apposite. Yet forests are not properly industrial spaces either, since forests follow the rhythms of nature rather than factory whistles, and as a result, foresters frequently clashed with managers and private landholders regarding yields, schedules, financial targets, and realistic expectations. Finally, foresters must balance their agricultural and industrial obligations with scientific inquiry. Unlike farmers or owners of mines, they are expected to advance the understanding of the land they tend.

Linked to many groups but belonging to none, foresters found themselves constantly struggling with the very groups they sought to help: the rural population, noble landowners, industrial concerns, the state, and the society as a whole, no matter how much apathy they encountered. One forester educator bemoaned the pervasive indifference to their efforts: "The public, unfortunately, is not accustomed to thinking about either our forest activities or about forestry; they see the forest as an object from which it is possible to take money, possible to abandon it in a difficult position. It is indubitable that the lack of familiarity of the public with the forest . . . serves as the cause of the misperceptions. For this ignorance perhaps we foresters are guilty."[30]

The contradictory position of the prerevolutionary forester mirrored the complicated system of forest ownership and management. No fewer than five different forms of forest ownership prevailed in the prerevolutionary period, each with its own regulations and methods of access: privately owned forests, state forests, peasant forests, crown forests, and monastery forests. Professional foresters were, to varying degrees, dissatisfied with all of them.[31]

In 1914, 21.7 percent of Russia's 5.6 million square kilometers of forest was privately owned, but this number was shrinking annually.[32] Privately owned forests were technically subject to the Forest Protection Law of 1888, a law that aimed at regulating the use of privately owned forests and preventing them from destruction without the permission of local committees.[33] However, the law in practice worked haphazardly, as one participant at a 1911 forest conference noted: "The law, according to its very essence, may only be enforced pursuant to denunciations, which leads to a series of injustices; one forest is cleared without interference while another owner pays an enormous fine, because not just different committees, but the same committees decide similar matters differently."[34] Lacking consistent guiding regulation, private forests were, in the best cases, managed for a steady income, sometimes with privately hired foresters overseeing the logging operations, but more often with police patrolling the boundaries. In the worst cases, the forests were sold off for timber and then converted to agricultural land; it was possible to buy groves "from penniless nobles for peanuts," one account relates, and then destroy them, for "it [was] always easy to obtain the permission of the forest-protection committees for clear-cutting."[35] At other times, private forests were the object of a peculiar deal struck between landowners and the surrounding peasantry, whereby peasants took de facto control of a landowner's forestlands in exchange for an unspoken agreement that tragedy would not befall the landowner's home and property, a situation common enough to have been acknowledged by the influential forestry professor Aleksandr Rudzskii.[36] In these cases, private forests either came to resemble peasant forests (described below) or were cleared to sate the land hunger gripping Russia after the emancipation of the serfs.

As a result, the total amount of privately held forests indisputably decreased in the late nineteenth century and early twentieth centuries, and it was precisely this trend that led most foresters to support nationalization of the forests. To take but one representative example, in Vilna *guberniia* total forest cover decreased from 1,439,000 *desiatins* at the beginning of the 1860s to 917,000 in 1911, nearly all of this at the expense of private forest.[37] As awareness of this phenomenon grew, support for nationalization among forest professionals grew and then crystallized at the All-Russian Congress of Foresters and Forest Technicians, held in Petrograd in late April and early May 1917. Seven hundred twenty-one foresters, professors, and students gathered under the presidency of Georgii Fedorovich Morozov to draft recommendations for Russia's next government. Morozov laid out as the four main objectives of the newly created union of forest workers "the recognition of forests as government property, the wide and planned satisfaction of the rural population's need for timber, the promotion of the slogan 'protect the forest,' and the provision of the needs of the foresters themselves."[38] Morozov, during his remarks, asserted that "the forest should belong only to the state, and the state should be its caretaker," because only the state could manage the forest in the interest of the community.[39] After some discussion, the congress agreed with Morozov and resolved that, because "the forest is a people's possession of high cultural value . . . it is necessary to place logging and the allotment of firewood and forest materials under the careful oversight of the government."[40]

Not all forest workers, however, supported nationalization. Many foresters agreed with the influential scholar Mikhail Mikhailovich Orlov, who, although not in attendance at the May 1917 conference, objected in print later that autumn that "the rapid nationalization of the forests without fair compensation is an action unthinkable among civilized humanity."[41] As a representative of that broad stratum in Russian society who defended private property rights and lost out in the revolutionary struggles of 1917, Orlov argued that the "seizure of the forests, by the state or by individuals, is the same act of force" and that any state that would commandeer the forests would have lost sight of "truth, fairness and civilization."[42] Orlov also perceptively noted that nationalization was unlikely to improve conditions so long as the term *nation* was defined in the way that many revolutionary parties chose: "If multiple, self-defined nations are allowed to coexist within one state, then the idea of the nationalization of the forests . . . will lead to the splintering of the forests among regional lines," thus undermining the hope for a centralized and rationalized forest management.[43]

Other opponents of nationalization at the conference went beyond a defense of private property rights and instead raised a troubling argument in circulation since the nineteenth century: if the state owned all the forests, who would protect the forests from the state? Morozov had participated in just such an argument with his fellow student Aleksei Nikolaevich Sobolev long before, during their grand tour of German forests in 1896. According to Morozov's biographer, "Georgii Fedorovich maintained that the forests should be almost entirely owned by the government, but Aleksei Nikolaevich defended the domination of private landowners."[44] Sobolev worried that if the sole owner of Russian forests was the government, then in times of trouble, the state could, for the sake of filling the treasury, be tempted to conduct unrestricted cuts. In addition to those who shared Sobolev's misgivings, a sizable minority at foresters' congresses was always ready to argue that Russian state intervention always ended in a confused muddle and that only private landowners, driven by financial incentives, could be relied upon to manage forests responsibly. Often heard were arguments doubting, in essence, the state's ability to legislate morality: that "protecting forests from their owners is not possible," that "the forest will be protected only when forest management becomes profitable," and that "police protection alone will not reach our objectives."[45] These opinions, however, like many of the opinions of the fading Russian aristocracy, carried little weight, since most voices in the periodical press and at conferences seemed to agree that the free market was not functioning to conserve forests and that the state needed to take firm action.

However, even those who supported the decree of the 1917 foresters' congress did not necessarily share the same concept of "nationalization."[46] For the academic professors at the 1917 congress, nationalization implied central control and the subjugation of provincial agencies to scientific opinion, but deputies from the Union of Peasants and Workers supported a very different nationalization, a more anarchic one that would bring a reversal of the "antifolk" policies of the tsarist Forest Department, that "favorite of forest industrialists and kulaks," for whom the peasants were "stepchildren."[47] These ambiguities moved to the fore after the Bolsheviks began to formulate their policies, but in the revolutionary summer of 1917 the groups in favor of nationalization were generally willing to overlook them. Nationalization seemed the wave of the future, the perfect method to remedy the excesses of private ownership, provided that the details were left unspecified.

If private forests were indeed nationalized, then these lands would ostensibly join the 65.9 percent of Russia's forests already under state control by 1917, but how to best manage these lands remained the subject of an acrimonious dispute. Experts debated whether the state's market-oriented methods could remain in place without permanent damage to the forest. Over the course of the nineteenth century, the tsarist government had moved away from the original use of state forests—sequestering the best forests to provide masts, ship staves, and pitch for the navy—and had taken active control of increasingly large swathes of Russian forestland, with the emphasis swinging to managed logging for the export market.[48] This shift to managed logging rendered tremendous profits to the state: between 1909 and 1914 alone, timber exports brought 825 million rubles into the treasury.[49] But the effort to maximize income led to the adoption of ever more aggressive methods of extraction, including clear-cutting, as well as high-grading, the removal of only the most valuable trees from a stand. To determine which practice would be applied in a given location, the tsarist forest department developed an organizational system that tied the method of logging to the marketability of the plot's timber above all other considerations; forests were divided into six classes, with class I forests consisting of "especially valuable woodlands" subject to clear-cut in full, class II forests of lesser quality but still worthy of clear-cutting, and lower classes from which only the best trees would be removed.[50] This policy meant that as demand and prices for timber rose, clear-cutting increasingly dominated forest management at the national level. In 1900, the ratio of cubic *sazhens* logged selectively to those logged by clear-cutting was 1.5 to 1.[51] Ten years later, the ratio had reversed, and twice as many cubic *sazhens* were obtained by clear-cutting.[52] However, in the remote north of Russia, where the forests were farther from markets and the wood of poorer quality, the practice of high-grading remained the preferred method.

The consequences of demand-based logging, clear-cutting, and high-grading were unpredictable, but almost always negative. Some forests, especially in the north, became swamps after clear-cutting, because the trees previously serving to transport moisture from the soil to the air were removed. Plots in the south, on the other hand, tended to become sandy dust bowls when the roots that had held the soil in place were torn out. Clear-cut plots also alarmed foresters because of the effects of what Russians called *smena porod*, or species change, whereby undesirable softwood species such as aspen, alder, and birch spread into the spaces left after valuable oak, pine, and spruce were removed. High-grading produced similarly poor results, since high-graded plots frequently underwent devolution: when sickly trees and "weed" species were left in place to act as the parents of the new forest, each subsequent generation of forest drew from weaker genetic stock. Both methods were recognized as problematic, but during the latter half of the nineteenth century, foresters in vain relied on the hope that the next slight adjustment to their formulas would provide a remedy: "Forest organizers of the period from 1849 to 1912 altered the system of cuts with each revision of the forest organization instructions, but all the attempts turned out to be fruitless, because regardless of the methods, the logged plots eventually came to be covered in birch, aspen, and oak."[53] Faced with such unpromising results, and recognizing that Russian forest groves suffered from a grave labor shortage (the state groves of Kurland *guberniia*, for instance, employed 120 workers to patrol a space where 967 would have worked if in neighboring Prussia), reform-minded foresters came to believe that a reconceptualization of the forest and a fundamental reworking of forest science, rather than mere tweaking of details, were necessary.[54]

However, just as some foresters rejected the call for a revolution in the forest, many rejected the call for a revolution in the forestry textbooks. Foresters with industrial leanings, along with their allies in industry and the government, argued that logging should adhere as closely as possible to demand, since forest management was, after all, for humans, and that any organizational program that prioritized the forest's "needs" over economic realities put the cart before the horse. As one author writing in the prerevolutionary Russia's industrial journal *Lesopromyshlennyi vestnik* put it, "Industrially oriented research should precede the research of the forests themselves, and focus on what is needed by the economy," rather than the preferences of professors.[55] Others found the prospect of rejecting German authority and embarking on an experimental flight of fancy too risky.

Nevertheless, given the revolutionary tenor of the times, the prevailing trend moved toward diversifying the considerations that underlay forest policy, to rally around the pluralistic vision that D. K. Sazhen voiced in 1905: "The government should not forget about the other needs the forest can fill and might deemphasize fiscal attitudes to the forest and forgo part of the income, in order to reach other worthy goals."[56] It was this notion—that economic prerogatives should not determine forest policy or forest science, because Russia's unique biological, social, and cultural considerations needed to be respected— that more than anything else distinguished early twentieth-century Russian forestry from its predecessors and that lay at the heart of the dispute about state forest management in the prerevolutionary period.

The belief that the state should actively encourage usages other than industrial ones occasioned even more controversy when applied to the 7.9 percent of Russia's forests owned by the country's peasants, because informed opinion held that peasant management squandered the country's resources.[57] According to nearly all published accounts, peasant forests were among the worst managed in the country. A typical account in a 1910 article from *Lesopromyshlennyi vestnik*, entitled "Forest Organization in Peasant Forests," claimed that as a result of haphazard management, peasant forests were riddled with barren spots and littered with brushwood, bringing permanent threat of fire and infectious diseases from rot—"in a word," the article concluded, "one sees a picture of the disappearing vast forests of our fatherland."[58] The trend of destruction, coupled with a booming rural population, meant that in the first decade of the twentieth century, peasant forests were satisfying less than one-quarter of the peasant demand for timber.[59] Only compounding this problem were rampant timber poaching and widespread forest clearing occasioned by land hunger. When taken together, these problems lent peasant forests a menacingly anarchic appearance.

For many foresters, the solution to this problem lay in forcing peasant society to adopt the methods of scientific forestry. One popular proposal would have expanded the Forest Protection Law of 1888 so as to regulate peasant forests like private forests. Delegates to the first All-Russian Agricultural Congress (held in Kiev in September 1913) adopted just such a resolution.[60] Looming behind the resolution of the congress and others like it was the widespread belief that the peasant was either unable to understand the concept of property rights in the forest or simply chose not to do so. No shortage of peasant folk sayings backed up this opinion: "In the forest even the priest is a thief," "He who is not a thief in the forest is not a master at home," "Water is not measured and the forest is not counted," "Drag what you want, no one is offended," and most important, "The forest is God's, so the forest is no one's." Stories in which peasants behaved in exactly this fashion abounded in the forestry periodical press. For instance, when one group of peasants was asked why they had chosen to break the law by felling state timber and constructing a hunting lodge on state forestland, they answered (with no lack of guile), "Why did we build a shelter here? Well, in the summer, after all, you can spend the night in the forest—but in the winter, you will freeze!" When the ranger pointed out that the rub lay not in the season, but in the fact that the timber belonged to the state, the hunters remained unperturbed: "Never mind—," they replied. "That's what the state is good for!"[61] In general, peasants working in the forest had a habit, according to one ranger's account, of behaving in a "simple-hearted, even naive" fashion, their "spiritual darkness" preventing them from understanding their own legal rights, much less those of the state, for in such rights they were "completely uninterested."[62] Rather than abstract legal privileges and obligations, the ranger reported, the peasant placed his faith in the logging ticket itself, which he usually could not decipher, but that he nevertheless wore "like a talisman in a pouch around his neck"—unless he happened to use it to roll a cigarette.[63] The conclusion that flowed from observations such as these, that the peasant was simply too ignorant and backward to participate in proper, scientific forest management, was all too easily corroborated by a brief visit to a peasant forest, shocking in its disarray to those trained to value regularity. The implication was clear: those who could not properly relate to the forest should forfeit their right to manage their lands as they saw fit.

A few dissenters (as well as lower-level foresters, who were closer socially and physically to peasants) saw in the accusations of peasant opacity, however, a harmful misunderstanding. They countered that any backward behavior of the peasant was the result of social alienation and marginalization—that it was the state that had failed in not reaching out to the peasantry and incorporating them into the national economy, since the peasant was quite capable of responsible action if the state would adjust expectations to fit real needs. The result was a protracted and sometimes angry debate on the pages of the forestry journals, and especially in *Lesopromyshlennyi vestnik,* between those who argued that the peasant could and should be made part of the daily working of forest management and those who saw no evidence for this belief. One prominent forest owner, Baron Tisenhausen, having apparently lost his patience with the steady stream of articles in *Lesopromyshlennyi vestnik* demonizing the peasant, set out the views of the first group in a May 1911 article: "Until recently it has been customary to think of the peasantry as implacable enemies of the forest and foresters. They say that the peasant has a special psychology, and that the theft of timber lies in the very nature of the peasant. But it is simply not true that thievery lies in the nature of the peasant. This is offensive calumny. Forest depredation is a phenomenon of recent times and not a consequence of some view among peasants that the forest is a 'gift from God.'"[64] Tisenhausen argued that the strained relationship between the peasants and organized forestry was entirely the fault of the foresters, since the burden of establishing proper relations should fall first of all on the state representatives intervening in the daily life of the population. If the prevailing situation was to be remedied, a "thoughtful attitude toward [the forester's] neighbors, self-restraint, tact, and the sincere study of the peasant's methods of forest use and his relationship to the forest" were required.[65] Tisenhausen described the experience of a forester in his area who had tried to improve relations by calling meetings to explain the state forest policies and programs. "At first it was very difficult and awkward," Tisenhausen admitted, "but then after a year it became easier. Over this short period of time the cuts, as though by a wave of a magic wand, almost completely stopped. The forest became peaceful—and popular morality was the victor."[66]

Tisenhausen's article spurred a flurry of dismissive responses. One representative reply, written by the influential and progressive forestry professor D. K. Sazhen, argued that Tisenhausen's approach was too subjective and vague —how could Tisenhausen know the nature of the peasants or their thought processes? It would be better, Sazhen maintained, not to speculate about the secrets hidden in people's hearts, but instead to base policy on observable facts, better still to "strengthen protection and organize punitive measures" to enforce those policies.[67] Sazhen did acknowledge that, at root, poverty drove peasants to make unwise decisions in the forest and that any serious long-term solution to poor peasant forest management had to include raising the living standard of the rural population, but this lay outside the sphere of the forest manager. The forest manager's job, until economic conditions improved, was not to bring the peasants more fully into Russian society, but to bring order to forests, order that was apparently wholly absent.

Order in the peasant forest, however illusory to most foresters, could be divined by perceptive observers, if they were so inclined. Most elite foresters, those trained in the universities or employed in the upper reaches of the bureaucracy, failed to see any system at all in the peasant forest. But a sizable minority believed that Russian peasants merely managed their woodlands in a different way, thereby providing themselves with that vast array of forest products without which "the peasant could not take a single step," as a common saying put it.[68] The state, and thus scientific forestry, esteemed high-quality construction timber, but the peasant needed large trees in only limited quantities. The rural household instead required tremendous amounts of brushwood and lesser grades of timber for firewood. In Novgorod province, south of Petrograd, each peasant household used 3 cubic *sazhens* each year for heating home and *bania,* but only 0.4 cubic *sazhens* for construction and 0.1 cubic *sazhens* of poles and stakes for enclosures. In Kostroma province, to the northeast of Moscow, these numbers were 4.0 cubic *sazhens* for heating and 0.8 for construction.[69] Peasants therefore logged their forests more frequently than was scientifically optimal for the production of saleable timber and instead encouraged the growth of "coppice," or adventitious woody shoots growing from logged stumps.[70] Coppice wood grows quickly and burns well but possesses a poor form, thus making it valuable for small tool-making, fence-building, and firewood, but not construction or sale. In addition to abundant coppice wood, peasant forests provided invaluable grazing lands for an economic group that never had enough, since pasture and meadow had been largely omitted from the emancipation land allotments. However, grazing livestock almost always prevented a forest from regenerating with tall, straight trees. As a result of the peasant-preferred practices of frequent logging, the encouragement of coppicing, and grazing, peasant forests presented a frightful picture to the trained forester: instead of orderly rows of valuable timber extending to the horizon, a low tangle of gnarled shrubs, infested with browsing hoofed animals. But from the peasant's perspective, such a forest provided an abundance of valuable goods: firewood, fence posts, pasturelands, berry patches, and mushroom nurseries.[71]

Moreover, only a sympathetic eye could discern that the typical species composition of peasant forests, so irritating to industrially minded foresters, resulted from the conscious efforts of the peasant. The softwoods that dominated peasant forests were in fact the desirable results of intentional practices. Specifically, the Russian peasant economy relied heavily on the linden and birch tree, although these trees had little industrial use and were considered by some to be weeds. Linden, in particular, played a crucial role in peasant life because of the usefulness of its inner bark (*mochalo*), and land populated with linden trees sold for much higher prices than cropland or even pine woodland.[72] Peasants processed *mochalo* into bast (*lyko*), which was in turn woven into sandals, mats, cloth, and toys. Because of the tremendous importance of bast products in daily life, and because of the ready cash that *mochalo* could bring at most times of the year, linden trees formed a cornerstone of the peasant economy.[73] In accordance with its value, the peasantry developed a remarkably complex method of extracting the *mochalo,* revealing how attuned to forest management the peasant could be. Families, after surveying the forests to find suitable trees, worked together to remove the outer bark of the linden at the end of May, during a brief lull in the agricultural calendar, when the wood held the greatest amount of sap and hence the inner bark was at its most pliable. After the outer bark was removed, the logs were left to soak in a common place until September, when the trees were apportioned back to the houses. The *mochalo* was then hung in the air to dry until the winter so that the indoor work of bast weaving could begin. As careful and profitable as linden processing was for the peasant economy, however, sales of *mochalo* brought little gain to the state treasury. Hence, peasant forests, bereft of pine, spruce, and oak, but filled with linden (and birch, which offered similar opportunities for peasant households), seemed from the point of view of the exchequer mere wasted land.

Keen critics also recognized that the historical relationship between the state and the peasants scarcely encouraged the peasantry to engage in the kind of far-sighted management that professional foresters generally preferred. After the emancipation of 1861, peasants formerly belonging to the state were generally allotted enough forests to satisfy their needs (1.0 *desiatina* or 2.75 acres in the north, 0.3–0.4 *desiatinas* in the less forested south), but when the liberated peasants, "fearing that the forests would be taken back from them," began to clear the forests for sale, their right to sell forest products from their own lands was curtailed, first outlawed entirely in 1877 and then regulated after 1900.[74] The peasants who had been emancipated from service to the nobility received even less incentive to think about the future. The 1861 and 1863 decrees almost entirely omitted any mention of forested land, with only the forests in the "more forested belts of the non–black earth provinces . . . not close to cities, railroads, rivers and so on," allotted to the noble peasants.[75] The 1863 forest organization decree completely deprived peasants who had belonged to the nobility of free forestland, and after 1870 even the few long-term leases granted to peasants were in the main withdrawn: by 1897 only 13,000 *desiatinas* of the original 96,000 leased to the peasantry remained in their hands.[76] Put bluntly, the peasantry had every reason to mistrust the state and very few reasons to conserve their forests as part of the larger Russian national project. Whether they were deprived of ownership or dubious that the forests they did possess would remain under their own control, peasants usually (and understandably) chose to adopt short-term, survival-oriented strategies rather than the strange and painful policies recommended by scientific foresters and their assistants, the police.

Such was the state of the Russian forest on the eve of the revolution—like Russian society itself, fragmented and ailing, the object of calls for drastic change. As was true for Russia as a whole, Peter the Great's decision to emulate Europe had brought tremendous gains but had also created terrific contradictions. The adoption of German forestry had greatly benefited the state treasury, just as the adoption of European military and government practices had allowed the emergence of Russia as European power. However, by the end of the nineteenth century, both adoptions were creating enormous strains and tensions. At the social level, the importation of Western philosophy had given rise to widespread support for democracy and liberal values, as well as a revolutionary movement that aimed to topple the monarchy. In the forest, the introduction of Western forest methodology was turning the forest into sandy barrens in the south, swamps in the north, and bleeding red forest in between—meanwhile alienating the vast rural population, which could not obtain the goods they needed through legal means.

In response, Russian foresters began to reassess their assumptions and theoretical foundations. The search for a more Russian forest management had already begun; the path was paved for the scientific and political movements of Georgii Morozov and forest democratization.

2   SEEDS

New Visions of the Russian Forest

A thoroughgoing reevaluation of forest management was just one small part of a deep wave of national self-examination disquieting nearly all aspects of Russian life in the nineteenth and early twentieth centuries. By the time the monarchy fell, educated Russians had been engaged for almost a century in a vigorous debate about Russia's relationship with Europe and the meaning of Russian history—at its core, a debate about the worth of Russian culture itself. The dispute, triggered by the publication of Petr Chaadaev's "Philosophical Letters" in 1836, pitted admirers of European civilization, or "Westernizers," against "Slavophiles," or defenders of Russian political customs. In the letters, Chaadaev argued that Russia had produced nothing of value in its history, that Russian culture was boorish and coarse, and that the country should emulate Europe to the fullest extent possible in order to escape from its backwardness. In short order an answer emerged, posited by writers such as Aleksei Khomiakov and Konstantin Aksakov, celebrating the unique quality of Russian culture and its foundational concepts of obedience, piety, and social unity. For the Westernizers, Europe represented freedom, progress, and economic growth, whereas for the Slavophiles, European society offered only amorality, disorder, social friction, excessive rationality, and excessive individualism. Due to the fundamental nature of the philosophical divide between Westernizers and Slavophiles, nearly every important national question of the nineteenth century, including serfdom, absolute monarchy, and liberal constitutionalism, related back to this debate directly or obliquely, and the most prominent voices in Russian arts, including Dostoevsky, Tolstoy, and Gogol, addressed it in their works. Russian forestry, too, with its many connections to German methods, required any reformer to engage the question of Russian identity, however reluctantly.

Thus, as they built a response to the growing evidence indicating that German forestry was not well suited for domestic conditions, Russian foresters added an environmental dimension to the Slavophile question, a centuries-old argument about the correct relationship of Russia to the rest of Europe. At the same time, they spurred new debates about proper boundaries of scientific inquiry and the correct balance among industrial growth, environmental quality, and social equity. The resulting schisms splintered forestry experts and government officials into numerous fiercely antagonistic camps—the two most important led by Georgii Fedorovich Morozov and his opponent, Mikhail Mikhailovich Orlov—but also led to the creation of a remarkably original and culturally resonant intellectual tradition that, entwined with its supporters' sense of Russian identity, continued to surface again and again throughout the twentieth century.

Georgii Fedorovich Morozov, the "patriarch of Russian foresters," as the docents at the Moscow Forest Museum call him today, never set out to critique Russia's relationship with Europe, as did the philosophers and poets who framed the Slavophile debate, but the history of Russian forest management drew him, nevertheless, to do precisely that. The path that Morozov followed to become the leading reformer of forestry therefore was a convoluted one, requiring at least two dramatic and reluctant reorientations. The first was from bookish urbanite to champion of nature. Morozov was born into a St. Petersburg merchant family on 7 January 1867, his father a city council commissioner of Russian provenance and his mother a member of the so-called Vasilevskii Island Germans, descendants of immigrants who arrived in the new capital during the reign of Peter the Great.[1] Morozov as a youth showed no special interest in the outdoors, adored mathematics, and was trained as an artillery officer in St. Petersburg, receiving his first commission at Dinaburg fortress on the western edge of the Russian empire, near present-day Daugavpils, Latvia.[2] There, Morozov's battery commander, seeing that the young officer's heart was not in soldiering and understanding that a lack of Greek and Latin blocked the path toward Morozov's preferred career in physics, urged the younger officer to consider botany. He recommended to Morozov a series of books about the plant world, at the time becoming classics: Timiriazev's *Life of the Plant* and Kaigorodov's *Conversations about the Russian Forest*. At about the same time, a fellow junior officer introduced Morozov to a study circle. The group's discussions broadened Morozov's horizons, prompting him, as he put it, to make his "first steps toward contact with the wider Russian economy and political economy in general."[3] As part of this acquaintanceship, Morozov felt motivated to familiarize himself with Russian law, including the recently promulgated Forest Protection Law of 1888. A meeting with the Dinaburg regional forester, originally intended only as a fact-finding interview, intrigued Morozov such that he decided to resign his commission and enter the St. Petersburg Forest Institute in the fall of 1889.[4] His father did not welcome Georgii's decision to leave the military and become a forester and told his son that he was no longer welcome in his home.[5]

Morozov's second metamorphosis changed him from orthodox nineteenth-century forester to twentieth-century scientific radical. After developing a nervous condition that afflicted him his entire life and delayed his final exams for a year, Morozov eventually took sixteen A's out of twenty-two exams and graduated in September 1893 with the rank of forester, second-class. Next came an assignment at the Khrenovskii forest district in the south-central Russian province of Voronezh, during which time he was promoted to forester, first-class, upon presentation of his first scholarly work, and then a tour of Germany, where Morozov worked personally with many of the brightest lights in German forestry, including Adam Schwappach, Heinrich Mayr, and Karl Geyer.[6] Morozov, who had learned to speak fluent German from his mother and was inclined to regard German culture as superior, found his allegiance to the German approach to forestry only strengthened.[7] It was not until his return to Russia in 1899 and his assignment to Kamennyi Steppe, an experimental forest founded by the celebrated soil scientist V. V. Dokuchaev, that Morozov's views began to shift. Morozov, whose duties revolved around establishing forests on the steppe in accordance with Dokuchaev's theory that the hydrology of Russia's southern borderlands had been harmed by human activity, confessed that Dokuchaev's books had played such a decisive role in his life and brought "such joy and such light," and such "moral satisfaction," that he could not imagine life without his views on nature.[8]

Morozov's enthusiastic embrace of Dokuchaev only becomes comprehensible once the unique spiritual content of Dokuchaev's philosophy is understood. Vasilii Vasilievich Dokuchaev is most famous for founding the study of modern soil science, and to this day, the names that soil scientists around the world use to describe many of the objects of their study—terms such as *chernozem, podzol, gley, solonets,* and *solonchak*—are Russian. It is no exaggeration to say that Dokuchaev's contribution to soil science is as great as that of any other Russian to his or her field.[9] But frequently omitted from discussions of Dokuchaev's legacy is his mysticism, despite the fact that Dokuchaev's scientific writings often bled into topics metaphysical, if not wholly religious. For example, in affirming the existence of soil zones in nature and advancing a holistic interpretation of nature, Dokuchaev argued that science had up to that time been conducted on isolated bodies, such as minerals, plants, and animals, and that despite the positive results, it had missed the "the genetic, eternal and natural ties that exist among energy, natural bodies, and phenomena, between the dead and the living in nature," which he said should be "the building blocks of human life, including morality and religion.[10]

Dokuchaev's fervor was indisputably contagious. Normally staid academicians, when reflecting on Dokuchaev's ideas about the land, lapsed into poetry, as did perhaps Russia's most illustrious botanist, Andrei Nikolaevich Beketov: "For the first time, soil zones merge and correspond with the zones of natural history in such a tight and intimate nature, that one could hardly suspect such love from a faithful spouse or the most exemplary children and parents. In these zones we see the highest manifestation of the universal law of love."[11] Similarly alive to Dokuchaev's passion was Morozov, but Morozov took Dokuchaev's ideas further and used them to do something even Dokuchaev did not: attempt to build a new science with holistic considerations at its base.

This Morozov did upon his return to the Forest Institute in St. Petersburg, where he assumed a spot as professor in December of 1901. In that year, Morozov began to produce a series of articles and books that changed the landscape of Russian forestry, crowned by his masterpiece, *Uchenie o lese* (The Theory of the Forest). Morozov set out and refined in these works his primary concept, the "stand type" (*tip nasazhdeniia*). Despite its unassuming name, the stand type proposed a radical solution to the problems plaguing the Russian timber industry, for Morozov asserted that the Russian forest could (and should) be divided into stands, these stands classified into types, and these types managed according to what the forest required, rather than what humans desired. As Morozov understood the concept, a stand was not merely a group of trees present in a given locality, but the sum total of the trees' properties, the climate, the soil and geological properties, the geography (including relief and hydrology), and the activities of humans, plus the changes wrought by the mutual interactions of all these factors. Proper forest management, Morozov argued, would recognize landscapes as unified wholes rather than agglomerations of disparate parts, for forests, like individual organisms (or human societies), represent living communities and should be treated as such.

Thus, Morozov gave tremendous importance to forest organization, since he believed that the true cause of Russia's fading forest was the improper classification system that divided forests into private and public, profitable and unmarketable. Although seemingly an esoteric endeavor, forest organization was in fact recognized at the time as the "queen of forest sciences," because, as the nineteenth-century Russian forest organizer Mitrofan Kuz'mich Turskii noted, "forest organization embraces all aspects of forestry: during the organization of management it is necessary to take into consideration forest regeneration, forest protection, forest use, and forest appraisal."[12] Over the course of the nineteenth century, forest organizers had been asked to master an increasingly complex set of skills, synthesizing geometry and trigonometry, dendrology (or the study of the trees themselves), surveying and mensuration (the study of estimating a plot's wood volume), soil science, hydrology, macro- and microeconomics, and sometimes even sociology, if the disposition of the surrounding population merited consideration. Morozov raised the importance of the forest organizer to even greater heights, since in his scheme it was the forester organizer's job not only to survey allotments, to pay attention to the extant species both in the canopy and on the ground, and to analyze the soil layers that Dokuchaev had developed, but also to peer into the history of the stand to determine how human interference had changed the vegetation and then make a prognosis about the future of the stand by assigning it to a category. For example, a northern forest with dry soils, a predominance of pine in the canopy, and white moss as ground cover would be classified as a *bor-belomoshnik,* whereas a similar forest with a predominance of berries as ground cover would be called a *bor-iagodnik,* as a portion of a chart from one of Morozov's essays, reproduced here as table 2.1, shows.[13]

The very terms that Morozov chose reveal another important aspect of stand types: their populist component. So impressed was Morozov with the peasantry's intimate knowledge of the forest and their ability to orient in northern Russia's vast trackless woods that he chose names drawn directly from peasant rather than scientific usage.[14] The northern peasant, wrote Morozov to his colleague P. P. Serebrennikov, knew well that the *bor-belomoshnik* offered the best trees for collecting pitch; that the *bor-iagodnik* and the spruce *kholms* provided the best construction timber; and that wood taken from the *suradok, subolotok,* or *sogra* forests would be knotty, weak, and prone to rot.[15] Morozov's choice of terms lent a folkish feel to his stand types—one ally of Morozov wrote that the "popular nomenclature of stand types is very comforting for our national self-esteem"[16]—and although detractors derided Morozov's terminology as confusing and unscientific, workers accustomed to navigating in the forest found it very easy to relate stand types to their subjective experience of the woods, as this appraiser indicated: "A trip across the *parma* [a kind of spruce forest] in the evening is especially difficult and unpleasant. The spruce forest depresses everyone, evoking gloomy thoughts about mortality. . . . The spruces list over as though in endless melancholy, sparse and pitiful, wrapped in a shroud of cold gray fog." But a few steps away, in the *belomoshnik,* the forest felt completely different: "The air changes; one hears joyfulness

TABLE 2.1.
The Most Common Stand Types

	Pine	Spruce	Larch	Mixed Forest
Dry soil	*Bor-belomoshnik* or *Bor-iagodnik* or *Bor-ostrovnoi*	*Kholm*	*Novina*	*Bil'* or *Chernichnik*
Damp soil	*Suradok* or *Subolotok*	*Sogra*	*Uita*	

Source: Reproduced from Morozov, *Uchenie o tipakh nasazhdenii,* 147.

in the voices of the workers. How much light, air, and easiness in the palette of the landscape! When they walk through such forest, the workers become more alert, and repeat admiringly, '*Now, this is a sensible forest!*'"[17]

The degree to which Morozov depended on just such feelings and subjective judgments in classifying forests marks it as perhaps the most distinctive aspect of Morozov's typological approach, and this was simultaneously its strength and its weakness. Morozov expected his followers to see past the apparent and intuit the essential. This expectation, electrifying though it was for some workers, presented a real problem for those who failed to grasp Morozov's heuristic; the famous botanist Vladimir Nikolaevich Sukachev remembered many years later going on an excursion with Morozov and his students through a grove of aspen trees. Morozov asked the students what type of forest they were walking through, and one of them answered, reasonably, that it was an aspen forest. But Morozov disagreed: "No, it's a spruce forest. The soil here is a moist *suglinok,* and therefore, there should be spruce trees here.[18] Morozov wanted a new classification system that would codify not just what was present, but what *should* be present. His organizers had to analyze the natural world, but then compare their observations with an ideal world that not everyone could see.

A mere improvement of classificatory systems, however, was not Morozov's aim. His deeper aim was to tie his new classificatory system to improved, more highly adapted forest management methods, an endeavor summarized in his pithiest aphorism, "The cut and the regeneration are synonyms." This deceptively simple claim possessed immense ramifications for forestry. If a tract of forest, for instance, was changing from pine or spruce to birch and aspen, as was happening all across Russia at the time, then, according to Morozov's theory, the prevailing management did not accord with the nature of the stand. Indeed, regeneration was one of the best ways to determine whether a certain set of practices fit the forest: clear-cut red forest that regenerated with spruce or aspen, ipso facto, was being managed incorrectly. The key to proper management in Morozov's scheme, then, was finding the proper set of practices for each stand, which would allow the forest to regenerate as it naturally should. Any practice was theoretically possible. Morozov offered no proscription even against clear-cutting, if a given stand responded well to such treatment, although in practice, clear-cutting rarely produced the desired objectives. The real enemy, in Morozov's words, was a "formulaic approach" to forestry, which he linked with the Germans, and especially Georg Hartig and the *General-Regeln* outlined in his text *Lehrbuch für Förster*.[19] Morozov's ambition, then, was novel, incredibly simple, and incredibly difficult: to forge a partnership based on empathy with the landscape rather than routine, to determine what the forest itself wanted and cooperate.

Attentive readers perceived in the empathy so central to Morozov's approach something more than cold, scientific reasoning at work and discerned a connection between stand types and Russian Orthodox religious beliefs. From this point of view, Morozov's call for empathy contrasted sharply with the more authoritarian tack taken by the Protestants to the west. "In Lange-brück forest district [in Saxony]," observed an author identified only as "Les-nik," the forest manager "gives orders according his own desires, not asking nature if cultivating spruce is suitable and not basing decisions on the natural conditions of growth."[20] In comparison, Lesnik argued, Morozov's proposed relationship to the forest was more akin to the method of interacting with the world recommended by the Orthodox philosopher Vladimir Solovëv in his book *Opravdanie dobra* (The Justification of the Good). According to Lesnik's interpretation of Solovëv's ethics, Morozov's stand types manifested a suitably Solovëvian moral attitude to the external world because Morozov eschewed "passive subjugation to nature as it exists"—inequitable to nature and humanity alike—but also an antagonistic "struggle against nature, its subjugation, and its use as a tool," which robs nature and humanity alike of their spiritual dignity. Instead, Morozov's forestry resembles Christian ethics because it harnessed humanity's ability to alter nature not for selfish gain, but to benefit humanity and nature alike by fostering an ideal state wherein nature and humanity work to improve one another.[21] This, Lesnik claimed, was a more Russian, more Orthodox, and more moral state of affairs than that which prevailed in Germany, which was stuck in a primitive, active struggle with nature, with its preference for artificially controlled landscapes. Thus, Morozov's approach inverted the cultural hierarchy in place since Peter the Great, if not longer. Morozov's breakthrough revealed that, in contrast to widely held belief, Germany was not in fact superior to Russia, but only more successful at dominating nature. According to Lesnik, a truly cultured people would bequeath to their descendants "a forest having an unimaginable usefulness," achieved through the application of an "*authentically* cultured attitude to the forest."[22] For Lesnik, a cultured attitude meant an Orthodox religious attitude, an attitude that granted agency and respect to the natural world.

The link between spirituality and Morozov's science is not quite as farfetched as it might at first seem. Morozov belonged to a prominent religious subculture that thrived at the St. Petersburg Forest Institute while he studied there. Although positivism and atheism commanded widespread popularity among many scientists, and Russia's most prominent botanist, the plant physiologist Kliment Arkad'evich Timiriazev, publicly proclaimed that the very existence of science decisively disproved the existence of God, there persisted at the Forest Institute a small but influential cohort of professors who encouraged a contemplative, reflective approach to their studies by promoting a synthesis of science, spirituality, and aesthetics. For example, one of Morozov's teachers, and later one of his colleagues, Ivan Parfen'evich Borodin, loved to begin his lectures on plant physiology by declaiming the Russian patriotic poet Tiutchev and once interrupted a conversation with the startled Morozov with a strophe from Tiutchev's poem "Tol'ko vstrechu ulybku tvoiu" (I Only Encounter Your Smile):

> Only the song needs beauty
> Beauty does not need the song

Borodin followed by asking Morozov, "Is it really so that science does not need beauty? And that you and I, sir, are engaged in a heartless enterprise? And is it really so that this heartless enterprise conceals in itself a threat to all mankind?" Morozov then stammered, more to himself than to Borodin, "Then, this means that science should be like a song . . . . Science is able to include in itself poetry, just as poetry undeniably carries in itself scientific value, only at a higher spiritual level."[23] Borodin was not the only professor at the institute to promote a synthesis of science, aesthetics, and spirituality. Perhaps the most famous exponent of synthesis at the time was another institute professor, Dmitrii Nikoforovich Kaigorodov, tutor of the tsar's children in natural history, author of the most popular works about nature in late nineteenth- and early twentieth-century Russia, and organizer of the springtime reports about bird migrations.[24] Kaigorodov, a deeply religious man who never missed a service, who believed that the "soul should be warmed in prayer" before beginning scientific work, and whose remarkable career as a popularizer of natural science began with a public lecture entitled "The Flower as a Source of Enjoyment" at a gunpowder factory, worried in print that the Russian people were becoming "torn from nature," that they "had ceased to feel it and ceased to love it," and that they were thus losing their physical and spiritual health.[25] The remedy, in Kaigorodov's view, lay in "spiritual closeness to God, as well as to nature," for only this closeness would "open for Russia the path to general prosperity."[26] Positing that the "spiritual world of the Russian people is tightly bound with nature," Kaigorodov propagandized widely (and ostensibly directly to the tsar) in favor of what would now be called environmental education, believing that exposure to the natural world creates a setting in which morality, religious faith, an appreciation of beauty, and a love of science would be mutually reinforcing. Morozov later took active part in this endeavor.

While some saw connections between Morozov's philosophy and broader cultural trends by linking stand types with Russian Orthodoxy, more commonly observed (or charged) was a tie to modernism, an amorphous but tremendously significant philosophical and literary movement ascendant in Russia in the decades before 1917. Although Morozov's detractors intended the term *modernist* as a criticism, the accusation has with the passage of time lost nearly all of its asperity and now sounds both complimentary and appropriate for Morozov's scientific approach. Silver Age modernism, as it is now called, was a heterogeneous blend of symbolism, futurism, mysticism, impressionism, and other avant-garde trends and accordingly lacked a strong unifying character, but in the broadest possible terms, Silver Age modernist works tended to emphasize metaphysical approaches to social and technological challenges of the period, evinced a fascination with the mystical or supernatural, and mused about the potential perfectibility of the world.[27] "It is not a coincidence," Morozov's colleague V. I. Perekhod declared, "that almost simultaneously with the appearance of new streams in literature, art and technology, the study of stand types has emerged."[28] Perekhod saw a similarity between the experimental forms of perception advanced by early twentieth-century poets and philosophers and Morozov's view of the forest not as a mere assemblage of trees, "but as the sum total of organized communities, subject to common laws of sociology."[29] However, in Perekhod's view this modernism made stand types too off-putting, too unfamiliar to serve as the sole basis for forest organization. What if, he asked, the terminology suited to northern forests seemed absurd to workers in other parts of the country? Was this not "pure futurism," centrifugal democratization run amok?[30] Whether or not Perekhod was correct in arguing that Morozov's philosophy was too far ahead of its time to be useful, Perekhod's objections reveal how attuned Morozov was to the intellectual currents swirling about him. Arguments crafted in 1910 to condemn Morozov as a modernist now only illuminate how timely Morozov's stand types truly were, how they connected with the sense among Russia's intellectual elite that some kind of dramatic change was on the horizon.

The connections between stand types, Orthodox Christianity, and modernist literature and poetry movements demonstrate how closely linked Morozov's scientific teachings were with the cultural setting that produced them, but the cultural force with the greatest influence on stand types was nationalistic thinking. Morozov's ideas captured the imagination of supporters for a variety of reasons, but likely the most important was the appeal to Russian pride and the potential to invert the well-established hierarchy with Europe and Germany in the leading position and Russia as follower and imitator. As such, forest management deserves to be thought of as an artifact of cultural expression, since so many other leaders in Russian artistic, intellectual, and scientific fields were, especially in the nineteenth century, crafting unique, Russian versions of disciplines invented in Europe. Indeed, Morozov, whose romantic nationalist forest management was first publicized in 1905, may have been the last of these leaders.

An awareness of Russian distinctiveness, and a concomitant desire to find expression for that uniqueness, largely drove Russian culture in the nineteenth century. Perhaps more so than any other country at the time, Russia focused its artistic energies intensely on establishing a national identity, a quest made all the more difficult by the nobility's fondness for European culture.[31] The quest began in literature, in Pushkin's poetry and the rediscovery of the earthy charms of the Russian language in the wake of Napoleon's invasion, and then proceeded outward in every direction. Almost immediately, a distinction arose, between European artificiality and affectation on the one hand and simple, humble, Russian organicity on the other. In architecture, the building restrictions that produced St. Petersburg's European facades were repealed in 1858, allowing a neo-Russian style to emerge, represented by folk-inspired buildings like the Russian Museum on Red Square and Tretiakov's gallery across the Moscow River. In the world of music, Russian composers, first Glinka and later Borodin and Rimsky-Korsakov and many others, integrated peasant melodies into their works to create a distinctly national mood, while another group, the *kuchkists,* led by Modest Musorgsky, employed unusual whole-tone and octotonic scales to evoke an unique otherness.[32] A parallel development occurred in art, where Russian painters invented and then implemented a humbler, plainer version of the European Romantic aesthetic, conveying with open, airy landscapes a sense of transcendent liberation, provided the viewer was properly predisposed to see the Russian landscape that way.[33]

This process of appropriation and alteration of European cultural forms accelerated and expanded throughout the nineteenth century and eventually found expression in Russian scientific theories. For example, a Russian sense of otherness made its way into ideas about food, nutrition, cooking, and agriculture.[34] Because the Russian climate and soil conditions differed so clearly from those of Europe, agricultural science represented a logical place for self-consciously nationalistic ideas to emerge. The agronomist Ivan Palimpsestov, as early as 1853, was arguing that Russian agricultural experts should avoid relying upon German recommendations, since Russia's environment differed so strongly from that of central Europe.[35] Dokuchaev, a colleague of Palimpsestov, reached a similar conclusion by grouping the prime Russian agricultural area, the Black Earth region of the Russian south, into a category with the steppes of Hungary, Asia, and America, rather than with Europe, a supposition that, if true, required different agricultural techniques, possibly different crops, and perhaps even dramatically altered land-use patterns.[36] Given the profound influence of Dokuchaev's thought on Morozov, it is probable that this idea of regional difference requiring adaptations in theoretical approach ultimately helped give rise to stand types.

The nationalistic trend in Russian creative thought, of which Morozov's forest management theories were only a part, did not consist of a simple rejection of Western standards. In all of these cases, Russians adapted Western forms rather than inventing new ones, resulting in a syncretism, an expression and an attempted resolution of the deep cultural tension between Russia and the *Kulturträger* to the west. Just as Musorgsky wrote for ensembles of Western musical instruments, and artists such as Ivan Shishkin gave a Russian gloss to a genre of painting developed in the West, Dokuchaev and Morozov used a European methodology, and championed the usefulness of that methodology, in fashioning a Russian version of it.

From the moment of their publication, Morozov's essays about stand types created an immediate sensation. A cascade of enthusiastic endorsements (and acerbic objections) followed, and the furor did not die down in the forestry press until Stalin's "Revolution from Above" put an end to the debate twenty-five years later. In 1913 and 1914 alone, almost a decade after the initial publication of Morozov's paper, 130 works on stand types were published.[37] For many, the overwhelming emotion upon reading Morozov's ideas was one of relief: "Finally," wrote the St. Petersburg Forest Institute professor D. M. Kravchinskii in *Lesopromyshlennyi vestnik*, "we, Russian foresters, have found firm ground on which to base our technical activities."[38] An anonymous supporter concurred, claiming that "with stand types, forestry has truly found that guiding principle that it has long sought."[39] If it proved true that an objective foundation for conservation had been finally found, then forest management might shed its reputation for backwardness, and many thanked Morozov for turning Russian forest management into a science, when before it had a reputation for being little more than brute law enforcement. Henceforth, appeals for more moderate practices in the forest might be justified scientifically rather than purely aesthetically.

Equally exciting was the thoroughly Russian quality of Morozov's new science. For the first time in memory, a Russian had made a meaningful, even revolutionary, contribution to forestry, a science previously dominated by foreigners, and the uniqueness of the Russian landscape had been recognized and placed at the foundation of the new science. Morozov himself had stressed the importance of Russian identity in his theories: "Our slowly advancing science of forestry," he wrote, "arose in Western Europe, beginning with the Germans . . . but our forestry, without discarding . . . the idea[s] of the West, will make an attempt to allow for the unique properties of *our* forests and *our* country."[40] A new era, it seemed to at least one forester, had dawned: "The period of admiration, imitation, and borrowing of foreign works—a pseudo-classical period—has given way to a period of authentic knowledge of our domestic forests; foreign practices have proven too constraining to suit our gigantic Russian forests."[41] The Germans had long squabbled about general principles in forestry, with the dominant Hartig prescribing a crucial handful and Pfeil denying their existence, but suddenly a Russian had solved the riddle by constructing general principles on the foundation of local variations.[42] How intoxicating was the thought that this breakthrough was made not by a foreigner, but by a native son. "It is worthwhile to note," wrote a warden stationed in the southern mountains of the Caucasus, "that the study of stand types is the result of almost exclusive observations and studies by Russian foresters— for they have laid the beginning of a foundation of a general philosophy of the forest."[43] Indeed, it was argued that only a Russian could have seen what Morozov described, since the wildness and vastness of the Russian forest made the true character of the forest more apparent: "It is well-known that the forest has been used intensively in Western Europe for centuries, and therefore the forest there has such a 'cultured' appearance, so different from our primitive type, that for Western foresters it is difficult to recognize the more or less permanent types of woody vegetation. Lacking this distraction, Russian foresters have been able to lay the basis for Russian forestry in the future."[44] Morozov later explained that Russia's geographical peculiarities had indeed formed his ideas: "the classification of stands according to type," he once argued, "is necessary for the study of Russian forests, given our enormous forest expanses."[45]

The promise of atoning for the past also strongly inspired Morozov's supporters. "I dare think that everyone who loves our Russian forest grieves from the bottom of his heart," wrote one convert to Morozov's theories, "about those unintentional blunders committed by our ancestors as they pursued expedience in the forest." But because it was these very mistakes that laid the foundation for stand types, the destruction had not been for naught: "They did what they could; they conducted new experiments and moved closer and closer to the precious goal, the truth of the nature of our Russian forest, revealed by the study of stand types, on which the salvation of our forests rests."[46] Again and again in articles extolling stand types, there appear references to ancestors and descendants, to Russian forests and the Slavic spirit, as foresters seemed to see in Morozov's proposal not just mere forest organization, but the regeneration of the national culture.[47]

Perhaps most influential of all, however, was Morozov's felicitous and almost magical way with the written word. *Uchenie o lese* has been described as a prose poem masquerading as a scientific work, and Morozov's contemporaries seem to have been transported by his articles as though by literature. "Morozov's masterful style," one devotee asserted, "breathes life into every phrase; he irresistibly seizes the reader, forces him to underline each word, and creates the impression of entirely new and profound understanding of the forest."[48] Morozov's students often felt the same attachment to their professor's words as did his readers, as one of his pupils recalled: "His listeners were together with him in that forest. The unconnected, laconic phrases were the words of a prophet; the listeners could see what he saw, far beyond the walls of the auditorium—they could see that place where his interests, his thoughts, his spirit were transported."[49] The spell that Morozov cast with his words inspired hundreds of articles and books organizing this grove or that forest district according to type. Talk of a "new school" grew up, its membership determined by the contents of its adherents' hearts. If it was true, as one convert claimed, that "the distinction between old and new foresters is most of all internal and subjective," that a deep understanding of the forest "was a stumbling block for the foresters of the old school," then the future belonged to those able to see and feel at the same time.[50] The members of the old school, however, did not shrink away from the challenge, and there soon appeared contentious and well-founded objections to Morozov's ideas.

The most outspoken critic of Morozov's philosophy was his fellow professor at the Forest Institute Mikhail Mikhailovich Orlov, and the two men became rivals for the rest of their lives on the basis of Orlov's promotion of a completely different organizational system that grouped forests according to *bonitet* (from the German *Standortsbonität*), or soil productivity. If Morozov looked at a pine forest with sandy, damp soil and a certain assemblage of ground cover, and then dubbed that stand a *svezhii bor*, necessitating a certain management tailored to that type, then Orlov instead determined the rate at which trees on a given stand grew—how tall the largest trees of a given stand were at thirty years of age, fifty, and so on—and assigned that stand a *bonitet* from I (highest) to V (lowest), with more productive stands to be logged more often. The reductivist system that Orlov recommended thus possessed a greater connection with the natural world than did the late nineteenth-century method of focusing logging operations on the most marketable trees, but nevertheless made no allowance for regeneration. If *bonitet* I forests in a certain region repeatedly regenerated with much less valuable *bonitet* III forests, Orlov's management of other *bonitet* I forests would nevertheless not change a bit. A considerable advantage of Orlov's system, however, lay in the fact that *bonitets* were undeniably objective and almost instantly measurable, requiring only a few minutes to assess, if the organizer knew how old the forest was. It should be noted that Orlov was no tsarist-era reactionary—he once expressed in print his belief long before the Bolshevik revolution that Russian forestry needed to "eliminate old norms incompatible with the new order and to rework those propositions that are at present obsolete in their particulars"— and he did not immediately oppose stand types. When Morozov's first articles appeared, Orlov welcomed the new concept.[51] But when it became apparent that Morozov thought that forest organization should be predicated solely or primarily on stand types, Orlov voiced impassioned dissent.

Orlov, like many others, derided stand types as "modernist," but his main criticism was that stand types were too subjective, too confusing. They were impossible to identify in real life, and they codified only the observer's impressions, rather than objective reality. Orlov warned that the adoption of stand types, because they "lack a strict definition and engender misunderstandings," would lead only to bewilderment and that any resulting forest organization reports, if actually produced, would be impossible to interpret.[52] Some early attempts to categorize forests bore out Orlov's warnings when they produced frustratingly useless results: "One observer goes into a grove and describes five types," wrote one correspondent who had participated in a trial, "but you go to another who finds twelve there, and a third says, 'This is all nonsense—there are only two or three here!'"[53] This problem was strengthened by the fact that Morozov himself never presented a comprehensive list of Russia's stand types with definitive signs of the respective types. (One of Morozov's adherents did produce such a list, but this effort was not completed until after the war commenced, when attention paid to forest organization had waned.) Morozov's defenders pointed out that the study of stand types was still at a very early stage of development, receiving explicit articulation only in 1903, and that more research would iron out the wrinkles in his ideas, but Orlov early expressed his doubts that anything could ever come of such muddled beginnings.

Even if Morozov or his followers were to produce an exhaustive list of stand types, Orlov argued, they could not overcome the fact that the concept at the base of their theory was fundamentally flawed. The "fruitlessness" of modern typology, Orlov wrote, led him to analyze closely Morozov's precepts, and this analysis revealed a simple truth, that "the stand type is not the consequence of geographic conditions."[54] The same conditions, he insisted, were capable of producing any number of different formations or types, undermining the very idea that the forest organizer could identify the actual nature of the forest.[55] Essentially, Orlov was rejecting Morozov's implicit Platonism, since Morozov believed that the tangible world offered only manifestations of ideal types (not unlike the climax communities of the American ecologist Frederick Clements), and Orlov wholeheartedly repudiated any such claim.[56]

Others found Morozov's theory theoretically unsatisfying for its failure to explain change in the forest. If a given plot was of its essence a *svezhii bor,* why and how would it change into something else? It was a question "they do not try to ask," one critic noted, and "in the best case they dedicate a few phrases that, although pretty, explain nothing."[57] Morozov held that human interference triggered the creation of so-called temporary types, a forest's inherent response to perturbation, but exactly why this occurred was either left unexplained or at best attributed to the land's intrinsic properties, an explanation that some found unacceptable.

Finally, philosophical and scientific disagreements aside, Orlov and other critics of stand types opposed making the forest's biological properties the guiding consideration in forest management. "Is it really possible," V. I. Perekhod asked, "for a serious forester to accept the old school, to accept the cultivation of species that do not have a market, just because they comprise a 'fundamental type'?" Perekhod concluded that it was not. Forest use, he felt, "should be rational in the economic sense, to give the highest income . . . to base forestry on mathematical, scientific-historical and economic laws."[58] Orlov agreed, asserting that "the criteria for evaluating the suitability of a management decision lies in its financial maturity, defined according to the correlation between income received and capital invested . . . determining the age of financial profitability decides the question of whether a stand should be cut or left at the root."[59] It is important to note that Orlov always insisted on the importance of sustainable use, but he nevertheless insisted that financial considerations, rather than metaphysical or ecological ones, should be the operative criteria when making forest management decisions. This insistence served to endear him to industrial leaders and was probably the factor that ensured that his voice exerted more influence than any other, including Morozov's, when the time came to craft new forest policies.

Orlov's criticisms implied that Morozov advocated a romantic preservationism disconnected from practical considerations and interested more in nature for its own sake than in maximizing output from Russia's forests, but such an impression would be mistaken. Morozov was essentially a conservationist who insisted that forestry was a "child of necessity," and he encouraged the development of practices that would make possible truly sustainable use, so as to ensure that forests would survive for future generations to exploit.[60] He at no time argued that forests should be placed off-limits for human use. Morozov merely kept a longer time frame in mind than his opponents did. Like any industrialist, he wanted to maximize forest yields, although over the course of decades or centuries rather than just one logging rotation. Morozov's brand of conservationism featured an admixture of what might be called ecological conservatism, because forests where birch historically predominated deserved to remain in that state regardless of the profit potential, but wedded to a utilitarian ethic maximizing the greatest good for the greatest number for the longest period of time.

The ultimate goal of Morozov and his supporters was not to refine a classificatory scheme, but to remake national forest policy. To do so they needed to change the state's official forest organization instructions. The state forest organization instructions, the single most important document in Russian forestry, established the methods by which the state's forestland was divided and managed by determining which lands would be logged, at what age, and in what manner. Throughout the nineteenth century, the instructions had shifted abruptly from one management method to the next as practices fell in and out of favor, mirroring the German pattern. "The first Russian instructions," according to one historical review, "established the area-mass method as the basis for forest organization," but after fourteen years, a new method— the division of the forest into exactly equal areas—was adopted, only to be rejected twenty-five years later.[61] As the twentieth century approached, this trend only accelerated. New instructions were issued in 1887, 1888 (in coordination with the Forest Protection Law), and 1894, as organizers sought the one perfect formula that would produce positive results throughout the country. Four more sets appeared in the first fourteen years of the twentieth century, pushing some, including a forest organizer named Grekov, to the outer reaches of their patience: "Why do we see such a frequent change in the state forest organization instructions? Are they really necessary? The instructions, rapidly following one after another, do not present any sort of even, consistent development, as one would expect, but instead frequently contradict one another."[62] There was, however, a very simple reason for the rapid-fire editions of 1908, 1911, and 1914 that so aggrieved Grekov: the frequent changes in the instructions reflected the struggle between Morozov and Orlov, a struggle played out at meetings of the St. Petersburg Forest Society, at irregularly held foresters' congresses, and in behind-the-scenes negotiations between foresters and government officials. At issue was not, as it was in the nineteenth century, which formula to apply, but whether formulas in forestry should be rejected entirely.

The first round of the debate went decisively, albeit briefly, to Morozov. Stand types found their way into the national forest organization instructions and were endorsed soon thereafter by Russia's national forest congress. On 6 February 1908, there convened a meeting of the St. Petersburg Forest Society where many of the most famous foresters of the country, including many professors from the Forest Institute, gathered to formulate the recommendations they would make to the government special committee then revising the forest instructions. D. M. Kravchinskii, a Forest Institute professor who had worked on organizational schemes resembling Morozov's but whose writings never quite captured the imagination the way that Morozov's writings did, opened the meeting by emphasizing the importance of incorporating stand types into forest organization: "If we are going to promote stand types, it is necessary to apply them practically and not just theoretically. . . . Otherwise we will repeat the errors of the 1900 forest organization instructions, which treated pine forests on swamps and on sands in the same way."[63] The participants agreed with Kravchinskii, and a call was circulated to request that Kravchinskii and Morozov work together to compose a proposal introducing stand types into the instructions. Kravchinskii eagerly seconded the idea but then went further. Because it was "important to strike while the iron was hot," as one participant maintained, the society should advise the state special commission to change the forest organization instructions so as to make stand types the basic units of the Russian forest. The assembly supported the motion, but ironically, after years of relentless campaigning, Morozov objected, arguing that it was "better to influence public opinion with reports and articles than to make recommendations, for there is no certainty that we will even be listened to if we do send a direct appeal to the forest department. It is more worthwhile to try to influence public opinion—and doing so is the real task of the Forest Society."[64] The society ultimately agreed with Morozov and resolved only to issue a report, so as to sway the public to Morozov's side. This the society did, and when the 1908 forest instructions appeared, they included a section indicating the importance of stand types and the desirability of noting the stand types during the process of organization. This was scarcely the sweeping reform that Morozov had hoped for, since the methods of exploitation were still not tied to stand types, but only a scant five years had elapsed since the publication of Morozov's first essays about stand types in *Lesopromyshlennyi vestnik,* and already they had made their appearance in the national forest organization instructions. There was reason to believe that time was on Morozov's side.

The 1908 instructions, for all their best intentions, pleased almost no one when they became public, like those that came before. For proponents of stand types, they did too little, and for Morozov's detractors, they went much too far. Most foresters could at least agree that the government's proclaimed rededication to forest organization merited approval, since in recent years the amount spent by the state on forest organization had dropped precipitously and forest organization had almost completely ground to a halt as a result.[65] The state declared its intention, as it published the new forest organization instructions, to reverse this trend and to organize 517.7 million *desiatinas* of forestland by 1929, almost sixteen times more than all the land organized in the previous two hundred years of Russian forest management.[66] Beyond this plan, however, the forest department's new direction tended to either tantalize or frustrate. Supporters were cheered by the fact that stand types had found a "worthy place in the new instructions," as the instructions specifically referenced Morozov's *vereschatnik* and *belomoshnik* stand types. For at least one organizer, the new instructions offered nothing less than intellectual and spiritual liberation: "After 1908, a brilliant light shined on me, resulting in a striking change. In place of the previous indifference, I felt such a lifting of the spirit, usually reserved for life's greatest events. The year 1908 removed the scales from the eyes of the forest organizer."[67] Nonetheless, Morozov's supporters generally felt that the application of types was too restricted to merit their full approval. Most crucially, vague wording diminished the usefulness of the stand types concept. Groves organized for selective cutting were to be divided into types "in full correspondence with the relevant signs," though what these relevant signs actually were was left unstated. Though Morozov's *ramen* forests and *subor* groves were mentioned explicitly, these terms were applicable only to so-called special parcels—certain high-demand, selectively logged forests that in practice occupied an area too small to be meaningful.[68] For some critics, however, even this limited endorsement was excessive. Morozov's old friend A. N. Sobolev argued that stand types were too prominently featured. Still too new and insufficiently studied, stand types deserved no place in the forest organization instructions at all. It was Orlov who responded to the limited endorsement of stand types in the most resolute fashion: he immediately embarked upon a two-week trip to the north of Russia to see the new instructions in action, and upon his return he reported to the Forest Society the confusion that reigned in the forests he had visited.[69]

Morozov's popularity, however, was surging so strongly at this time that Orlov's activities could not immediately reverse the tide. The Eleventh All-Russian Forest Congress, held in Tula in 1909, represented to some degree a referendum on the instructions of 1908, and Morozov's influence reached its all-time zenith there. His ideas dominated the proceedings. The first three resolutions approved by the delegates recognized as urgently necessary

1. The thorough study of the influence of geographical factors on forest groves, with the goal of eliminating formulaic approaches in forestry and the development of a natural classification of forest stands in Russian forests
2. The thorough research of the biological characteristics of all stands, in order to establish the proper classification of stands
3. The thorough study of the various ways that humans interfere with the life of the forest.[70]

Nearly all of Morozov's motions were carried unanimously by the congress, and the remainder passed after a minor alteration of language.

Orlov objected insistently at the 1909 congress, accomplishing little aside from prolonging the debate before Morozov's resolutions were approved, but he did not capitulate to the majority, and his subsequent activities were more successful. At the meetings of the St. Petersburg Forest Society in 1909, for instance, Orlov assumed a confrontational style that helped to galvanize Morozov's opposition. Repudiating a report given by one of Morozov's allies, Orlov asserted that typology was "superfluous" and claimed that if stand types did become the new standard, they would "create great confusion, bear poor fruit," and most dangerously, overshadow *bonitet,* "which is the greatest harm of all."[71]

Perhaps more important than his direct oratory was Orlov's decision to disseminate freely the forest organization reports gathered during his trip to the north, reports that revealed that "the very same stands with the same geographic characteristics were organized differently in different places, and given different local names in different reports," and thus made impossible any attempt to create logging plans at the provincial level.[72] Orlov's reports were tremendously persuasive, both because they targeted a real weakness in Morozov's approach and because Morozov at the time was refining his definition of stand types and thus could not refute Orlov's charges.[73] Morozov's defenders answered feebly that first trials are always difficult and that the organizers had been inadequately trained, but Orlov could all too plausibly counter that, given his well-documented criticisms of stand types before their trial in the northern forests, the confusion was no coincidence.

All this, though, was merely argumentation, and the real coup came when Orlov was appointed to author the 1911 forest organization instructions. Orlov's accounts of the period, published in the late 1920s, do not indicate why the state decided to authorize a new set of instructions only three years after the most recent edition, nor why Orlov was chosen to compose them, but given Orlov's fierce and public opposition to stand types, one might safely assume that it was he himself who lobbied the government to publish new instructions so that he might better influence their contents.[74] The 1911 instructions, edited by Orlov, indeed differed significantly from the 1908 instructions. References to stand types were almost entirely eliminated, as were measures to ensure the "reliable regeneration of logged plots and . . . to improve the forest."[75] Instead,

Orlov's instructions linked logging directly to *bonitet*. Drawing upon earlier instructions, Orlov divided the forests into six classes—from I to VI, with the best forests assigned to group I and the worst to group VI—but rather than grouping forests according to the marketability of their lumber, he used *bonitet* as the guiding criterion. Hence, forests that grew fastest would fall into groups I and II and thus be clear-cut. Less productive forests would be added to groups III and IV and be logged selectively, and the relatively unproductive forests of groups V and VI would not be actively managed.[76] Although another iteration of the forest organization instructions followed in 1914, Orlov composed these as well, ensuring that stand types received no further practical application in tsarist-era Russian forest management. To crown his victory, Orlov published an obituary in *Lesopromyshlennyi vestnik* entitled "The Fate of the Concept of 'Stand Types' in Russian Forest Literature." Judging by the triumphant and unequivocal tone of the article, Orlov apparently believed that the threat posed by Morozov's upstart philosophy had been exposed as a fraud and would soon vanish.[77] Short-term economic considerations were again recognized as the sole basis for forest organization.

Morozov's stand types did not disappear or lose their popularity as a result of having been displaced from the forest organization instructions, but the excitement of a few years before palpably dissipated. A special session of the 1912 foresters' congress was devoted to stand types, and although Morozov again eloquently defended his theories, the congress responded weakly, concluding only that "in correspondence with the constantly growing significance of the Russian forest, a thorough scientific study of forest biology is urgently needed . . . and also needed is study related to the natural classification of stands."[78] No resolution calling for the application of stand types was issued, but instead only a vague call for research into the biology of the forest—a resolution even Orlov could endorse. Morozov continued his promotion of stand types in *Lesnoi zhurnal* and his 1912 classic *Uchenie o lese,* but war soon gripped the country, and the thoughts of foresters turned away from regeneration and toward survival.

As Russia's second time of troubles approached, it seemed that Orlov had prevailed. Firmly installed as the central authority on state forest organization, he could grant as much or as little official sanction to stand types as he pleased. As Morozov himself suspected might happen when he tried to limit the influence of stand types in the 1908 forest organization instructions, the very popularity of the new approach brought about its downfall. Its appeal led adherents to push for too much, too fast, and then centrifugal forces destroyed all chances of a coordinated evolution of key concepts. The resulting disorder provided Morozov's opponents with ample evidence proving that stand types were impractical. Predicated on subjective experience, intuition, and local knowledge, the earliest application of stand types suffered from a surfeit of all three. Morozov's supporters retreated into the background, but they did not surrender. Instead, they occupied themselves by organizing nearby forests and improving their definitions and waited for a more auspicious time.

At the same time that academic foresters were vying for control of national forest policy, their humbler colleagues in the provinces, the foresters who directly oversaw the quotidian tasks of surveying, logging, and planting, were quietly altering high forestry by inviting Russia's peasantry into the day-to-day functioning of forest management. This decision made sense for a number of reasons. First, peasants constituted an enormous untapped workforce able to help with the growing responsibilities of twentieth-century forest management. Second, peasants greatly outnumbered forest workers and thus wielded great influence over the success of state policy. Third, an alienated peasantry could undermine any effort with benign neglect or hostile antagonism. Fourth, threats of imprisonment did not deter peasants from committing crimes (often driven by necessity) in the forest. And finally, peasants worked with plants and possessed (some hypothesized) firsthand knowledge about how best to cultivate new forests. Over time, the trend that began by providing peasants with incentives to help reestablish forests eventually grew into a larger project of forest democratization, wherein economic decisions at the local level, especially in Russia's "forest-steppe" zone (a transitional area south of Moscow, dominated by Tambov province), often privileged local populations over distant consumers so as to promote social equity.

Foresters first invited peasants to participate in forest management in order to counteract the infuriating tendency of artificial forests to die in their first or second year, victims of the May beetle (*Melolontha hippocastani*, or in English, the "forest cockchafer"). The propensity of expensive planted forests to wither and vanish became apparent almost immediately after state-prescribed clear-cutting made artificial afforestation necessary. The state began to conduct widespread clear-cutting and replanting in 1850, and already by "the beginning of the 1860s . . . the harm caused by the May beetle began to attract attention; especially strong infestations were noted in 1859, 1864, 1869, 1874, 1879, 1884 and 1889."[79] The reason for the infestations was simple. New pine plantations offered an ideal habitat for the larvae of the beetle, a pest capable of transforming fields of carefully tended seedlings into scenes of desolation. The depredations of the beetle, this forester reported, had decreased the value of the land he managed from thirteen rubles per *desiatina* to five and a half. This trend, widespread throughout Russia but most prevalent in the forest-steppe region, obviously demanded some action, but lacking the pesticides that twentieth-century forest managers have adopted to defeat insect predators, Russian forest management turned to the rural population.

The most primitive method employing the rural population against the May beetle was to hire peasants to remove the beetle and its larvae by hand and pay them for the insects they captured. In some places schoolchildren were conscripted to hunt the beetles before school for pocket money, and in other places the boiled beetles were sold as pig feed. In the end, though, all of these proved too expensive for practical use, especially considering that even generous estimates put the percentage of beetles captured at roughly half.[80] Russian forest managers then gravitated toward a different method, based on the theory that plowing agricultural crops, perhaps melons, potatoes, or grain, could kill the eggs of the May beetle hiding in the soil. There thus arose a popular policy of leasing forest plots to peasants for temporary agricultural use, usually two or three years, after which the plots would be returned to the state and planted with trees. This practice gained currency in the 1890s and then evolved by requiring the peasant lessor, as part of the lease, to conduct the sowing of pine seeds at the end of the term. If peasants agreed to sow three kilograms of seeds on each plot at the end of the lease, the land was rented to them for as little as fifty kopecks per *desiatina*.[81]

The evolution of peasant involvement continued when forest managers noticed that even when the peasants sowed the proper seeds conscientiously, the roots and stumps from the previous timber crop hindered proper regeneration, and accordingly, by 1899 peasants were expected to remove the stumps.[82] In this way, peasants came to exert control over state forests throughout Russia at the most critical time in the forests' life cycle, the transitional years when a new crop is established. At the same time, as a result of the struggle with the May beetle, peasants became integrated into the ordinary work of forest cultivation. Although state forest management prior to emancipation had little place for peasant participation, by the turn of the century peasants were not only buying timber rights and conducting logging operations for themselves but also assisting the regeneration of state-owned plots by clearing the land of logging remnants and often actually sowing the seeds for the next generation of trees.

This integration of the rural population into daily operations went hand in hand with the broader movement of forest democratization, the name given to a set of policies meant to reduce the influence of large timber merchants and syndicates by favoring independent loggers, and more specifically, peasants. The beginning of the trend toward democratization can be traced to 26 February 1896, when the forest department issued a rule extending twelve months of credit to peasants wishing to gain logging rights to state land.[83] Logging tickets, even for small plots, represented a significant investment that poorer peasants could seldom afford. Instead, they were forced to buy firewood and timber from middlemen (often referred to in the forestry press as *kulaks*) or driven toward poaching. "One of the main obstacles to the democratization of the forest market," wrote an author named Naumov (possibly the minister of agriculture, Aleksandr Nikolaevich Naumov), "was the need to provide the masses with circulating capital." After 1896, this hurdle was significantly lowered.[84]

The rule of 26 February was quickly followed by another on 16 April 1896 that created different procedures for establishing the price of a logging ticket depending on the buyer's social background. The new rule instituted the practice of selling logging tickets to peasants "without bargaining"—that is, offering plots to peasants at preset prices, rather than auctioning them off to the highest bidder. The rule was motivated by the beliefs that timber syndicates, although delivering tremendous sums to the exchequer, were bidding prices higher than was optimal from a social point of view and that "to restrict the meaning of state forests to one exclusive role—that of source of revenue—[was] a mistake . . . given the benefits brought by sale without bargaining to the well-being of the peasants."[85] Although some protested that this practice gave an unfair economic benefit to those peasants lucky enough to live near dense forests, a benefit that peasants in the south did not enjoy, the April 1896 rule was reinforced with a third regulation issued on 4 May 1905, which gave to foresters, rather than St. Petersburg planners, the right to set prices for timber plots below market value, if the economic situation of nearby villages merited this.[86] These policies, strongly supported by Russia's senior land organizer A. V. Krivoshein, remained in place throughout the tsarist era and indeed were systematically strengthened.[87]

The new programs did not operate flawlessly, but on balance they achieved their desired ends. Cash-strapped peasants often found the installment payments onerous, despite the fact that the state did not charge interest, but the local ranger stations, unwilling to seize a delinquent peasant's belongings, could do little but allow the debts to float.[88] Nonetheless, the regulations did succeed in bringing significant numbers of smallholders into the forest market and appeared to deliver considerable benefits. In Tambov province's Fashchevskoe ranger station, for instance, the number of forest buyers increased by 25 percent between 1908 (when the forest districts in Tambov province began to sell logging tickets at below-market prices) and 1911, while the area actually cut decreased from thirty-one *desiatinas* to slightly more than twenty-one—changes that the rangers there attributed to the democratization measures.[89] (The decrease in area logged was related to the boost in efficiency associated with small allotments. Forest syndicates tended to lease large areas and preferred high-grading, while peasants made do with the plots they could afford and worked their allotments more intensively, clearing the land and better preparing it for regeneration.) "Individuals, small forest traders, and the peasantry in villages and hamlets adjoining the ranger station," the ranger claimed, "are more promising elements for Fashchevskoe, because of their bona fide relationship to the forest rangers and their careful fulfillment of the conditions attached to the lease."[90] In Sokol'nikovskoe ranger station, also in Tambov province, the percentage of buyers purchasing or borrowing five hundred or fewer rubles' worth of timber rights increased by more than 16 percent between 1908 and 1911, while the number of buyers spending more than three thousand rubles decreased by more than 25 percent. Peasants represented more than 90 percent of logging ticket buyers, and the ranger there concluded that it was "clear

TABLE 2.2.
Forest Plots Managed by Peasants in Raevskoe Forest District, Tambov Province

	1909	1910	1911	1912	1913
Total	46	127	194	236	246
Peasants	32	57	152	194	223

Source: Compiled from Naumov, "Znachenie," 5

that forest trade in Sokol'nikovskoe ranger station lay almost exclusively in the hands of the peasants, and this was an extremely pleasant phenomenon."[91] In Tambov province's Raevskoe forest district, the number of ticket buyers increased, as seen in table 2.2.[92]

Utilitarian considerations (timber not offered at suitable prices would be poached) and concerns about social justice (the rural population deserved to buy timber crucial to their way of life at affordable prices, even if below market value) motivated the policy of forest democratization, but other ideas underlay the regulations. Some saw democratization as the antidote to market-based forest management, a set of practices that victimized woodlands and peasants in related and equal measures. One forester raised awareness of the fact that in Arkhangel province, for instance, "the local peasant population, for whom the forest is a daily requirement, has begun to voice concerns about the destruction of the forest, to raise claims that the forest is retreating into the distance, changing into mossy swamps."[93] Where the land had recently been covered with forest, elders remembered, "a kind of storm of tree felling had taken place," and they subsequently could not find "even a good fencepost." Nearby foresters recognized that the old-timers near Arkhangel understood all too well why their best timberland was shading into tundra, crumbling in landslides, and supporting only low, gnarled shrubs: industrialized forestry had reached the north, denuding the land and emptying the larders of people dependent on forest trades for their livelihoods.

The report from Arkhangel province reflects the belief, popular at the very least among those forest department officials responsible for issuing the rules of 1896 and 1905, that Russian forestry had lost its way and become too European. Much preferable was a system that allowed peasant use of the forest to be balanced with industrial use, fostering an economy predicated upon millions of smallholders competing with each other, generating comparable revenues for the state while making a smaller footprint in the forest.[94] This concept resonated with the Slavophile approach to Russian history and politics and the position that Russian economic development fundamentally differed, and should differ, from that prevalent in Western Europe. The academic forester G. N. Vysotskii, writing in *Lesnoi zhurnal* in 1906, spoke out against analogies that compared Russia with the "leading European countries": "Over the last forty years Russia has lost sight of its guiding star. We are marching in place and being sucked into a swamp. The economic conditions of European countries, their historical foundations, and their rate of historical development, all radically differ from those of Russia; lessons extracted from their histories do not conform to *our* ideals."[95] Vysotskii argued that Russia was of its essence an agricultural country; that Russia had been "artificially directed" toward European industrialism; and that Russia should, as soon as possible, "set out on a different path of development and embrace our agrarian roots, so as to evolve in our own way." Thus, industrialists represented (for like-minded Slavophiles) the true reactionaries in Russia's political scene, since true progressives ought to embrace national differences and chart a new trajectory, rather than emulate past successes of others.[96] This new trajectory would eliminate or reduce the number of logging leases given to timber syndicates and would give preferential treatment to peasants and independent renters of state land. To some degree the rules of 1896 and 1905 set Russian forest management on this path.

It should not be thought that the 1896 and 1905 rules, or the regional foresters' efforts to implement them, engendered a sudden or dramatic change in peasant behavior. Unauthorized felling continued to plague state forests, as it would well into the Soviet era. But forest democratizers, inchoate though their efforts may have been, made a real attempt to draw the peasantry into the operation of the economy, into urban culture and Russian society at large. Democratization acknowledged the reality of Russia's cultural differences and therefore made concessions to the peasant way of life, attempting to involve peasants in a scientific understanding of the world and interacting with them as partners in a common program, rather than as hindrances or *corvée* labor. If, as some have suggested, the Russian peasantry in the years before 1917 was an alienated, brutalized mass, alternatively the object of scorn or unrealistic idealization, then forest democratization represented an alternative vision of social relationships, one that rejected coercion and operated on the assumption that peasants could behave responsibly if given responsibility. Embracing Russia's peculiarities, forest democratizers sought to solve the "accursed problem" by making allies of the rural population in a program at once modernizing and traditionalist. The attempt had only begun to take effect when war and revolution intervened, with the earliest rules issued in 1896 and results beginning to appear only in 1908, and thus provides only a hint at what might have been had circumstances been different.

Morozov's soulful new forest science and a push for forest democratization thus rose to prominence as two alternative visions of forest management in prerevolutionary Russia, each comprising a self-described "new school" and both akin to Slavophile ideas about Russia's true essence. They shared a common recognition of Russia's peculiar ecological conditions, as well as a common sensitivity to Russia's cultural traditions. Both were based on the belief that proper environmental management should be founded on local differences rather than regional generalizations, on personal interaction with nature rather than abstraction, on granting agency to nature and forest actors alike rather than dictating results. In addition, both were examples of the "Russian idea" made real: both were practical, workable syntheses of Western and Russian ways of understanding and interacting with the external world. It should be noted that the two visions were neither closely related nor truly compatible with one another. A synthesis of the two might have been possible if organizers schooled in Morozov's methodology had determined the boundaries of stands and instructed peasants in how best to work their plots, but in practice no one espoused this point of view. Instead, Morozov imagined a forest patrolled by highly trained foresters and put little store in the peasant's ability to carry out his recommendations, while supporters of forest democratization said almost nothing about how exactly the peasants should treat their plots so long as the parcels were returned to the state in suitably sanitary conditions at the end of the logging period. Instead the two approaches coexisted in parallel. Although both fell into deep disfavor in the Soviet period, both survived to exert a profound influence on Russian natural resource policy long beyond the revolutionary period.

3 🌲   GROUND FIRE
The Russian Forest and the Bolshevik Revolution

Forests and revolutions are implacable enemies. Revolutions are radicalism made real, whereas forests are nature's hereditary monarchs, conservatism in landscape form. As they stabilize soil, moderate air temperature, and regulate water flow, they create conditions favorable for their continued domination of a landscape. Without relatively constant conditions, forests would not exist at all. Forest management, as an economic discipline, proceeds from the conservative assumption that this stability is a desirable quantity and devises strategies to ensure that expected yields and regular, predictable conditions will prevail as far into the future as possible. Politically, managed forests (like other objects of environmentalist concern) exist primarily to sequester resources for future uses deemed appropriate by elites, and thus they stand as living embodiments of ruling-class privilege. In short, forests both demand and reflect the kind of continuity—ecological, economic, and social—that revolutions struggle against.

This antagonism had serious ramifications for the Russian forest after February 1917, when the Russian Revolution began and the chaos of the revolution leveled swathes of woodlands, but it also placed Morozov and his supporters in an awkward position, since they wanted to revolutionize forest management by greatly increasing its long-term stability. Advocates of reform knew they were navigating an awkward path between forestry's inherent traditionalism on one hand and hopes of modernization on the other, as a December 1917 editorial from *Lesnaia zhizn' i khoziaistvo* makes clear:

There is no more conservative branch of the economy than the forest. Not in any other branch of the economy does capital accumulate so slowly; the seeds of the pine planted today will be harvested only after 100–150 years, and a birch stump will give a crop of new branches only after forty to fifty years. But as a consequence of a misguided approach to forest affairs, we have created a significant decrease in the forest fund of the country along with a significant increase in the demand for forest materials. Forestry, as a consequence of these facts, cannot hold with its former methods.[1]

Protecting the forest while effecting the kind of fundamental change imagined by the editors of *Lesnaia zhizn' i khoziaistvo* would have required impeccable skill even in the best of times. The twin revolutions of 1917 made Morozov's task impossible.

The prospects of successfully remaking Russia's forests were diminished even further by the breakdown of order in the countryside, since success for Morozov meant convincing the rural population about a management scheme that was decidedly nonpopulist. The typical response of European peasantries in times of revolution has been to run with axes to nearby woodlands to satisfy pent-up demand, rather than to consider new silvicultural theories. The revolution of 1789, it is said, destroyed 25 percent of France's forests, and Jonathan Sperber goes so far as to distinguish the period of European revolutions between 1848 and 1851 as "a time when the peasants could do what they wanted with the forest."[2] Russia proved no exception to the rule, with peasants across the country chasing away forest wardens, sometimes using intimidation to do so, and then establishing management plans that suited their own short-term needs.[3] By the late spring of 1917, the mayhem had progressed to the point where Georgii Morozov could do little but plead for restraint and public education: "God does not want chaos in the countryside, or for dark forces to whisper ignorant slogans, to sow hostility and fear, to sign a death warrant for the forest. . . . We must show the peasants that the protection of the forest does not mean restricting all use, but cutting it in such a way that the forest can reproduce itself again and again."[4] Given the terrific "timber hunger" that accompanied the "land hunger" afflicting rural Russia in 1917—the consequence of fifty years of tremendous population growth—public education was unlikely to dissuade anyone from taking needed timber.[5] Morozov's plea to the rural population to resist revolutionary excesses underscored the deeper weakness of his position: the difficulty of calling for order while simultaneously advocating change.[6]

Morozov's appeal for calm passed by ignored, and he found himself quickly outflanked, as advocates of even greater change seized power in the October Revolution. The fall of the Romanov dynasty in February 1917 left behind a provisional government that proved unwilling to make any large policy decisions until a properly constituted constitutional congress could be called, and Lenin's Bolsheviks capitalized upon the disorder by mounting a coup. By the time the December editorial in *Lesnaia zhizn' i khoziaistvo* about conservatism and change was printed, the Bolsheviks held the reins of government, at least in Moscow and Petrograd. Just a few weeks later, the Bolsheviks disbanded the Constituent Assembly and began to dictate forest policy. It soon became clear that Bolsheviks sought to nationalize the entire Russian forest and manage each parcel according to the German approach. The cautious optimism that had reigned among Morozov's followers in the summer of 1917 collapsed, and many reformers, including Morozov himself, chose to flee Russia entirely.

The strain of life under revolutionary conditions, combined with a chronic nervous condition, compelled Morozov to flee Petrograd for the Crimea, from whence he observed the development of Soviet forest policy with increasing alarm. In December 1917, just a few weeks after apologizing to the assembly at the Second Foresters' Congress for an address that had been "so sad, as though his soul was deprived of cheerfulness," he departed for Yalta and a stay at a sanatorium.[7] Although Morozov did not leave the capital for political reasons, he soon found that Bolshevik-style nationalization did not live up to his expectations, and he fell in with the Whites. His decision to accept employment at Tauride University meant that he was officially in the pay of the rebel government, since the Crimea was held by Wrangel in 1918, and he advised the temporary government about its forest policies in 1919.[8] Moreover, Morozov is rumored to have authored a book while living in Yalta entitled *Kak borot'sia protiv bol'shevikov* (How to Struggle against the Bolsheviks), although no copies have survived and some regard the volume as apocryphal. Morozov died on 9 May 1920, soon after purportedly completing the book, having taken a sleeping pill and never awakening.[9]

Peace did not accompany Morozov's death. Toward the end of his life, Morozov remained troubled by what his efforts had wrought in the forestry world. A lingering source of pain for Georgii Fedorovich, his friend V. V. Matreninskii remembered later, "was the gradually widening schism among foresters, the division into two mutually hostile camps and the terrible lack of sympathy of one group for the other."[10] Still more tragedy followed: Morozov's wife died soon after her husband, and Morozov's most recent biographer hints darkly that she was poisoned.

Morozov's most accomplished ally at the time of the revolution, Artur Arturovich Kriudener, left Russia soon after Morozov, having lost everything as a result of his noble background.[11] Kriudener had done more to develop stand types than any scholar aside from Morozov and published just before his emigration the first complete list of Russian stand types, but his efforts to popularize stand types in his new home of Germany (the very country whose traditions stand types sought to correct) proceeded extremely slowly. At first, Kriudener could not gain better employment in Germany than that of "master stump remover," despite his impeccable Russian qualifications and skill in multiple languages. Only in 1928 did Kriudener find a job as a soil scientist.[12] After gaining his scientific footing in Germany, Kriudener published more than sixty articles and books dedicated to stand types and gave innumerable speeches at German forest conferences on the subject. But in the words of his biographer, "Russian typological classification never received widespread acceptance in Western Europe, since the forests there had been so strongly changed by humans."[13] He eventually moved away from stand types and found a measure of renown in Germany by pioneering a new science that he called "engineering biology," which drew insights from forest management and ecology to solve engineering problems such as reservoir construction. Kriudener's memoirs demonstrate that although he never lost his love for Russia, he was never allowed to return nor able to popularize abroad the insights he gained in Russia's forests abroad.

With Morozov's voice silenced, it fell to his followers to promote the concept of stand types, but none immediately stepped forward. Morozov had other students willing to carry his banner, but in the early days of the revolution, they were either too young or too marginalized to exert any influence. The first years of Soviet power, a period marked by aspirations of firm centralized control and maximized output, were not the time to advance stand types, even had their leading exponents not suddenly disappeared.

The foresters who remained found themselves in a disorienting ideological territory, where older environmental attitudes scarcely mapped at all onto the new political landscape. The most politically radical voices spoke out for old-fashioned, imported, and exploitative forest practices, while those who had long been pushing for innovative methods based on Russian uniqueness heard their views described as backward and counterrevolutionary.

The ground shifted because the Bolshevik seizure of power and the subsequent imposition of Bolshevik ideology completely altered the terms of the debate about forestry, reviving a model that the reformers thought they had defeated. The dispute over nationalization of the forests came to an abrupt end, with Morozov's position winning out. However, Morozov's true aim, the installation of new forestry concepts in the newly nationalized forests, became a dead letter, once it became clear that the Bolsheviks had no sympathy for romantic, nationalist conservationism. Instead, the discussion shifted to the Bolshevik initiative to turn Russian forests into German ones. In the first years after the revolution, the Bolsheviks sought to improve the performance of the forest sector by championing the same abstracted, centralized, and universally applied principles, devised by Germans in the nineteenth century, that Morozov and his supporters had criticized for their inapplicability to Russian conditions. Any shortcomings of the approach, it was contended, could be remedied by more extensive, coordinated efforts to artificially regenerate felled forests—efforts that were beyond the scope of a capitalist country, but well within the abilities of a socialist economy. In other words, the first Bolshevik forest policy was actively transformationist, in the sense that it dismissed the concerns of trained experts about the importance of unique social and geographical circumstances and instead asserted the ability of humans, working in concert, to remake landscapes according to will. This approach fell in line with the general outline of the revolution as a whole, because, as was also the case with Marxism, the Bolsheviks planned to solve the country's problems by importing a nineteenth-century German ideological construct and promising to apply it stringently.

Thus, each of the influential factions seeking to reshape forest management in the revolutionary period was pursuing goals at odds with the times: Morozov and his allies had sought to harness a revolution so as to install a system aimed at stability, and the Bolsheviks attempted to remake the forest by applying a centralized, labor-intensive system at a time of tremendous upheaval. Both ambitions failed. The reformers saw the revolution quickly pass by without the implementation of any of their more substantive plans. The Bolshevik failure became apparent more gradually, but was in some ways more complete. The problems that Morozov had insisted were inherent in the German approach to forestry, when combined with the widespread unrest in the countryside, produced undeniably poor results. Once a few years had passed, the Bolsheviks changed course, and with the onset of the New Economic Policy, they relaxed centralization and invited the tsarist-era experts to join the government, thereby engendering a renaissance of prerevolutionary reformism. Morozov's ideas again regained relevance, Orlov's influence reached new heights, and technocrats took the initiative away from the transformationists. The first ten years of Soviet power were a period of disillusionment for all parties concerned, when hopes of an easy transition to the perfect forest, whether more ecological or more automated, encountered a complicated reality. The creation of a distinctively Soviet forest would have to wait until the plans of both the ecologists and the industrialists could somehow be reconciled.

Despite the immense problems facing the nation as a whole, and the Russian forest in particular, foresters maintained a cautiously optimistic attitude at the frequent conferences and meetings held before and after the Bolshevik coup. "Russia is embarking upon a great reconstruction," an article from *Lesnoe khoziaistvo* claimed at midyear, "and the constricting walls of old wisdom are collapsing. The space for the construction of the new is being cleared."[14] An end to the war, and thus an end to increased demand for timber and logging damage inflicted by amateur conscript workers, seemed nearer.[15] But more important, the full nationalization of the nation's forests grew from distant dream in 1914 to virtual certainty after the February Revolution. One forester looking back on the revolutionary era remembered immense excitement about the "destruction of accursed private property, the implementation of the dream of dozens of generations of foresters, the achievement of the main condition for the protection of the forest."[16]

Early revolutionary events seemed to justify the foresters' optimism. At their national congress held in late April and early May 1917, after the abdication of Nicholas II but before the Bolshevik seizure of power, the provisional government's deputy minister of agriculture, A. I. Shinsarev, acknowledged the "difficult situation in Russia's forests and the lack of proper management in many forests," but predicted "with good cheer and certainty" that "all of this [would] disappear when the forest truly becomes the people's property."[17] In the meantime, he asked the assembled workers to maintain order until the provisional government could transfer power to a duly elected legislature, which would then enact more perfect structures. Morozov himself seemed reluctantly amenable to the bargain, suggesting in his opening address to the same audience that, troubles and doubts aside, Shinsarev's idea held promise, since "the idea of nationalization of the forests and the exploitation of them in the interests of the population already has support in the consciousness of the people in the provinces and in the government."[18] The All-Russian Union of Foresters and Forest Technicians agreed, proclaiming in its resolution that its main task was "to protect the forest by any means necessary in recognition of them as national property" so as to "help the motherland organize forest management according to correct foundations."[19]

As previously mentioned, however, the concept of "nationalization" was fraught and highly contested. No fewer than three mutually incompatible visions of a fully nationalized Russian forest circulated in 1917. Morozov and his allies saw nationalization as the key to introducing fundamental reform and establishing regeneration as the guiding consideration in forest management, and only a state apparatus liberated from short-term economic considerations could implement the far-sighted policies they desired. For the Social Revolutionary Party (the political party with the strongest link to the peasantry and the most populist political program) nationalization meant, according to their manifesto, that "the government should implement equal rights of all citizens in the forest," that state interference in rural matters should be strictly limited.[20] Finally, there were industrially oriented forest managers who believed that nationalization of the forest deserved support because it would facilitate Western-style economic efficiency, that the "general law of production proves that the wider the established industrial concern, the greater chance for the decrease in the cost of production."[21] For such supporters of nationalization, the state promised to be the most efficient structure imaginable.

The Bolsheviks chose the third option. In 1918, they developed their first forest law, the "Basic Law on Forests," ultimately deciding to ignore the decentralizing trends of 1917 favored by the Social Revolutionary Party and entrusting instead an overwhelming majority of power to the central apparatus.[22] (In so doing, the Bolsheviks also rejected the decentralizing experiments of the prerevolutionary period, since both Morozov and forest democratization invested a great deal of authority in local structures.) Rather than indulge in utopianism in the forests, the Bolsheviks attempted to impose on forestry the same structure they favored for nearly all other branches of the economy during the earliest years of Soviet power: rigid central control. Although the provisional government during its brief tenure in power had approved a set of policies (the "Temporary Rules on the Cutting and Conservation of Forests") that gave provincial and district land committees the power to approve or reject logging requests, by January 1918 the Bolsheviks had abolished these land committees. Subsequently, other potential centers of authority were systematically liquidated or subjugated to the highest Soviet authority, the Council of People's Deputies.[23] The trend culminated with the 30 May 1918 publication of the "Basic Law on Forests," a document that created a Central Administration of the Forests of the Republic (TsULR) under the People's Commissariat of Agriculture (Narkomzem), an organ "solely responsible for assessing and setting the scale of demand for forest products by all users throughout the country."[24] The power grab came with no apologies. According to the state-owned journal of forestry *Lesa respubliki,* the Basic Law on Forests aimed to do nothing less than "centralize the forest economy of the country, to dictate its will to the localities, and to demand from them absolute economic obedience."[25]

After centralizing the political structure, the Bolsheviks appointed industrially oriented foresters to the leadership of TsULR who formulated policies that treated Russia's woods as an industrial resource to be controlled, more akin to coal mines or oil wells rather than biological entities or social commodities. The Bolsheviks' early efforts took two forms: at the same time that official planning in Narkomzem focused almost exclusively on control and exploitation, the state steadily pushed into the margins all organized voices calling attention to the other uses and meanings of the forest. The publication of Morozov's *Lesnoi zhurnal* was terminated in 1918 after an eighty-five-year run, as were *Lesopromyshlennyi vestnik* and *Lesnaia zhizn' i khoziaistvo.* (An article in the one remaining independent journal, *Lesnoe delo,* expressed puzzlement about what was happening, ultimately concluding that it was "possible that the central administration has refused material support for *Lesnoi zhurnal,* although this would hardly correspond to the professional dignity of forest workers.")[26] Dignified or not, *Lesnoe delo* had to shut its doors the next year, leaving the stridently pro-Bolshevik *Lesa respubliki* as the only national source of forest management news in Soviet Russia. *Lesa respubliki* used its position as official organ to accuse Morozov of treason and to rain incessant criticism on independent bodies such as the Union of Foresters until the union was eliminated in 1921.[27]

During the same period, TsULR began using the powers enumerated in the Basic Law on Forests to dictate a forest policy greatly resembling the German form of management that so many foresters in the prerevolutionary period had argued was ill-suited to Russia. TsULR's direction was largely determined by a section of the Basic Law that stipulated that Russia's forests should be managed with two goals in mind: the "extraction of materials for the satisfaction of state needs" and "the extraction of monetary profit from the sale and allotment of forest materials."[28] Through its Forest Organization Collegium, TsULR enforced the Basic Law by reviewing each of the hundreds of survey and management plans produced at the local level and pruning any plans that did not promote maximization of output and profit.[29] The result was a group of remarkably homogeneous plans for all the far-flung forests of Russia. Perhaps the predominant characteristic of early Soviet forest policy was an emphasis on great size. TsULR's (and Soviet Russia's) earliest published technical guide to forest management asserted that organizational units should be as large as possible because, the guide maintained, "forest management is never successful in small groves . . . and accordingly, small groves have gradually disappeared from the face of the earth."[30] Word came down from TsULR that "the division of forests into ranger districts should be based exclusively on creating conditions for convenient administration of the new units and according to the market demand."[31] Although new ranger districts were created as private forests were nationalized, the central apparatus worked to keep this number low. In 1919, for example, Novgorod province foresters proposed the creation of 721 new ranger districts, but received funding for only 41.[32] Large management units, it was contended, would allow for more efficient replanting efforts, and the forest would become more regular and productive as a result.

Grouping forests into large management units almost completely eliminated any opportunity to manage the forest according to small variations in geographical conditions, as Morozov and others had advocated. Instead, the plans focused on large spaces and dominant species, favoring pine and spruce monocultures in the forest and taking measures to create them artificially when they did not arise naturally. The first head of TsULR, N. I. Kuznetsov, while planning the new courses of study in the country's forest schools, urged instructors to "concentrate predominantly on forest planting work, on the artificial regeneration of logged plots, on the creation of different types of forest nurseries, plantations, and so on."[33] The early records of TsULR's Forest Organization Collegium show that Moscow expected local foresters "to secure the dominance of red forest [krasnyi les] by applying the most careful measures of protection to these species," implicitly mandating that all species aside from pine and spruce held no importance.

The earliest Soviet forest policy also harkened to nineteenth-century methods, and invoked German professional prejudices, by denying the peasants right of access in all but the rarest exceptions and simultaneously removing them from the operation of the ranger districts. The Basic Law on Forests accorded peasants the right to buy fuel and construction material from the state and to go for sojourns in the forest, but they were only allowed to work directly in the forest in those places where there was a "surplus of annual growth." (Additionally, they were allowed to keep bees.) Otherwise, they were to leave forest management to the experts.[34] The authoritarian attitude of TsULR was expressed well in a set of instructions sent in 1918 to forest guards (themselves usually of peasant background): "Often the rural population, according to ignorance or the strength of its established customs, permits use of the forest that undermines the very existence of the forest, slowly but surely leading to the elimination of the forests."[35] Seeking to construct a solid wall between the peasantry and professionalized forest management, the Forest Organization Collegium of TsULR time and again rejected petitions from peasant communes that might have blurred the distinction. On 25 October 1918, for instance, the citizens of a village named Raznezh in Nizhnyi Novgorod province issued a petition for permission to cut an additional one hundred *desiatina* for timber, but the collegium refused to consent. A decision came down from Moscow, stiffly proclaiming that "the needs of the local population can be satisfied by the state organs according to the established norms" and that, moreover, "for questions about the harvest of timber in every specific case, a violation of the general plan may not be allowed."[36] This pattern was repeated over and over, with peasants asking for authorization to take wood from nearby forests, and the Central Administration of Forests invariably declining.[37]

Thus, in the span of a few of the most radical months the world has ever known, the Bolsheviks sought to revolutionize and modernize their forests using nineteenth-century techniques. Soviet forest management gravitated toward familiar forms: large monocultures treated more like factories than living forests, landscapes managed for profit at the expense of other considerations, the rural population excluded from daily operations. Although the results of these policies were no different after the revolution than they had been before, the Soviet government pursued them nonetheless.

The earliest Bolshevik reforms did, however, introduce one innovation to Russian forest management, one with profound ramifications in the coming decades: the division of forest management (*lesnoe khoziaistvo*) from forest industry (*lesnaia promyshlennost'*). According to this arrangement, the cultivation of forests was considered an agricultural activity and given over to the People's Commissariat of Agriculture (Narkomzem), while logging and processing were deemed industrial pursuits and assigned to the Supreme Soviet of the Economy (VSNKh) and its complex system of overlapping subdepartments. Each year VSNKh had to send an estimate of its needs to Narkomzem, which then determined the amount of land needed to satisfy the demand and transferred a corresponding area to VSNKh.[38]

Whatever logical appeal this division held, it meant that two bureaucracies with very different economic objectives and targets were pitted directly against each other for control of the woods. VSNKh perceived any appeals for conservation from Narkomzem as mere obstacles in its effort to meet timber quotas, while Narkomzem saw VSNKh's practices as violating regularity in the forest. Consequently, both bureaus frequently argued that the other was best eliminated.[39] Many foresters, such as this delegate to a 1920 forest conference, felt that the selflessness of their work placed them in undesirable but unavoidable conflict with loggers: "The forester is a proletarian of the highest stamp; he creates forests knowing in advance that he will not use them. Instead he works for future populations, and his heart bleeds at the sight of the destruction of young stands. He always protects the forests as something precious to him. I repeat, the forester and the logger [as separate entities] are not compatible. Aside from the place of their work—the forest—these two kinds of forest labor have nothing in common."[40] This new division between forest management and forest industry also meant that the Bolsheviks created an institutional structure at odds with Morozov's fundamental insights: that the cut and the regeneration are synonyms, that the shape of the next forest is determined by the way that the old forest is removed, and that the means and ends in forest management are the same. So long as one bureaucracy was charged with cutting the forest down and another with raising it up, discord would reign.

The Soviet government was completely unprepared for the responsibilities implied in the Basic Law on Forests, and the result was chaos. No working government chain of authority actually existed, especially in forest matters. Instead, a dozen different national agencies with a stake in forest matters, including Narkomzem, VSNKh, the military, the commissariat of railroads, and innumerable local administrations of all varieties, implemented convenient policies regardless of consequences, while simultaneously protesting the tendency of other agencies and the local population to overstep proper boundaries.[41] As one manager admitted, "the People's Commissariat of Finance views the forest as its own, VSNKh views the forests as its own, Narkomzem as its own, and we foresters also as our own."[42] TsULR assigned forest parcels to one organization after another, without continuity or consequences; "khutors, sovkhozes, sundry firms with life spans no longer than the life of a butterfly, all [sharing] one goal: to take from the forest all that [was] possible at the moment, leaving ground where even grass will not grow."[43]

VSNKh, being the largest and most important state bureaucracy, was likely the worst violator of the sustainable practices that were officially required by the Basic Law on Forests. Its constituent administrations tended to regard restrictions based on ecological concerns as ludicrously irrelevant and employed any practice, including subterfuge, to meet quotas and escape logging limits, as this 1918 report from TsULR makes clear: "We learned that representatives [of VSNKh] demanded the right to log 600,000 kuby [cubic sazhens, a unit equal to 343 cubic feet] of firewood in parcels close to the railroad, although the annual demand had been set at 300,000 kuby. When asked whether they had logged such a quantity of firewood, they coolly responded that they were in a position to log no more than 40,000 kuby. However, they did not volunteer the fact that the remaining amounts were logged by contractors hired by VSNKh, individuals beyond the reach of Soviet power."[44] Narkomzem and its regional affiliates protested loudly that VSNKh's subordinate body, the Railroad Forest Committee (zheleskom) seemed bent on stripping each last stick of wood from the forests under their aegis (those within fifteen *versts,* or approximately ten miles, of any railroad), but to no avail.[45] Throughout 1919 and 1920, the TsULR sent repeated telegrams to the *zheleskoms* in various provinces, ordering them to halt unauthorized logging along the railroad paths, but in the end the *zheleskom* was able to appeal to a different chain of authority and obtain special permission from the province-level Interagency Commissions for Fuel.[46] A 1920 conference of forest organizers found that the lack of proper legal and technical oversight was only made worse by "the ignorance and thoughtlessness of the individuals in the State Logging Commission [the forestry arm of VSNKh], whose lack of expertise creates enormous waste," and the willingness of the State Logging Commission to "resort to insinuations, contrivances, political intrigues, and accusations of counterrevolution" to rid themselves of meddling foresters.[47] Similar complaints were leveled at the many other organizations that worked in the forest, outside the oversight of experts.

However, even if Narkomzem had possessed the political wherewithal to tame VSNKh and realize the ambitions spelled out in the Basic Law, its employees were in no position to carry out its program of widespread artificial reafforestation and state control of the timber market. Intensive, German-style forest management requires at the very least a well-developed infrastructure, extensive funds, and vast cadres of experts. Bolshevik Russia lacked all three. Russia's network of nurseries and plantations lay in utter disarray, often disrupted by migrating armies.[48] The budgetary crisis of the revolutionary era meant that ranger districts were receiving as little as 3 percent of the budgeted funds needed to conduct their work.[49] But the most serious problem was the lack of qualified workers, a function of Russia's low population density and its political instability. In November 1918, the director of the Petrograd Forest Institute, E. E. Kern, estimated that Russia needed seven million forest workers to carry out the tasks prescribed by the Bolshevik government, "excluding transport, processing, and trade," at a time when fewer than a tenth of this number existed and when many were abandoning forestry as a profession.[50] "One would need the legs of a moose," one critic grumbled, "to make the rounds."[51] The bureaucrats in the TsULR, accordingly, found themselves forced to make recommendations like the one issued on 7 June 1919, providing the whole of Kostroma province with 135 forest workers for ninety-one ranger districts, each district averaging roughly 44,000 acres.[52] In other places, the shortage was even more dire. The Ufa province forest department reported in 1920 "an extreme lack of technical resources from the very first moment of the organization of the department, with one forester assigned to two or three ranger districts all too common. At the present time only 2 percent of the required foresters exist."[53] The compensation afforded forest workers certainly did not encourage new workers to sign up. In 1924–25, even after a marked improvement of conditions of payment, salaries equaled only between a quarter and half of prerevolutionary norms.[54] With so few workers patrolling borders, the trees stood unprotected and uncared for, rendering unworkable the state's hope to manage its forests intensively, as well as its ambition to keep the peasantry out of the forest by supplying the rural population's needs itself. The outcome was expressed well in this 1918 letter from Narkomzem to VSNKh: "If during [World War I] predatory use of forests and speculation in forest materials reached catastrophic levels, then at the present time the affair is no better— and perhaps worse. Logging firms and organizations have developed in such numbers that it is impossible not only to approve of their actions, but even to observe them. All these organizations conduct logging independent of oversight and without a general plan, frequently concentrating their logging in the same places, and creating a terrible mess."[55] In a meaningful sense, however, Narkomzem and the drafters of the Basic Law were the parties truly responsible for the confusion, since they had advanced a vision of a highly professionalized, centralized, and intensive form of forest management that they could not reasonably hope to implement.

The rural population might have been drafted to assist in forest management, as experimenters in the tsarist period had attempted to do, but the peasantry brought to any such negotiations its own conditions, most notably a say in the decision-making process. In March 1918, for instance, an Extraordinary Congress of Land Departments, Committees of the Poor and Communes (*chrezvychainyi s"ezd zemotdelov, komitetov bednoty i kommun*), issued a decree proposing that every commune and village be "given the right to allocate forest plots for firewood and construction timber according to the desires of the population, while not deviating from the plan of forest organization."[56]

However, the Bolsheviks, mistrustful of the rural population, rejected this power-sharing arrangement in favor of forest professionals who did not exist, leaving peasants little choice but to take matters into their own hands. Nationalized forests offered a source of needed forest materials, but these were technically off-limits until they had been inventoried, and the inventorying effort ultimately took years instead of months, because of a lack of personnel.[57] In the meantime, the state failed repeatedly in its ambition to supply the population with forest goods, as the All-Russian Union of Foresters and Forest Technicians noted in 1920: "Having reviewed the condition of forest management, we see that a vast percentage of the population is deprived of using timber. Some of this is due to the fact that dividing the forest equitably is extremely difficult, and it may well be impossible to give each citizen only that which he really needs. If a citizen needs a log, he receives firewood (and vice versa), creating enormous hardship."[58] The rural population, understandably unwilling to freeze while the new government organized itself, responded with an epidemic of unauthorized logging. *Lesa respubliki* thoroughly chronicled the phenomenon in issue after issue, arguing explicitly that the failures of the Bolshevik state were actually the fault of the peasantry. The portrait of the inscrutable and malevolent peasant that *Lesa respubliki* liked to paint is, however, no more than half accurate, since peasants themselves worried about the destruction and sent scores of distressed telegrams to TsULR appealing for help. A peasant named Laptev from Vladimir province, for example, wrote to "request protection from the predation of our forests; there is no one to turn to—no power, no court. The forests are perishing by the axes of the local population."[59]

The effort to impose German-inspired management structures on the Russian forest, then, fundamentally ignored the political, economic, and social peculiarities of a vast country undergoing a revolution, and the result was a near-total breakdown of authority and scars on the forest landscape that lasted for decades. The nation's most valuable forests were stripped bare by competing agencies with overlapping duties, as well as by a rural population excluded from decision making in the forest and underserved by an insufficient apparatus. According to the minutes of the second conference of forest organizers held in Moscow in late April 1920, the area logged by state enterprises in 1918, 1919, and 1920 exceeded the amount designated for an entire decade, the direct result of "the collapse of forest management, which has brought the forest to its present ruinous condition."[60] The breakdown would be costly to remedy: in 1923, TsULR estimated that fifteen years would be needed to repair the damage done during the years from 1918 to 1921.[61]

Perhaps worst of all, better forests suffered more from abuse than lesser ones. As Morozov had once noted, pine and spruce woodlands with rich soils— those supporting the forests most attractive to loggers—tended to support thicker mats of grassy vegetation, denser shrubs, and more prolific patches of softwoods after their large trees had been removed, more so than woodlands with poor soils. The carpet of pioneer vegetation that grew more readily on better soils then hindered the appearance of new red forest. Indeed, the records of TsULR's Forest Organization Collegium show that even as early as 1918, the central authorities fully recognized the problems that resulted from their approach; a management review for Kazan' province from 1918 noted that foresters did not expect the best stands to return to their prior condition before thirty or forty years had passed and anticipated that the second- and third-class forests would regenerate with main species only 10 percent of the time.[62] In many places, the spruce and oak forests in Kazan' province were returning to their previous condition so infrequently as to be statistically insignificant. In the rich Dolgorukii grove near Moscow, "only 8 percent of the grove regenerated in a satisfactory manner, while 92 percent of forest regeneration did not occur at all."[63] By the year 1922, a national conference of forest department heads acknowledged that their plans had failed, since "concerns about natural forest regeneration had been relegated to secondary importance and placed in an impossible situation, while works on artificial regeneration moved along at a rapid tempo, [but] ultimately came to nothing."[64] The chaos in the forest accrued to the Bolsheviks' benefit by allowing for extremely large harvests of timber, and Lenin himself claimed that the wealth extracted from the Russian forest during the Civil War "saved the revolution," but the mounting destruction ultimately forced the Soviet authorities to reevaluate their policies.[65]

The Bolshevik emphasis on strict central control and maximization of output, which obtained not only in forestry but in all realms of the economy during the early years of Soviet power, underwent serious examination after the Civil War came to an end in 1921. Answering Lenin's call for a calculated retreat from full-scale communism, the Soviet Union reoriented its economy with a program called the New Economic Policy, or NEP. Aware that strict state control of every aspect of the economy had brought growth to a standstill and alienated broad strata of society, including groups once strongly allied with the Bolsheviks, the Soviet government embarked on a program of economic liberalization, including the legalization of private trade.[66] While retaining control of the "commanding heights" of the economy, including financial institutions, heavy industry, and ownership of land, the Soviet government pulled back from ideologically based dictation of every aspect of economic life to allow more outside input, as a concession to an angry populace.

The NEP had a direct and immediate impact upon forest management, bringing the same decentralization and pragmatism to forestry as it did to trade. N. I. Kuznetsov moved over to the industrial planning agency Gosplan, and a new leader, A. I. Shul'ts, a figure far more sympathetic to traditional forestry approaches, took his place. Under the direction of Shul'ts, Narkomzem reassessed its policies, accorded the opinions of experts new importance, and began to reconsider the ideas of Morozov and peasant democratization. Because the earliest Bolshevik forest policies and the Basic Law on Forests had been predicated on the concept that socialism would engender a healthier forest than capitalism had, an honest admission that the forest was faring poorly demanded a change in approach. Slowly but steadily, the Bolsheviks began to espouse policies greatly resembling prerevolutionary norms, with the most powerful voice in forestry being, as it was in 1914, that of Mikhail Orlov.

No one familiar with Orlov's activities during the revolution would have expected him to rise to a position of influence in a Bolshevik-led government. Orlov eventually reconciled himself with the Soviet regime as the "free choice of the people," but he spent the revolutionary years in Petrograd avoiding direct political entanglement and penning a number of works explicitly condemning socialism.[67] Orlov's works of the early Bolshevik era, the 1918 book *On the Foundations of Russian State Forest Management* and a long essay published in *Findings of the Petrograd Forest Institute,* echoed the positions of the liberal Constitutional Democratic (Kadet) Party, and expressed only disdain for revolutionary ideals. He bitterly opposed the socialization of Russia's forests and condemned the All-Russian Union of Foresters for socially irresponsible sloganeering. Orlov reserved his harshest criticism for the union and its twin aims of maintaining order in the forests and changing their management entirely, between the simultaneous conservative and radical impulses of the day: "What could possibly happen, when everyone in one voice is saying 'Protect the Forest!' while the same people's actions are endangering the forests more than anything else? What, after all, is threatening Russia's forests today? From what or whom need they be protected? The forests first of all need to be protected from the consequences of agrarian disorder, created by the whispering of ignorant slogans."[68] The most dangerous aspect of these whispered slogans for Orlov was the elimination of private property in the forest: "If you want to protect the forest," he claimed, "then first of all you must protect the right of private property in the forest, since such forests benefit not only the individual who owns the forest, but also society and the state."[69]

Such opinions put him conspicuously at odds with the populist direction of 1917 forest politics, as well as with the Bolsheviks' decree about the nationalization of land, but the passage of time convinced Orlov that his opposition to Soviet power could be overcome. He never endorsed the nationalization of state forests, and he heartily rejected the notion that "the rural population can control itself in the use of others' forests," but his strongest objection to Bolshevik rule was the trend he perceived toward anarchy.[70] He believed that forest work not carried out by trained foresters, by people who had vowed to "plant, guard, foster, and tend the forest themselves, working not only for themselves, but for society as a whole and for the state," could only end in failure.[71] When Orlov wrote his 1918 works denouncing revolutionary forest management and socialized forests, it appeared to him that the trend of the revolution was moving toward mob rule and decentralization.[72] But after the Bolshevik government adopted the Basic Law on Forests and Orlov saw that the expertise of specialists in Moscow would exert tremendous influence over policies in socialized forests, he reconsidered.

Orlov's rapprochement with the communists, a negotiation replicated innumerable times throughout the Soviet Union during NEP in various scientific disciplines, began with the acceptance of a number of honors and then developed into a meaningful (although brief) partnership.[73] In 1921, in recognition of more than twenty years of service at the Petrograd Forest Institute, Orlov received the title of "distinguished professor." Relations grew friendlier still in 1923, with the bestowal of the Soviet "Hero of Labor" award. Orlov became the most influential forester in Russia soon thereafter, when in 1924 Shul'ts invited him to draft the new forest organization instructions.[74] Orlov was simultaneously the most logical and the least likely choice for the job, possessing more experience than any other Russian by dint of penning the 1911 and 1914 forest organization instructions, although for a bourgeois government. Nevertheless, he consolidated his power still further the next year when Shul'ts named him chair of Narkomzem's highest convened body, the Forestry Scholar Committee (*lesnoi uchennyi komitet*, or LUK).[75]

In the period between its creation in 1921 and Orlov's ascension in 1925, LUK (and the professors who comprised it) gained steadily greater authority over Narkomzem's forest policy, until LUK wielded effective veto power, with no directive or instruction issued against its wishes.[76] Its first task was rather modest: to examine the sizes of the country's ranger districts, which in some cases exceeded 900,000 *desiatiny* (roughly the size of Rhode Island and Delaware put together), and to use its scholarly expertise to determine their ideal boundaries.[77] LUK's purview soon expanded to embrace the analysis of all department policies, including courses of study at forest schools; methods of allotting timber to the population; and ways to mitigate VSNKh's destructive influence on forest regeneration at a time when, in the committee's words, "the existing system of exploitation leads to the full collapse of forest management, so much so that forest industry as it currently exists is threatened."[78] Almost immediately, LUK heard accusations of disloyalty from VSNKh for trying to limit harvest sizes, but for the time being, LUK proved able to defend itself with explanations such as this, given at a 1922 forest conference: "When we move on to matters of loyalty, the matter is different. It is not enough to be a simple soldier and to do what is ordered. When you understand the essence of Soviet power, then you will see in our work not mere decrees, but creativity. They say we scholar foresters are doing nothing, but this is a thousand times incorrect. We are creating."[79] Thus, LUK's main ambitions were clear even before Orlov signed on: the committee attempted to satisfy VSNKh's demands while somehow preserving academic oversight and to maintain rule by experts without alienating the upstart communists.

LUK's capacity to reconcile technocratic oversight with the ever-growing demands of the state underwent its first real test just before Orlov's recruitment, when LUK assumed the task of reviewing the new national forest law. It had become clear to forest professionals as early as 1921 that the Basic Law on Forests had been a disaster, and at the second All-Russian Congress of Provincial Forest Department Directors, held in late December of 1922, the director of Moscow province department complained that the forest law had "had its day" because "no one takes it seriously" and that without proper norms, foresters had "no foundation on which to base our activities."[80] The new law bounced back and forth between various agencies before receiving final approval, but the body most responsible for drafting and finalizing its clauses was Mikhail Orlov's LUK.[81]

Critics of the Basic Law most often bemoaned its excessive centralization and the fact that experts far from the forests were making uninformed and inappropriate decisions about distant local conditions, with negative consequences for the forests as well as for the rural population. The chair of the forest organization committee at the 1922 conference claimed that forest management under the Bolsheviks so far had been, somehow, excessively influenced by capitalism, since the localities had been subjugated to the center, and such centralization equaled bourgeois centralism. "We want to organize forest management around the regional level, rather than the national," he claimed, and his colleagues agreed.[82] The Murmansk province director contended that "only the provinces can conduct this work, that only they can regenerate the forest . . . because the center is not in a position to consider all the complexities of the localities," while another attendee asserted plainly that "outsiders do not know how to work in the interests of forest regeneration."[83] Moreover, delegates argued that local control would deliver economic benefits as well ecological ones, because, as the TsULR had noted in its 1922 annual review, "the centralization of logging [in VSNKh] did not yield the expected results due to organizational shortcomings," whereas local agencies, if "given the greatest possible initiative and independence," could attend to details better and produce higher output.[84]

However, the provincial forest organization plans submitted to TsULR in 1923 show that, more than any other change, the regional administrations used their newly acquired authority to implement Morozov's ideas. For instance, the forestry plans for Gomel'sk province (an area on the border of Russia and Belarus) stated that "the forest organizers will study the growth of the forest and the conditions of its regeneration. They will establish management stand types requiring different management methods. In so far as a comprehensive system of types still does not exist, the following primitive classification will be used: 1. dry pine forests [*belomoshniki*]; 2. damp pine forests [*zelenomoshniki*]; 3. swampy pine forests [*torfianiki*]; 4. *nazemistye* pine forests, those that possess spruce in the first layer and linden in the second."[85] The 1923 report for the northern province of Vologda 1923 sounded a similar note, charging that the present management regime "divides stands exclusively according to *bonitet*, ignores natural-historical conditions, and is insufficient unless stand types are brought in."[86] In choosing to base their prospective management plans explicitly on Morozov's concepts and terms, Gomel'sk and Vologda province joined a growing consensus that the Basic Law did not take proper account of local ecological variations, something only local authorities could do well.[87] By 1924, the upper reaches of the central administration had come to agree. In its organizational plan for 1924–25, TsULR asserted that "the highly variable natural-historical conditions across the broad territory of the forests of the RSFSR require the instructions to reflect better local variation and the importance of stand types."[88]

A related critique of the Basic Law on Forests focused on the suffering dealt to the peasantry by the law's provisions. The head of TsULR, A. I. Shul'ts, recognized all too well the problems the Basic Law's approach to rural politics had caused: "We got too carried away with nationalization and took so many small parcels from the peasants that we produced colossal irregularities in the provinces. They lacked the groves they needed to support their existence. And even worse, we had to increase the number of forest guards to concentrate attention on mere shrubs completely lacking in significance, meanwhile ignoring forests with real value."[89] Relinquishing some authority over the forests would, a regional department head added, "give the peasants the opportunity to obtain the materials they need directly, rather than getting them from us; we will eliminate unauthorized cuts as well as the extensive conflict in the villages."[90] TsULR's executive body (which included Orlov) acknowledged that the economic meaning of the forest had occupied an overly privileged place, to the exclusion of other meanings, when it established as a guiding principle the assertion that "the new forest law should have as its goal not fiscal, but cultural aims."[91] In practice, economic concerns never took second place in Soviet forest management, but the LUK and the TsULR under Shul'ts worked as hard as any agency to balance them with creative solutions to Russia's forest problems.

The Soviet government issued a new law in 1923, aimed at correcting all the shortcomings of the Basic Law on Forests identified by TsULR, LUK, and Narkomzem: the Forest Codex of 1923. The greatest change made by the Forest Codex was the creation of "forests of local significance"—forests given in perpetuity to peasant communes.[92] At least initially, the forests of local significance possessed more symbolic importance than economic, since the transferred forests were by definition the poorest in the country and because they were most often merely returned to the communes that had used them before and after the revolution. However, the forests of local significance reflected the changing forestry debate in the Soviet Union. If henceforth there were to be different forests with different levels of state intervention, then strict centralized control did not represent a universal mandatory policy. At the very least, the new categories of forests signified the trend of NEP forest policy toward the devolution of power to lower-level bodies. TsULR recommended that the "leadership and direction of forest organization work in the provinces should be entrusted to the local inspectors," officials often ready to implement practices more attuned to population and the landscape.[93]

Orlov helped steer the LUK toward policies better attuned to the realities of rural Russia, but at the same time his leadership brought to the fore the still unresolved debates in forest politics, since he remained a fierce critic of socialism and decentralization. While reviewing the work that his new agency had performed just prior to his joining, Orlov concluded in an internally circulated document that "the experience of forest organization activities in 1922–1924 shows the necessity of the centralization of these tasks," at the same time that the chief of Narkomzem, A. I. Shul'ts, was emphasizing the necessity of "a fundamental review of the entire system . . . with the goal of decentralizing authority and bringing the population closer to the forest."[94] Yet because Orlov was the dean of Russian academic foresters, the most accomplished specialist, and the most experienced author of forest organization instructions in the country, Shul'ts deemed his cooperation indispensable. Indeed, Orlov's inclusion in the decision-making process illustrates the tendency during the NEP era for expertise to trump ideological unanimity and highlights the conflicted nature of Soviet forest management in the 1920s, still caught between the various meanings of nationalization.

The conflict came out undeniably into the open with the next task put before Orlov and Narkomzem: the composition of a new set of forest organization instructions, the creation of the document that dictated how to divide and manage the nation's forests. The existing forest organization instructions had by 1925 become a source of irritation for anyone who thought the revolution should have changed forest management, whether in a populist, industrialist, or scientific direction, since the instructions in effect after almost a decade of socialist rule were essentially identical to those formulated by Orlov in 1911. TsULR, for instance, declared in its 1924 operating plan that the instructions did not "correspond to the policy of Soviet power and are inapplicable given the nationalization of the nation's forests."[95] The economic and social foundations of the country, nearly everyone could agree, had changed completely, so why had the methods of forest organization remained static? The next forest organization instructions were expected, like the 1917 revolution, to usher in a totally new order in the Russian forest, although the shape of this new order varied greatly depending on who was speaking.

The views of rank-and-file forest workers, as expressed in *Lesovod* (the journal of the Union of Land and Forest Workers), tended toward a variety of technocratic holism, forest management embracing all aspects of the forest, rather than merely industrial ones. "In the past," said a forester named V. Savich, analyzing Russian forest organization methods in 1924, "research in the Russian forest was conducted almost exclusively focusing on wood mass, but that emphasis, borrowed from the practice of Western European forest management, may not be considered correct here in the Russian forest."[96] Instead, Savich wrote, ideas like those of Morozov deserved to be reconsidered, since Soviet forest management should strive to "understand the nature of the forest as an organism, to comprehend the forest's vital qualities, its sensitivity, its structure, its durability, its regeneration and so forth," or in other words, "the nature of the forest in all its fullness."[97] Other field workers saw in this holistic view of the forest a reflection of a new view of the forester, liberated from the past by the Bolsheviks:

> In tsarist times, I studied in a higher forest school; there I studied natural science, economics, and political economy. Then I fell into the ranger districts. The forester immediately advised me to forget everything I had learned and studied. He told me, "No chemistry, no botany, no geology. Learn how to fill out a forest-cutting ticket." Instead of a laboratory, I wound up in a marketplace. Then came Red October, and the pawns were turned into citizens, builders, and social workers. Now we are training a new cadre of forest specialists, not divorced as before from the scientific way of life.[98]

The import of the Soviet project, for workers like those who published in *Lesovod*, lay in its ability to transform wardens into scientists and lumberjacks into experts who saw the forest not as standing timber, but as "a complex biological formation, a geographical and social phenomenon, subject in its life and development to definite rules"—a formation not unlike a human society.[99]

Academic foresters tended to agree with these views, and many felt that the drafting of new instructions provided the perfect opportunity to revive and implement experimental ideas such as those of Morozov. In 1924, TsULR conducted a survey of prominent academic and professional foresters to ascertain what they wanted to see implemented, and a significant number responded that stand types deserved a larger place in Soviet forest management. Professor Aleksandr Korsh of the Leningrad Forest Institute, for example, after recounting how "Morozov had devoted enormous attention to 'geographical signs in forestry,'" claimed to see evidence that "the ideas of the great teacher are beginning to appear in reality, as a result of today's forest management regionalization—despite the fact that the very opponent of the 'modernism' of stand types, Prof. Orlov, plays such an important role in contemporary forest policy."[100] A group of regional foresters together sent in a survey emphasizing the importance of methods "providing for natural regeneration" (code words for Morozov's prescriptions) in light of the "vast expanses of barren forestland and the difficulty and expense of regenerating such forests."[101] The head of TsULR agreed, though perhaps not with all the particulars, by affirming the need for a "new forest instruction with its center of gravity on natural regeneration, rather than artificial, which is very expensive and difficult."[102]

Industry, too, eagerly anticipated the new instructions, though not because they promised to heighten social mobility or restore ecological balance. Industrial leaders agreed that a new set of instructions, departing radically from existing approaches, was needed, but only so as to maximize industrial output, still hamstrung by the biological considerations. The journal *Lesnoe khoziaistvo, lesopromyshlennost' i toplivo* (the forestry monthly of the VSNKh) frequently gave vent to this point of view: "The copying of earlier methods from the old forest organization instructions," an article from 1923 maintained, "will satisfy no one; our forests do not allow further forest organization according to the old model. Especially outdated is the provision that harvests should not exceed the annual growth of the forests."[103] Orlov's 1911 and 1914 instructions had erred, VSNKh's representative I. I. Iatsenko asserted, in making "forestry considerations rather than economic ones the predominating principles of management," since only the concepts of demand and value could rationally determine the optimal amount of timber to harvest.[104] In addition to rejecting the growth rate of the forest as an upper limit to exploitation, VSNKh dismissed as old-fashioned the division of forests into traditional groves and ranger districts, units built to a more-or-less human scale, preferring instead

larger units predicated upon mechanized modes of transport: "With the expected rebirth of forest organization, a return to the old methods of forest
organization built around grove and ranger district would be a large error—
not a step forward, but back."[105] In sum, VSNKh wanted "forest organizers,
speaking vulgarly, to work as merchants" and wanted the new forest organization instructions to allow the removal of timber in the amount VSNKh requested, regardless of forest conditions, previous treatment, artificially drawn
boundaries, or academic calculations.[106] Only management based on demand,
VSNKh's representatives argued, would facilitate "tight links between forest
management and forest industry."[107] If indeed a new era had dawned, the old
understanding of forest function needed to be reformed into something more
profitable.

Orlov had the unenviable task of reconciling the expanding industrial demands of VSNKh with the renaissance of support for Morozov, while at the
same time remaining true to his own somewhat conservative, German-influ-
enced belief that *bonitet* was the only suitable basis for wise forest management. Complicating the debate was the fact that each side had a valid critique
of the other, and Orlov knew them both well. Experimental ideas about forestry such as stand types were exceedingly difficult to implement in the field
and tended to produce confusion, while unchecked exploitation resulted in ru-
ined forests. So long as sustainable yield and high industrial output remained
explicit aims for Soviet forest management, the status quo, and management
according to *bonitet,* represented the likeliest outcome.

The instructions that Orlov ultimately produced, unsurprisingly, were a
virtual mimeograph of his 1914 instructions, so much so that when they finally
emerged in the summer of 1926, they were presented not as a new set, but as a
mere revision. The changes would have been slighter still had it not been for the
efforts of Morozov's most faithful followers. At the March 1925 Forest Organization Conference, the prominent ecologists Vladimir Nikolaevich Sukachev
and Mikhail Elevfer'evich Tkachenko had openly criticized Orlov for ignoring stand types. Tkachenko argued that organization according to *bonitet* was
a terrible mistake and that only types could provide the basis for sustainable
management. Orlov replied coolly that "the bitter experience of the application
of typology in 1908 had brought even the most eager supporters to reject it"
and asked why anyone would want to repeat that debacle.[108] Sukachev then explained the advantage of stand types, that they contained all the information
that *bonitets* conveyed but added natural-historical considerations that were
too important to ignore. The convention, having heard the two sides, resolved
"that *bonitet* should be the basis of classification of stands during forest organization," but also that "along with *bonitet,* the forest type should be noted by the
forest organizers, and therefore a corresponding general classification of types
should appear in the instructions."[109] Sukachev received the unenviable task of

fulfilling his own request to compile a comprehensive classification, but after a year of work, he informed the Leningrad Forest Society that "in view of the insufficient elaboration of the classification of types, the organization of forests according to type would be at the present time to difficult to implement."[110] Instead, he suggested that the new instructions should require workers to collect data to create maps and tables to help determine their boundaries, so as to provide for the determination of stand types later. When his suggestion was ratified by Narkomzem, stand types again appeared in the forest organization instructions. They occupied, as always, a distinctly secondary position, since Orlov did his best to diminish the importance of "that botanical abracadabra, that strange muddle of *suborevykh suramenei* and *suramennykh suborei.*"[111] Orlov's final instructions allowed only a box for stand types on the organizer's worksheet, but did not contain explicit guidelines about how to fill in this blank or indications of what should be done with the information. Nevertheless, the mere presence of the box on the worksheet kept stand types in the minds of forest organizers—and many found that box most intriguing.[112]

And so, with the publication of the 1926 forest organization instructions, the first effort to Bolshevize the forest reached a dead end. Two decades had passed since Morozov first published his ideas about stand types, two wars and a revolution had brought unimaginable disruption to the forest, but still fighting for acceptance were romantic conservationist ideas about the forest as a social organism, and still opposed were industrialists who wanted to extract maximum value, allied out of convenience with Mikhail Mikhailovich Orlov, who most of all wanted a well-ordered, mathematical forest. Perhaps Morozov's ideas had gained some popularity because of the enhanced social position of workers, who saw in Morozov's teachings a chance to elevate themselves from lumberjacks to scientists, but industrial interests never suffered for lack of support in the Soviet Union.

Likewise, the prerevolutionary dispute about the correct role of the peasant in forest management remained alive. Although NEP-era policies brought about a shift away from the traditional European model that entrusted forest management exclusively to trained professionals, the momentum of the times promised even more peasant involvement. After granting the peasantry their own woodlands in the form of the "forests of local significance," Narkomzem and TsULR adopted the slogan "Turn to the village" and tried to effect a *smychka,* or alliance, with the rural population so as to involve them in the life of the forest.[113] In 1922, even before the forests of local significance were turned over to the villages, the head of TsULR was stating publicly that "the reason for unauthorized cuts in the village is not the 'basic criminality of the people,' as some think, but economic conditions in the village; when our administration moves toward the people, the results are perfect."[114] The "hero bees," those countless anonymous but dedicated local forest workers, were called on to cooperate in this endeavor, "to overcome one's fear of the masses and help the peasants understand proper forest management, for only by means of persistent social work among the peasantry will the active protection of the forest be possible."[115] The TsULR and the Union of Land and Forest Workers, hoping to win the "confidence of the broad peasant masses," encouraged foresters to "abandon the formal letter of the law and become 'public representatives of forestry'" and leaders of a new village intelligentsia that "spoke the peasants' language and worked to find ways to satisfy the peasants' needs."[116]

The efforts of the TsULR, however, reached beyond mere rhetoric about a friendly rural technocracy and toward meaningful action. Peasants were once again invited to take temporary control of forestlands directly after logging, in the belief that agricultural use killed off pests in the soil and inoculated future forests against infestation. After three years of cultivation, peasants were required to "plant in the last year the seeds of coniferous species, instead of grain," and return the land to TsULR.[117] Perhaps, it was hypothesized, even the peasant habit of grazing animals in the forest, which had long been taboo among foresters, might actually be integrated in forest regeneration, since "many foresters had occasion to notice that the pasturing of cattle can bring about an abundance of new growth, because cattle eat the grassy cover that hinders forest regeneration, pigs turn the soil with their snouts and fertilize the soil, and dung beetles (following after the cattle and swine) stir up and make available soil nutrients."[118] In 1924, peasants in the southern and southeastern provinces of the RSFSR were offered government assistance for the crop failure of that year in return for participation in afforestation work, and the work, it was reported, was completed in full with "half of the work done without pay."[119] Beyond direct participation in afforestation work, peasants were offered tax incentives to cooperate in forestry work and free timber in exchange for clearing state land from logging rubbish and brushwood.[120]

Perhaps the most charming element of the proposed *smychka* between commune and ranger district was the invention of a new holiday for the village: Forest Day. Forest Day first appeared in Russia in 1898, imported from America by the Southern Russian Society for Acclimatization. The earliest Russian efforts, focused more on increasing the leafiness of Russia's southern regions than public education, enjoyed their widest success in the years directly preceding World War I.[121] TsULR revived the holiday in 1922, but changed its emphasis so as to "lay the foundations for a proper relationship between the peasantry and forest workers, to engender a protective attitude toward the forest, to propagandize the forest's economic and natural-historical significance, and to encourage a desire to associate with nature."[122] In many places, Forest Day merely offered children a pleasant break from their schoolhouse routines, a chance to spend a lovely spring day outside planting trees in gardens and around communal buildings, but the planned lectures and activities often reached more broadly: "Both old folks and young listened in silence, and it was clear that they understood every word and each made a great impression. Accidentally one seedling fell from a wheelbarrow, and a gray old man found it and brought it to the planting site with the words 'This tree I will plant for my grandson.' It became clear that these new forests would be valuable to those who had created them, for he who plants a forest will not hurt it with his own hands."[123] The nominal head of state of the Soviet Union, Mikhail Kalinin, endorsed the attempt to alter the peasantry's perception of nature, writing that people "accustomed to planting trees will develop a different attitude to the destruction of the forest, a psychological feeling we should develop to a maximum degree," and the state, in backing him up, relied on materials both written by Morozov and inspired by him.[124] In the book *Den' lesa* (Forest Day), published in 1924 to publicize the new holiday, readers learned how important it was "to recognize that the forest is not a simple gathering of trees, but a very complex social organism, constructed according to its own social laws and consisting of tight and permanent bonds between everything living there."[125] For the entirety of the 1920s, the most popular guidebook used by teachers planning Forest Day field trips was a pedagogical pamphlet written by Morozov, his 1909 work *An Excursion into the Forest*.[126] Thus, at the local level, the *smychka* between city and country also provided a conduit for the most challenging conclusions of scientific thinking to reach forest workers thrust into positions of authority and through them the rural population.

Despite the renaissance of interest in Morozov's ideas, his followers feared that his legacy would become, like the forests themselves, another casualty of revolutionary chaos. In June of that year, a worried note appeared in the journal *Lesovod*: "Near Simferopol there is a precious but forgotten grave, that of our teacher Georgii Fedorovich Morozov. We cannot allow this grave to be lost, and yet this could occur, since the gravesite has already fallen into decay; it is not fenced, and wandering cattle graze nearby. We propose opening a subscription for the construction of a monument at the grave of Morozov, and hope that foresters from across the Union will respond to this call."[127] The subscription went poorly, and only enough money to construct a humble, low fence was collected. But the contributors met at the grave the next spring to mark the completion of the fence and the seventh anniversary of Morozov's death. An impromptu speech was read aloud:

> To your grave, our teacher-creator,
> We haven't brought thoughtful speeches or garlands.
> But we have gathered as one, as a family,
> Illuminated by the light of love.
> All of your ardor, all your great passion for creation,
> Shines like a bright star, showing the path
> Along which we must walk without doubt.[128]

The gathered pledged not to allow the grave to remain forgotten, but little did they know that even more serious challenges awaited them. The revolution that Morozov had cautiously welcomed unleashed the same fury that revolutions always bring to forests, driving him to his grave in the process. And yet the revolution was still not over.

CLEAR-CUT

The Forest Felled by the Five-Year Plan

Pioneer species thrive on disturbed ground, places where the rapid destruction of the prior occupants has freed up resources for new inhabitants. Soon after colonizing an area, they begin to compete aggressively with one another and crowd each other out. In the absence of further disturbances, they will then recede into a secondary role in a forest under members of "climax species"— that is, larger, slower-growing trees that need stable conditions to germinate and survive. Climax species cannot live in the unsettled places where pioneers thrive. Every human-wrought clear-cut is thus a kind of revolution in the forest, destroying the evolved environment that allows climax species to generate and thrive and making space for pioneer species.

The disturbance that struck the Russian forestry community at the time of the Bolshevik revolution was more ground fire or windstorm than clear-cut. The nation's most stately oaks—true rarities of world significance—were lost, and much of the ground cover burned off, but the ideological ecosystem regenerated much as it had been before. Structures and relationships similar to pre-revolutionary ones reappeared within a few years. The crackling, unresolved tension between Russia's agrarian *demos* and its cosmopolitan ruling class, between rural and urban culture, between Old Russia and the West—the tension that underlies the works of Tolstoy, Dostoevsky, and Morozov—persisted and continued to influence government decisions, including forest policy. The forest maintained its important cultural, economic, and historic position in daily life and the national consciousness. No real attempt to change the forest's meaning had been introduced; universities and forest schools offered at least as much latitude for heterodox scholarship as did the tsarist system, and Morozov's philosophy survived, sheltered among populations of enthusiasts who embraced his brand of *modernizm*.[1] Moreover, his ideas had fallen on fertile soil and spread in the years following the revolution, since many forest workers pulled into positions of authority by the disappearance of the old tsarist forest guard found his holistic forest science more appealing than the clerical drudgery of traditional forest work. As traumatic as the era of war and revolution had been, the soil of Russian culture continued to support a diversity of opinion about the meaning of the Russian forest.

This survival of conflicting viewpoints frustrated advocates of industrial might, who feared that their chance to remake the Russian forest had been lost. Those in charge of meeting quotas wanted to convert the forest into something more strongly resembling a machine, but the revolutionary era had come and gone without establishing mechanism as the dominant approach to forestry. Even more discouraging for the industrialists was the fact that conservation had not merely survived the revolution—its proponents had climbed back into positions of power, and thus by the mid-1920s, the political situation favored conservationism and peasant control. The tsarist-era forest professoriate, with its insistent emphasis on biological limitations, had come to dominate Narkomzem, and as the 1920s drew to an end, VSNKh saw Narkomzem invading ever more of its institutional territory, assisted by allies at higher levels of the government. Meanwhile, a vast swathe of forests near the villages had been given over to the peasants to manage as they saw fit. Clearly, the Bolshevik revolution had not brought radicalism to the forest, and a different approach would be needed to alter the balance if the industrializers were to win a resounding victory.

Fortunately for the radicals, Stalin's "Great Break" provided a perfect setting to bring a second revolution to the forest. Beginning in 1929, the Soviet Union announced its first Five-Year Plan, an aggressive campaign of industrialization, with enormous targets set for iron and steel output, coal and gas production, and new factory construction. New industrial complexes were planned and built throughout the country, sometimes in previously uninhabited areas, requiring huge amounts of timber for construction and fuel. Accompanying the industrial push was a renewed propaganda campaign that championed the power of humanity, if properly organized, to surmount the limitations that constrained the bourgeois world—"there is no fortress that Bolsheviks cannot storm" was the slogan of the day. The industrialists fully capitalized on the opportunity: if the ground fire they set in 1918 had failed to remove the existing ideological ecosystem, then in 1929 their methods would be much more aggressive. They lobbied for and won complete control of the forest, chased their opponents from their jobs, imported and installed a completely new and untested forestry theory, and succeeded in making assertions of biological limitations on economic growth politically untenable. Yet despite these successes, the Politburo gave clear signs throughout the entire episode that the maximalist program of the industrialists was not the leadership's preference, as though the Communist Party were harnessing radicalism more than initiating it. The second revolution in the forest was more radical and much more successful than the first, and it succeeded in permanently altering the course of Russian forestry, although at a cost that even the Politburo recognized was much too high.

It was the publication of the 1926 forest organization instructions that spurred the industrialists to renew their push for a mechanical forest. For the first two-thirds of the 1920s, the imminent publication of new forest organization instructions encouraged most observers, conservationists and industrialists alike, to wait for changes rather than engage in polemics. A conference called by the Central Administration of the Forests of the Republic (TsULR) in March 1923, for instance, "foundered on a series of fundamental disagreements about the best basic organizational unit . . . but decided to table the matter until the publication of the new instructions of Professor Mikhail Orlov."[2] When the first drafts of the instructions began to circulate in 1925, however, and all concerned parties saw that the rules presented a compromise and would not usher in the new era of forest management that they had expected, the patient waiting came to an end. The editors of *Lesovod*, the journal of the Union of Land and Forest Workers, noted with frustration that "forest management, regardless of nine years of the dictatorship of the proletariat, has scarcely changed at all" and urged the union of forest and agricultural workers to address the question of "sovietizing forest management in general, of the maximal rationalization of all branches of the economy."[3] However, *Lesovod*'s "rationalization" was entirely compatible with conservationism, and the criticisms leveled by the Union of Foresters remained mild. In contrast, the journal *Lesnoe khoziaistvo, lesopromyshlennost' i toplivo,* the organ of the VSNKh, began to print ever sharper critiques of the 1926 instructions. Direct attacks on Orlov and his forest theories, based as they were on concepts of sustainable yield that industrialists believed were outmoded, appeared with greater frequency, and a push for a completely new, Bolshevik forest science coalesced.

This new Bolshevik forestry was primarily the work of a colleague of Orlov's from the Leningrad Forest Institute named Sergei Alekseevich Bogoslovskii.[4] Bogoslovskii contended that Orlov (and Russian forest management in general) had arrived at a dead end not because of excessive German influence, as Morozov had claimed, but rather because the German trend of abstraction had not been followed closely enough. Although Orlov had almost single-handedly popularized the German forest management concept of *bonitet* in Russia in the late nineteenth century, his research since then had focused on applying *bonitet* more than on importing additional foreign techniques.[5]

In the meantime, however, much had changed in German forest management. Territory lost in World War I reduced the size of the German forest from 14.2 million hectares to 13 million, and the concomitant economic collapse and impoverishment of the country, according to one Russian observer, "forced German foresters to search for new paths to restore the productivity of their forests, since the old methods turned out to be excessively scholastic and timid."[6] In February 1923, Bogoslovskii first drew attention to one such promising German innovation, a method called "flying management," which promised to allow much more intensive harvesting of timber while maintaining sustainability, or at least the outward appearance of sustainability. Bogoslovskii explained that eastern Prussia was much more heavily wooded than western Prussia, yet less populated, and thus there was a shortage of timber in the west and a surplus in the east. In order to maximize output without overtaxing the resource on a national level, Prussian foresters suggested preserving the western forests while increasing the take of timber in the east. Provided that the unit of analysis was large enough to encompass unexploited forests, this approach allowed individual groves to be logged at levels far exceeding annual growth. In recommending flying management for Russian forestry, Bogoslovskii again raised the question about Russia's relationship with Europe: "If the idea has been accepted in such a densely populated and industrialized country as Prussia, then why should we keep with our old methods?"[7]

Flying management held such great promise for Bogoslovskii because its adoption would allow Russian forest managers to use the immense untouched forests of Siberia in their calculations of sustainable yield, still a guiding consideration for Soviet forest management throughout the 1920s. To provide an example, a forest grove with an annual growth of one hundred cubic meters, according to the conventional understanding of the concept of sustainable yield, cannot yield more timber than that in any given year. The advantage of flying management lay in the realization that managers could, for the sake of convenience, combine two different forests (even if separated by hundreds of kilometers) and concentrate the logging scheduled for both forests in just one; one forest could thus supply two hundred cubic meters if another were left untouched.

Flying management offered limited utility in the Prussian setting, where "credit forests" existed only in restricted quantities, but its possibilities staggered the imagination in Russia, where immense Siberian forests lay completely untapped. If an entire region, or the country as a whole, were accepted as the unit of management, then truly stupendous harvests were possible, since annual growth could be taken from only the most accessible regions of an enormous area, without violating—from this perspective—the demands of sustainable use. For example, in 1923, Soviet loggers gathered 62 million cubic meters of timber. The next year brought a significant jump to 74 million cubic meters, an increase of almost 20 percent.[8] This harvest likely exceeded annual growth in the forests where the logging actually took place, but the yields were far from excessive for the Soviet Union as a single unit, since annual growth for the nation's forests as a whole was estimated at 349 million cubic meters.

Bogoslovskii also claimed that the demographic realities of the Soviet Union favored focusing logging in large, contiguous spaces, rather than small, isolated ones. "Given the vast unpopulated and roadless regions of the USSR," he argued, "only cuts concentrated near capital investments such as suitable roads and workers' living quarters offer realistic chances for profitable development."[9] Soviet foresters, Bogoslovskii proposed, should broaden their horizons as the Germans had and look beyond the boundaries of the ranger districts, for such units were far too small to allow for a properly industrialized forest. "Luckily," he wrote, "more and more accepted is the thought that forest management should not restrict itself to the composition of self-contained cutting plans and methods of regeneration, but strive for the solution of much larger problems"—namely, the "fullest possible interlinking of interests of forest industry and forest management."[10] In practical terms, "interlinking of interests" meant subjugation of the interests of forest management to the demands of forest industry.

Bogoslovskii developed his analysis of German forest management further in his 1925 work *Novye techeniia v lesoustroistve* (New Currents in Forest Organization), the book that placed him at the center of the forestry debate in the Soviet Union. In *New Currents,* Bogoslovskii reviewed an array of developments in German forestry and found that they shared in common a rejection of the "periodic method," the practice of dividing forests into relatively small, discrete, and homogeneous units and tapping them for resources at predetermined points in time. Unlike his earlier article from 1923, when Bogoslovskii recommended balancing large harvests from small parcels with lower harvests from other parcels, *New Currents* recommended using large units, on the regional or even national scale, as the basis for forest organization. Claiming that the Soviet Union faced "completely new problems, solvable only by seeing the entire economy as an organism, with all parts developing according to defined interrelations," he called for the "liberation of forest management from excessive regimentation in forest organization" and the formulation of new rules that would allow timber to be extracted in the needed quantities.[11]

Although Bogoslovskii offered a wide range of recommendations, all of them pragmatic and none of them even remotely inspired by Marxist theory, his readers seized upon his proindustrial claims to the exclusion of his other advice as the basis for a new proletarian forestry. Soon after the publication of *New Currents,* echoes of Bogoslovskii's arguments began to appear in *Lesnoe khoziaistvo, lesomprmyshlennost' i toplivo:* "If the earlier forest organization was based on ideas about independent forest groves and their independent forest organization, at odds with the approach of the rest of the world, then the new forest organization should be based on the idea of the unity of the country. . . . The practical application of these ideas leads to the division of the country's forests into zones, provinces, and regions."[12] Behind the scenes, the state economic planning commission (Gosplan) and VSNKh started exploring the possibility of implementing concentrated cuts throughout the union, although usually using camouflaged language. In January 1925, the head of the state planning agency announced that his agricultural experts had "raised questions about the necessity of linking forest management at the all-union scale," the first step "to revise the forest law of the USSR, permeated with attempts to protect the forest from depredation and to increase the forest area."[13] Three months later, VSNKh's organ in the northwest region "convened a conference to review the practices of the region, with the goal of increasing the income of forests and adjusting rotations to meet the changing demands of the market, including the overseas market."[14] Bogoslovskii's personal star rose, as well. After he urged the "rejection of the principle of regular harvests of timber according to groves and the acceptance of increased exploitation of regions" at the semiannual 1925 national forest organization conference, he was given the task of drafting a proposal to implement these ideas.[15] (Orlov, however, was present at the 1925 meeting and was able to avert a policy shift by convincing the conference that the existing norms and rotations were well-grounded: 120 years for pine and spruce groves of *bonitet* I and Ia, 100 for *bonitet* II and III, and 80 for IV and V.)

Orlov criticized Bogoslovskii's ideas for their myopia, but his comments only served to popularize the controversial aspects of *New Currents,* because Orlov held such an influential position in the forestry community and because Orlov wrote almost nothing about those aspects of Bogoslovskii's theory with which he agreed. Orlov, in fact, harbored no categorical opposition to most of the content of *New Currents,* including the concept of concentrated cutting, a practice he recommended in certain cases. Concentrated cutting had a place in Russian forestry, Orlov believed, especially in the far north, where most forests had aged such that their annual growth (and hence their annual economic productivity) had reached zero; these forests required concentrated cutting so as to again become productive.[16] Although special care needed to be taken when conducting concentrated cuts in the far north, since removing the tree cover quickly from a northern Russian forest often left behind a miry swamp, such exploitation belonged in the forester's repertoire provided that the loggers also dug canals to draw off the extra water. What Orlov objected to was Bogoslovskii's suggestion that concentrated cutting deserved universal application in Russia. The risks of this approach were all too easy to predict: Bogoslovskii's methods "can in no way be recognized as correct, since in practice half of his management units would be mature forest, and the other half be completely barren, conditions barely describable as providing for strict sustainable use."[17]

Orlov foresaw all too clearly what would happen if Bogoslovskii's recommendations were followed: forests designated for logging would be leveled, and reserved forests would come to shelter the only usable timber. Thereafter managers would be forced to tap the forests held in reserve. Even worse, in Orlov's opinion, was Bogoslovskii's rhetorical method, decidedly out of step with Orlov's conception of scholarly propriety. Bogoslovskii substituted "criticism and heaps of phantoms" for factual argumentation and wrapped himself in the "beautiful banner of freedom and independence of scientific thought, meanwhile placing his opponent under the old banner of dogmatism and scholasticism."[18] A new era of scholarly argumentation was just beginning in 1925—it was becoming sufficient, even in scientific circles, to label an opponent's idea as reactionary to gain the upper hand in a debate—and Orlov, clearly, was not prepared.

Rhetorical strategies aside, Bogoslovskii's prescriptions gained immediate and widespread support in part because they reflected a gnawing suspicion among some Soviet foresters that German forest management, and thus the most modern available technique, was leaving them behind. Perhaps the uncertainty of the NEP era drove Soviet foresters to seek an established example worthy of emulation, just as the founders of Russian forest management had done in the nineteenth century. Whatever the cause, Germany emerged once again as the standard against which a growing number measured the Russian forest. One forester lamented the condition of Russian forestry in *Lesovod*: "In the capitals of noise, a war of words is being waged: *Dauerwald,* forest aviation, the mysteries of Wagner, Muller, Viberke . . . but in the depths of Russia, an eternal silence. Moribund forest management formulas, cattle in the forest, the deadening yoke of office work. The chasm between the capitals and the depths of Russia, between forest science and forest practice, is just as enormous as ever."[19] The vitality of the forestry debate in Germany also inspired dispirited envy in Russian observers. After returning from a visit to Germany, for example, Professor E. P. Damberg argued in a January 1925 report to the Leningrad Forest Society that "remnants of tsarist practices" were blocking the path to progress in the Russian forest and that "from the point of view of new currents in Germany, contemporary Russian forest management is characterized by obsolete concepts, technical backwardness, inertness, and a formulaic quality out of step with new German forestry ideas."[20]

Other contemporary critiques suggested that Russian cultural habits were to blame for the situation, since they encouraged passivity and emulation, rather than the feverish originality that drove German forest management ever further ahead. One forestry professor asked, "We with our pure Russian kindheartedness laugh at German foresters and their passion to publish their smallest conclusions, every little trifle, . . . but does this not provide a clue to the secret of German progress?"[21] "Immediately it strikes you," another professor just returned from a 1928 sabbatical to Germany reported, "the high level and wide distribution of new ideas in the sphere of organization and care for the soil"; if matching the productivity of German academia lay beyond the bounds of realistic possibility, he suggested, then perhaps the USSR could borrow and apply some of Germany's best achievements, so that "eighty years hence socialist Russia will not be in a position to rue the imprudent management we are about to implement."[22] For Bogoslovskii and many of his readers, the revolution had not liberated Russia from its innate conservatism or imparted the dynamism that the modern age required, but perhaps Germany could show the way.

Some worried about where all this Germanophilia might lead. A 1926 article in *Lesovod* recommended paying heed to the old Russian saying "What is good for the Russian is death for the German" (*Chto russkomu zdorovo, to nemtsu smert'*), arguing that "forest management conducted in Russia according to these new German rules, especially in the north, would bring only harm."[23] Morozov's students, most notably Mikhail Tkachenko, continued to stress the importance of stand types for regions such as the Russian north—the region that had inspired Morozov in the first place, since only stand types recognized the special requirements of spaces like the tundra and the taiga. At the 1925 forest organization conference, Tkachenko maintained the "impossibility of applying a single formula for the support of all of the north's varied forms . . . when only management connected with the natural-historical conditions of each region is warranted."[24] Others wondered why they had studied Russian conditions at all, if industrial demand was to be the only focus: "Why did I graduate from an institute, why did I need a higher education? Why do we need a forest organization . . . if we recognize only clear-cuts, which we took from the Varangians? Why do we need forest science, . . . entomology, dendrology, or botany at all? We need only to cut and sell, and you need not be a genius for this—this could be done by a miller, a hairdresser, or a jurist."[25] The German track record also prompted serious doubts: "Where has the Saxon enthusiasm for financial considerations brought them?" one follower of Morozov asked. "Where are the results, the brilliantly regenerated forests? On the contrary, their enthusiasm has brought only negative results."[26] German yields were higher than Russian yields, but whether this was due to better ecological conditions, more intensive forest maintenance, unsustainable practices, or German superiority remained a matter of bitter dispute.[27]

Thus, the shape of the Soviet forestry debate in the late 1920s came to mirror innumerable other clashes between intellectuals of the tsarist era and younger radical communists, although with one crucial difference: in the forestry debate, Europe represented the progressive force. In most other intellectual conflicts of the 1920s, older intellectuals were charged with "spreading ideologically dangerous doctrines of Western origin among Soviet youth" or with promoting "bourgeois pessimism and fatalism about the future."[28] Especially in arguments related to economic production, experts were frequently accused of citing European methods in order to undermine Soviet industrial progress.[29] In the contest for control of forest management, however, the roles were reversed: reformers, with their allies in the industrial bureaus, agitated

in favor of the adoption of German methods that deemphasized local variation so as to increase output, while their opponents, who hoped to retain (and
strengthen) forest laws that recognized the uniqueness of Russian conditions,
were accused of obstructionism. Orlov, as always, found himself caught some-
where in between.

German forest management in the 1920s was itself undergoing a period
of critical self-evaluation. Morozov was not alone in disliking the mechanistic quality of classical German forestry, with its reliance on clear-cuts, even-
aged management, and vast plantations of biologically undemanding Scotch
pine (*Pinus sylvestris*) and Norway spruce (*Picea abies*); as early as 1824, prominent German foresters had expressed personal dissatisfaction with the "wood
factories" that their methods engendered.[30] The profitability of German high
forestry ensured that no serious alternative emerged for the duration of the
nineteenth century, and indeed, the approach proved so successful that not
only Russia but England, France, and the United States adopted it in whole or
in part. Nevertheless, the turmoil of the postwar period drove German foresters to reevaluate all their assumptions, including those about the way that forests should look.

The most significant product of the reappraisal was *Dauerwald,* or the
"continuously productive forest," certainly the most important development
in German forest management of the early twentieth century. As *Dauerwald*'s
formulator, Alfred Möller, first explained in 1920, stewards seeking to create
continuously productive forests should make choices based upon a concep-
tualization of the woodland as a "living whole consisting of many thousands
of independent parts, each with its own defined significance in equilibrium
with the others."[31] Disturbances to this equilibrium, such as those occasioned
by logging, damaged the organism measurably by removing certain nutrients
from the soil but also harmed it subjectively by making an unpleasant impression upon the human visitor. Möller equated a forest's beauty with its health
and, basing his conclusions on the experiments of a previously unknown forest
owner named von Kalitsch, showed that management emphasizing aesthetics
could substantially improve the soil quality and even double the annual yield
of timber. The key to such dramatic improvement lay in encouraging "har-
mony" in the forest, but unlike Morozov, who focused on fashioning a distinct approach to every forest, Möller felt that all forests required the same
basic treatment to achieve their ideal states. He prescribed for all forests the
"abandonment of the idea of the normal forest, the normal distribution of age-
classes, and rotation," and instead aimed to improve the forest's health by removing individual trees with poor growth rates, leaving the robust remainder
to seed the stronger future forest.[32] If the forest was indeed an organism, then
Möller believed that humans could improve it—they could make it tougher by
making it more beautiful.

Möller's ideas spurred a vigorous debate in German forestry circles in the

1920s, with some hailing *Dauerwald* as a panacea and others dismissing it either as fraud or as old wine in new skins, but it might have faded into permanent obscurity if not for the Nazis and their *Reichforstmeister,* Hermann Göring. Möller's experimental forest, Berenthoren, was the target of sixteen hundred pilgrimages in 1921 alone, but the ardor for *Dauerwald* rapidly cooled, such that by 1925 the All-Union Congress of German Foresters accepted a resolution stating that "failures of *Dauerwald* will lead, undoubtedly, to the destruction and spoliation of the German forest, cultivated with labor and love." By the end of the decade, no state institution and very few private forest owners adhered to the theory's precepts.[33] In 1933, however, shortly after the Nazi accession to power, Göring visited one of the few forests in Germany still following Möller's prescriptions and immediately saw the tremendous propaganda potential of *Dauerwald.* He subsequently mandated *Dauerwald* as the official silvicultural system for the Third Reich. *Dauerwald,* one recent account argues, appealed to Göring and the Nazi sensibility in general because of its "'organic structure,' [because] it comprised only native species, and [because] it was a collective and perpetual entity that had no fixed morphology or life span"—or alternatively, in Göring's words, because "eternal forest and eternal nation are ideas that are indissolubly linked."[34] Soon, though, the demands of the war economy, as well as Göring's preference for forests that offered greater hunting opportunities, made *Dauerwald* inconvenient. The Nazis moved on to a more accommodating system in 1937.[35]

Dauerwald's popularity in Russia followed a different trajectory. Although many of the same impulses drove *Dauerwald* and Morozov's proposed reforms, including the belief that native forests were growing sick because of forestry's insistence upon imposing an artificial, mathematical, and overly rigid regimen on nature, *Dauerwald* developed its own distinct constituency in Russia in the 1920s. The Leningrad Forest Society heard a report on 26 September 1924 "expressing the hope that the importance of this new revolutionary idea in forestry—the uninterrupted forest—could as soon as possible be appreciated among specialist foresters and that its suitability and applicability for the forests of the Soviet Union be verified."[36] Later that year the Leningrad Agricultural Institute began testing *Dauerwald* at its Pashe-Kapetskoe experimental forestry station. Although some disputed whether the haphazard practices there could be described as *Dauerwald,* the trials went well enough that five years later one of Narkomzem's advisors claimed that the "path toward raising the productivity of the soil is the path toward *Dauerwald.*"[37] Even Orlov, who largely dedicated his career to the establishment of regularized forest management, seemed swayed by the tide, arguing at least once in print that "the guiding principle for Russian forest management should be the rejection of the periodic method and the gradual transition to parcel-based or free management."[38]

Russian interest in *Dauerwald* underscores, perhaps better than any other phenomenon, the wildly divergent forces in Soviet forestry in the 1920s. At the same time that Narkomzem was struggling with VSNKh to determine the extent of permissible logging, a related but discrete debate persisted about the role of German ideas in Russian forestry—and for the first time, in the late 1920s, the meaning of the German approach to the forest ramified confusingly. Whereas in the nineteenth and early twentieth centuries, German forestry had attracted (or repelled) Russian foresters for its aura of order and precision, by the late 1920s the unity had been replaced by a baffling cacophony of approaches, some reassuringly conservative and formulaic, others holistic and reminiscent of Morozov's homegrown forest sociology, and still others aggressively exploitative and industrially oriented. More was at stake than the allowable annual harvest of timber: Russians had to decide whether their forests should resemble those of their most prominent cultural influence—whether the Soviet Union would move toward the world or make a world of itself. As they had by adopting Marx, Russians did both, crafting an exceptionalism predicated on foreign ideas.

When the first Soviet attempt to resolve the conflict, the 1926 forest organization instructions, was released, and their cautious, decidedly nonrevolutionary content became evident to all, VSNKh and its allied bureaus, the People's Commissariat of Finance (Narkomfin) and the state economic planning commission (Gosplan), redoubled their efforts to check the influence of Orlov, Narkomzem, and the Forestry Scholar Committee (LUK). Voices from inside Narkomzem expressed dissatisfaction as well, but whereas foresters allied with Narkomzem wanted to refine existing concepts, VSNKh, Gosplan, and Narkomfin wanted wholesale change.[39] They wanted to abandon forest management based upon the ranger district and instead implement logging plans centered on the region or province as the unit of analysis, with the chips falling where they may, as an author in *Torgovo-promyshlennaia gazeta* (The Trade-Industry Newspaper) made clear: "We should not worry ourselves with fears about the deforestation of certain regions—even if this changes the character of regions such as Smolensk, Kostroma, Tver, Novgorod, and others entirely. If all the forests of these regions were to be cut down, then these regions could be converted into areas suitable for the development of grain crops. No one will suffer from such a change; on the contrary, those 'rotten places' on the map will disappear."[40] Here, the author uses the phrase "rotten places" to refer to forested land, providing some insight into the priorities of forest radicals.

Although industrialists demonstrated terrific enthusiasm for flying management, when they offered the theory to the highest levels of the Soviet government, they encountered remarkably little success. The struggle over flying management represented forestry's own version of the conflict between radicals and traditionalists that was playing out in many spheres of Russian society. In most cases, Party leadership supported the radical side of the debate, or the side that could successfully present itself as the more radical, proletarian, or industrial. But in the forestry debate, Party leadership consistently sided with the moderate group, the conservationists.[41] The reason for the difference cannot be known with certainty, but perhaps the symbolic value of forests, or perhaps a belief among the Soviet leadership that efficient resource use was a hallmark of communist economic planning, can explain why Party leadership repeatedly foiled the attempts to radicalize forestry in the 1920s.

In 1926, for instance, VSNKh asked the People's Commissariat of Peasants'-Workers' Inspectorate (Rabkrin) to investigate Narkomzem's logging performance over the past years, in the hopes that the inspectorate would find Narkomzem's productivity lacking and reduce its purview. "VSNKh," Rabkrin reported, "in its presentations to this body has attempted to prove that Narkomzem cannot satisfy in full the needs of transport and forest industry . . . and advances a claim about the necessity of linking the existing system with the fulfillment of industrial plans."[42] The industrial bureaus claimed that its various subdepartments required 2,487,293 cubic *sazhens* of timber, and that the Commissariat of Transport needed 755,585, but Narkomzem had only supplied them with 2,914,000, an 11 percent shortfall. If Narkomzem could not remedy this shortfall, VSNKh argued, then its authority over the forest should be curtailed. Rabkrin, however, did not see things this way. Dealing a harsh blow to VSNKh's aspirations, the inspectorate concluded that it was possible either "to satisfy the annual petitions of VSNKh in full, and consequently to travel further toward the destruction of the forest, as well as to ignore the needs of the rural population and the cities," or "to bring proper forest management to the nation's groves."[43] Noting that similar petitions had been reviewed and denied many times by many different bodies—including the Supreme Economic Council (EKOSO) on 18 May and 3 September 1925, the Council of People's Commissars (Sovnarkom SSSR) in May 1925, and the presidium of the Supreme Executive Committee (VTsIK) on 20 July 1925, Rabkrin sided with Narkomzem, endorsing Narkomzem's right to "determine which forestlands will be made available for exploitation and to balance the needs of the state forest consumers," thereby simultaneously spoiling VSNKh's designs for increased control over forestland and acknowledging that Soviet control figures had run ahead of reality.[44] In short, Rabkrin opted to support Narkomzem in its conclusion that "the demands of VSNKh exceed the available resources by more than one million cubic sazhens" and thus supported the policy that industry should accustom itself to work with less timber, in accordance with scientific limitations.[45]

When Rabkrin revisited the matter in October 1928, after the acceptance of the first Five-Year Plan, its disdain for what it saw as the wastefulness of the industrial bureaus had only sharpened. VSNKh again grumbled that its allotments were too low, since out of a possible 700 million cubic meters of annual growth, its bureaus had access to only 110 million, and that countries as small as Finland and Sweden had more success on the export market as a result.[46] But rather than assent that the answer lay in relaxing standards, Rabkrin provided VSNKh with a long list of improvements that would increase harvests without felling more forests:

A. The length of the workday and the season of labor in the forest should be lengthened;
B. Timber left behind in the forest should be reduced;
C. The use of small branches, treetops, and other refuse should be rationalized;
D. Loggers should be supplied with tools of best quality;
E. The technical qualifications of logging personnel should be increased.[47]

Rabkrin thereby reaffirmed its insistence on sustainable yield as a guiding principle; if this principle entailed timber shortages, then logging firms were expected to work toward increased efficiency.

Rabkrin's support of conservationism, and more specifically, Narkomzem's version of conservationism, carries special significance because the agency was close to the very pinnacles of Soviet power. E. A. Rees claims that although Rabkrin was initially intended to be "a party watchdog," it was later "ruthlessly adapted to the Politburo's needs" and over time became "a powerful instrument to control the party-state apparatus."[48] Rabkrin's directors (in 1925 Valerian Kuibyshev and from 1926 to 1930 Sergo Ordzhonikidze) were both Stalin's close colleagues, as well as future members of the Politburo. If it is true that Rabkrin functioned "as the party Central Committee's agent for the control and supervision of industry," then it is unlikely that it would have published a major report whose findings irritated the members of that body.[49] And because Rabkrin specialized in finding ways to maximize industrial productivity without making new investments by exploiting overlooked resources and capacity, its decision to thwart VSNKh's plans by endorsing conservationism was entirely consonant with its mission.[50]

Like Rabkrin, the Union of Land and Forest Workers played an important role in countering the arguments of the forest radicals and steering the central government toward accepting ecological considerations as a guiding principle of forest policy. The central committee of the union, its reports and documents make clear, zealously endorsed sustainable practices in forestry and moreover hoped that the future would allow Morozov's ideas to gain traction. Its 1926 report to Sovnarkom SSSR expressed concern that

> fiscal goals overwhelmingly dominate our forest management. The damage caused by this approach, due to the insufficient attention to restorative processes in the forest, will be felt only after fifty to eighty years. . . . Too prevalent is the deeply mistaken view that the "forest grows itself" and that the state need only protect the forest and allot it to consumers. Instead, all work in the forest should assist the retention and restoration of the forests; in forest science there exists the indisputable argument that "the cut of the forest is the initial

process of its regeneration." In the future it will be necessary to move toward restorative processes in the forest, since only then will the industrialization of the economy be possible.[51]

Not only did the report warn against the dangers of unchecked exploitation, practices characterized as "backward and excessively conservative," but it explicitly proposed Morozov's teachings as a progressive alternative by paraphrasing his central dictum, "The cut and the regeneration are synonyms"—another indication that his philosophy had penetrated the rank and file of forestry workers.[52]

The opinions of the central committee of this union are noteworthy, beyond what they indicate about the forestry debate in the period before the announcement of the first Five-Year Plan, because they had a direct influence upon Soviet government decisions. On 16 May 1927, Aleksei Rykov, the chair of Sovnarkom and of the Council of Labor and Defense, called upon the president of the union's central committee, requesting assistance in drafting new forest legislation.[53] Gosplan had requested a review of conditions in the forest industry, and the Union of Land and Forest Workers was being consulted to provide balance. The union subsequently sent two documents to Sovnarkom, a report and a piece of draft legislation. The report largely reiterated its 1926 predecessor, especially in its prediction that Soviet forest management would heed the teachings of Morozov, both generally, as a philosophical inspiration, and specifically, by entrusting both logging and regeneration to the same entity: "We now travel along the path of linking cuts with regeneration. Gosplan spoke out against this; they say the function of the forester . . . is to walk around the *lesoseki* and see which logs and stumps are left. But we . . . believe the foresters should take onto themselves all productive functions."[54] The piece of draft legislation attached to the report attributed the failures of forest management to problems quite apart from those the industrial bureaus wished to highlight: "The basic shortcomings in forest management [include] . . . the irrational working of forest parcels, related to cuts that violate the bases of proper management . . . and the backward form of forest organization on an administrative-fiscal foundation."[55] To remedy these shortcomings, the union recommended "the replacement of the existing system of organization of forest management, gradually unifying the exploitation of the forest with its cultivation and care," and the "strengthening of Narkomzem's authority over administrative management and productive operating independence."[56] Although the union's draft legislation specified a few issues advanced by VSNKh, including the importance of decreasing the cost of logging, as a whole it strongly resembled a document that Narkomzem might have produced itself. The troubled emphasis on the "lack of attention paid to the water-protective, soil-protective, agricultural, strategic, and other properties of the forest for the USSR as a whole" lent the document a decidedly conservationist tone.[57]

When Sovnarkom published its November 1927 decree about forestry—one of the last major forest decrees before the epochal realignment in mid-1929—the influence of the union's document was everywhere apparent, while the demands of VSNKh scarcely received a mention. In isolating the causes of failures in Soviet forest management, Sovnarkom focused primarily on over-zealous and unwise exploitation, pointing to "the excessive exploitation of less forested areas; the insufficient exploitation of forests in richly forested regions; and the extremely unsatisfactory development of regenerative processes in forest management, reflected in the dangerous reduction in forest cover and the worsening of forests' general condition."[58] Sovnarkom made fourteen specific recommendations, including three that were drawn nearly directly from the union's report:

I. Raising of value and productivity of the forest fund . . . by means of the ratio-nalization of methods of exploitation of forests and the full coordination of ex-ploitation with forest regenerative processes; . . .
K. The introduction into forest management of water-protective measures; . . .
M. Reconciling and organizing forest industry with the actual raw possibilities of the forest.[59]

Sovnarkom did mention "strengthening the assignment of forest parcels and groves in long-term use to those loggers who have this right," thereby increasing the latitude of VSNKh in the forests given over in long-term leases, but it stressed VSNKh's "responsibility to conduct rational exploitation of the forests, to provide for restorative processes, and to raise the value and productivity of the forests."[60] Overall, the document represented a direct repudiation of the industrial bureaus, which had hoped for a drastic reorientation of forest management toward increased output via organization according to district or region rather than parcel or grove and around industrial demand rather than biological supply. For the time being, the principle remained "from each forest according to its ability," rather than "to industry according to its needs."

Sovnarkom followed the November 1927 decree with a similar but even more emphatic version, published on 2 February 1928. Again repudiating the claims of VSNKh, the document pinpointed the basic failures of Soviet forest management as "extremely insufficient development of regenerative processes in forest management, creating a dangerous decrease in the amount of forest cover; the fall in productivity of forestland; and the worsening of forest conditions."[61] As an analyst writing in Lesovod noticed, Sovnarkom had accurately identified the essence of the conflict—"whether forest management should be based on the natural-historical properties of the forest or on the needs of the population, industry, transport, and export for timber"—and decided resoundingly in favor of the former.[62] The 1928 decree contained perhaps the most categorical endorsement of Morozovesque principles ever found in a document published by Sovnarkom, making obligatory "the processing of all annual forest parcels in full correspondence with the quality of the forest" and "the application of such methods and means of cutting the forest and clearing logged plots, such that would maximally provide for natural regeneration and full use of the productivity of the forest soils."[63] The Union of Land and Forest Workers was thrilled with the Soviet government's endorsement of its prescriptions, asserting that "the decree of the Sovnarkom should be met with enormous satisfaction by all forest workers": "This proclamation of the highest state organ about strict care for the forest is, on the one hand, an indirect indication of and approval for the arguments of Soviet forest specialists; on the other hand, it arms them with a powerful weapon in asserting the principles of proper management."[64] In the period leading up to the first Five-Year Plan, it appeared that Morozov's *modernizm* would play a significant role in Soviet modernization, because the leadership believed that the application of Morozov's theories would reduce waste and maximize efficiency.

As the contours of the first Five-Year Plan emerged in the autumn of 1928, conservationists could look back on several years of nearly uninterrupted political victories and a steady expansion of Narkomzem's authority and funding, accompanied by repeated rejections of VSNKh's incursions. Soviet industrialization appeared ready to proceed on the basis of sustainable practices. There were, in addition, other reasons to believe that sustainable yield had earned an honored spot in Soviet policy. On 12 January 1927, EKOSO authorized Narkomzem to delineate general forest policy in the Russian republic and to review all plans of management, including ratifying the sizes of timber allotments.[65] That decision was strengthened on 29 December 1927, when all logging for the 1927–28 operating year was placed in the hands of Narkomzem, the fulfillment of an "ancient dream of foresters," according to one enthusiast, entrusting that body with the "conduct of all forest management processes from the cultivation of the timber to its primary processing."[66]

Moreover, the Soviet state was willing throughout the late 1920s to make timber more expensive if doing so would benefit forest management. On 19 May 1927, EKOSO agreed to a 30 percent increase in timber prices so as to finance increased forest organization and forest regeneration efforts, and on 28 May 1928, Sovnarkom decreed that 10 percent of all timber sales be set aside in a special "'forest planting fund' aimed at forest regeneration and forest planting measures."[67] Narkomzem's future seemed all the brighter by dint of its reputation as the most cost-effective source of timber, much more so than VSNKh's timber trusts. The People's Commissariat for Trade wrote to EKOSO on 30 June 1928 that "Narkomzem is one of the neatest and most conscientious suppliers of timber, which one cannot say about the forest trusts, and Narkomzem sells its products somewhat cheaper than the trusts." The Peasants'-Workers' Inspectorate for the Ural region agreed that Narkomzem was, "by its very nature, the most economical forest logging organization."[68]

As late as January 1929, when the last all-union forest conference before the

Great Break took place, the balance of power still favored Narkomzem and the maintenance of the status quo. Present at the conference were representatives from a broad selection of state agencies, including VSNKh, Narkomzem, the Academy of Sciences, and State Economic Planning bureaus from the union and republic levels, as well as Mikhail Orlov and Sergei Bogoslovskii. VSNKh's representative, S. A. Kallistov, reiterated the requests that industry had been making for years, although perhaps more baldly, calling for

A. Intensifying forest use, up to 100 percent of annual growth;
B. Widening the zones of exploitation; and
C. Using "above-estimate" harvests from forest parcels, understanding that these amounts exceed those indicated in point A.[69]

The transparently self-contradictory nature of points A and C—the simultaneous pretension to both observe and violate biological limits—irritated some members of the conference, such as a Comrade Verliuk from the Central Committee of the Professional Unions, who noted that VSNKh had asked to increase above-estimate harvests by 20 to 30 percent per year, even in regions that had no infrastructure, basing its current estimates on future estimates of forest growth that "do not reflect reality."[70] Another listener found in Kallistov's arguments no shortage of sophistry and legerdemain: "I do not understand the speaker at all! What is the basis for such intensification of forest management? There is no basis, and when we ask the speaker for answers to our questions, he replies that the solution to the problem is a task of the general plan of the economy! But if this is so, then in fact there is no general plan."[71] This speaker criticized Kallistov (and VSNKh in general) for advancing incompatible proposals, such as Kallistov's suggestion that logging rotations be shortened while continuing to satisfy the market for large timbers and his claim to reconcile these contradictions with the airy admission that "forest industry and forest management must undergo an extremely stormy and intense technical revolution."[72] Although Kallistov's position was strengthened by the growing demands of the Five-Year Plan, a policy many of the speakers at the conference mentioned, the conference refused to endorse changes in light of new national policies.

When the time came for the conference to make its resolutions, the assembled acknowledged that "at the present time mutual relations between forest industry and forest management are extremely tense" and that "the country's needs for wood creates the necessity of a certain deviation from the norms accepted by the government."[73] But to meet these needs, the conference resolved that the assembled considered it "most expedient to give over to [Narkomzem] those forest regions with the most intensive sale of wood" and to assign "the organs of forest industry . . . areas with larger parcels of forest for the provision of their raw material needs."[74] In other words, the conference recommended that the most important forests, those whose timber had already been exploited and made available for sale, remain within the purview of Narkomzem, while VSNKh was invited to tap distant, undeveloped forests, precisely the opposite of what VSNKh had hoped for. The most sweeping change that the conference could agree to was the support of "measures directed toward the elimination of above-estimate harvests of timber, by means of increasing the forested area under management and increasing the productivity of the forests." Still, taken together, the conclusions the conference reached offered no discernible change to the status quo.[75]

Narkomzem was able to use its political capital to win one last victory for conservationism before the dictates of the Five-Year Plan swept the bureau from its position of power in forest politics. The numbers contained in the first draft of the Five-Year Plan reflect the preferences of Narkomzem, rather than VSNKh. Although the 1928 quotas predicted a sharp rise in forest output, from 64.8 million cubic meters of construction timber in 1927–28 to 107.1 million cubic meters in 1932–33, a jump of 64.3 percent, and a 362 percent increase over 1925–26, the dramatic increase would have been still larger still if Gosplan's targets had been adopted. (See table 4.1, with all figures given in thousands of cubic meters). These numbers, which brought union targets in line with the requests of Narkomzem and not Gosplan, are yet another indication that, up until January 1929, conservationism remained an important force, and to some degree a dominant force, in Soviet forestry.

Things changed very rapidly in the spring of 1929, when the first logging totals of the Five-Year Plan began to roll in: the harvests clearly would not facilitate the rapid industrialization foreseen by the Party leadership. April control figures showed that by 1 January, only 17.3 percent of the annual target had been reached. By 15 February this number had crept up to 31.5 percent, and by 15 March (the end of the logging period) to only 48.7 percent.[76] Poor weather conditions were offered as an excuse for the disappointing results, since a lack of snow impeded skidding season, but in fact the harvest tracked very closely progress from the year before. The dismal performance of Narkomzem's logging apparatus immediately drew the attention of the plenum of the Union of Land and Forest Workers' central committee, which had always supported conservation in the past but now came to very different conclusions about the

TABLE 4.1.
Forest Harvests Projected for the First Five-Year Plan

Region	Gosplan Proposal	Narkomzem Proposal	Five-Year Plan
Leningrad	38,178	15,961	17,973
Middle Volga	11,995	8,186	8,232
Ural	53,382	29,804	33,200

Source: Compiled from Bogoslovskii, "Finliandskii metod ucheta lesnykh resursov," 4; Narodnyi Kommissariat Zemledeliia RSFSR, Materialy, 374–98.

problems facing Soviet forest management: "The plenum deems that the basic shortcoming of contemporary forest management is the insufficient development of forest exploitation, the backward organizational forms and extremely backward technique of forest management, and the contamination of the forest bureaus with foreign elements."[77] Matters, clearly, had changed. The Union of Land and Forest Workers mentioned for the first time sinister foreign elements, but also abruptly turned its back on Narkomzem, its conservationist approach, its small ranger districts, and its "petty-industry methods of production."[78] The time had come, according to union leadership, to organize factories for wood built along the lines of industrial concerns. The union's weekly newspaper, *Lesnoi rabochii,* claimed that its leaders had no choice but to initiate a purge, since the Soviet government, "especially in the village, is littered with bureaucrats, kulaks, sub-kulaks, and people torn from the working masses who do not understand or accept the essence of class struggle."[79] That same month, Rabkrin also performed an about-face and proposed the "subjection of forest management to the interests of the industrialization of the country."[80]

Yet still the Party elite dragged their feet. Important functionaries continued to express suspicion about VSNKh's competence. In June 1929, a plenum of the Party Central Committee held a meeting to decide the future of Soviet forest management, and in spite of the uninspiring numbers from the previous winter, a voice no less influential than that of Lazar Kaganovich spoke out against overreaction: "When we approach the question about who should be the master of the forest . . . then we arrive at a sticking point between two agencies—Narkomzem and VSNKh. VSNKh has a larger appetite—they say 'I will take it all and never be satisfied.' I am afraid that they will gobble up [*perevarit'*] the entire forest. So from the point of view of protecting the forests, from the point of view of observing the rules of forest management, oversight by Narkomzem should be left in place."[81] Comrade Velovich, an invited visitor to the plenum, agreed: "We need to toss aside the exploitative VSNKh approach to the forest, as well as the peasant-agricultural approach of Narkomzem. In a word, we need not just a more cultured attitude toward the cutting of the forest, but a more cultured attitude toward cultivation."[82] Kaganovich suggested that the real problem stemmed from the Soviet state's inherently exploitative outlook. In 1913, he noted, the tsarist regime had folded one-third of its forest receipts back into management operations, and the German investment rate in 1926 had reached almost two-thirds, but the Soviet Union regularly only reinvested between 15 and 19 percent of its forest receipts.[83] The plenum resolved that "the existing system of logging is satisfactory in neither the system of Narkomzem nor VSNKh," instead proposing a new administration dedicated to the "correct organization of forest exploitation."[84] The plenum seemed unwilling to abandon the hope that, given proper funding, the demands of the state could be reconciled with ecological limitations.[85]

The next month finally brought the decisive break that VSNKh had wanted for so long. On 12 July 1929, the Council of Labor and Defense (STO) divided the nation's forests into three categories—intensive zones, extensive zones, and reserve zones—and entrusted nearly all to VSNKh. Narkomzem was given two weeks to draw up the documents finalizing the transfer.[86] All forests of industrial significance were transferred to the industrial bureaus in long-term leases to expire in the year 1989. Until that time, all work, including "the protection of the forests, forest organization and ameliorative work, work for clearing old logging plots, work for the care and regeneration of the forest, and the composition of plans for exploitation and the determination of annual cuts," was to be conducted by VSNKh.[87] A few weeks later, on 24 August, Sovnarkom specified which forests Narkomzem would lose: VSNKh received 100 million hectares, or 89 percent of the forests of the Russian Republic, and the Commissariat of Transport received 2 percent. Narkomzem remained in charge of "the forests of the Central Black Earth region, the Western, Moscow, and Central Volga regions, and the Lower Volga," as well as small pieces of other regions, in all equaling 9 percent, or 12.5 million hectares.[88] Although this represented an enormous shift, Narkomzem's real holdings were factually smaller still, since almost 30 percent of its tracts were to be immediately leased to individual trusts.[89] VSNKh received one last concession in the new law: Bogoslovskii's pet project, flying management, received sanction, and henceforth the management units for VSNKh's forests were not individual groves, but greatly enlarged forest industrial tracts, or *lespromkhozy*.

Pressing his advantage, Bogoslovskii almost immediately set himself another goal: discrediting the concept of sustainable yield, for decades the bedrock of tsarist and Soviet forest management. Although the concept had frequently been violated in practice, especially during the Civil War, the principle itself generally stood above question. But its continued salience acted as a brake on increased exploitation, and in April 1929, Bogoslovskii published an indication that sustainable yield would soon come under attack: "In contemporary Russian forest organization, the principle of sustainable use has been accepted as an unshakable foundation, on which rests the entire edifice of forest management. But despite the exceptional significance of this principle, very little has been done to substantiate it. Apparently, we have here an axiom taken as truth, demanding no proof."[90] Bogoslovskii argued that the very concept of sustainable use had evolved in a bygone era, when forests provided only the immediate vicinity with timber, but because socialist economies focused on regional or national supply chains rather than local ones, the principle was at best quaint, at worst injurious. Sustainable yield, in other words, was a petit bourgeois concept, based upon creating artificial scarcity on the local scale and possessing little relevance for the Soviet Union. Bogoslovskii stepped up his rhetoric later in 1929, painting sustainable yield not only as misguided and dogmatic, but as worthy of scorn, insisting that "the time of the romantics, when small children were frightened by fairy tales, has passed irretrievably. In our epoch, we are within our rights to demand proof of threatened economic crises."[91] Bogoslovskii claimed that deforestation was at best a strange delusion held by foresters scared by visions of "rapacious steel teeth"; given the Soviet economy's lack of development, such predictions were, in his words, "bizarre."

Bogoslovskii's writings, previously influential primarily among forest industrialists, began to gain wider currency. M. G. Zdorik, an influential forest politician who had briefly chaired Narkomzem's forest administration in 1922, used Bogoslovskii's ideas to advocate the abolition of forest organization entirely. Zdorik's rationale possessed a core of iron logic: "Because the plans of forest management," he contended at Moscow's Central House of Specialists in the summer of 1929, "drawn up on the basis of existing forest organization, are not practicable given contemporary forestry, and because they are expensive to compose, they should be replaced with plans of forest exploitation."[92] Rather than costly surveying and measurement, which after eighty-nine years of work had organized only 17 percent of Russia's forests, Zdorik wanted fieldworkers to ignore the technical aspects of surveyed forests, including the *bonitet,* soil, and hydrology, and instead cut permanent, regularly spaced sightlines in the forest, allowing surveyors to determine quickly which forests could be logged in the next ten to twenty years. Streamlined plans for mechanized clear-cutting could focus on these lands alone. "The time has come," Zdorik wrote in mid-1929, "to review old academic methods in forest organization and to work out something new, more in step with the tempo of our socialist construction. . . . We need revolution in the forest, not evolution."[93] Opponents dismissed Zdorik's plans as mere "pompous phraseology, backed with foolish accusations and 'unmaskings,'" but Zdorik's faith in the country's ability to devise a new forest science lay much closer to the spirit of the Great Break than did the doubt of those who urged caution.[94]

Zdorik and Bogoslovskii saw most of their ambitions fulfilled in the autumn of 1929, when VSNKh's assumption of responsibility in the forest cleared the way for a new draft of the Five-Year Plan, which included a dramatic increase in logging targets for construction timber (see table 4.2).[95] The already aggressive targets found in the early drafts of the Five-Year Plan, including a near tripling of the 1925–26 harvest by 1932, were ratcheted up to astounding levels, to a six-fold increase over the 1925–26 take. The new quotas rose to such incredible heights that even VSNKh's main logging administration, the Main Administration for Timber and Paper (Glavlesbum), balked and announced that the targets were beyond its strength, "that any target beyond sixty million cubic meters cannot realistically be fulfilled."[96] But the autumn 1929 quotas nevertheless became the new standard, necessitating changes to existing forest management principles.

Bogoslovskii's victory was made complete with the legislation of autumn 1930, which completely eliminated Narkomzem as a forest manager. In De-

TABLE 4.2.
Growth of Timber Quotas during the First Five-Year Plan

	A	B	C	D
1928–29	58.1	196%	62	208%
1929–30	62.9	212%	108	362%
1930–31	67.2	227%	135	453%
1931–32	74.9	252%	162	543%
1932–33	81.1	275%	180	604%

A = Logging targets for construction timber contained in the spring 1929 draft of the
    Five-Year Plan, expressed in millions of cubic meters
B = Figures from column A, expressed as a percentage of the 1925–26 harvest
C = Logging targets for construction timber in the autumn 1929 draft of the Five-Year
    Plan, expressed in millions of cubic meters
D = Figures from column C, expressed as a percentage of the 1925–26 harvest

Source: Compiled from Lavrov, "Piatletnii plan," 9; Materialy po perspektivnomu planu, 400–403.

cember 1930, Sovnarkom entrusted VSNKh with "the planning and regulation of all forest management and forest industry of the USSR" and transferred to its administration "the entire state forest fund of the union republics, with the exception of forests of local significance and protective forests, all the property and credits of Narkomzem for the administration of [their] forests," and the scientific research and experimental forests throughout the country.[97] All the laws regarding state forest management dating back to 1924 were repealed, as were the rules regarding timber pricing that provided revenue streams for regeneration work. After repeal of the pricing rules, timber became essentially free for the producer.[98] By the end of 1931, VSNKh had achieved what it had lobbied for since its founding, and the path to unchecked exploitation of the forest lay completely open.

The attacks that Zdorik and Bogoslovskii leveled against sustainable yield and traditional forest organization also explicitly targeted the foremost exponent of these ideas, Mikhail Orlov. Orlov, whose preference for rationality underlay all of his proposals, was suddenly left unprotected when the very criteria for rational choices shifted. Pointed rhetoric was nothing new to Orlov, and he had been happy to aim sharp words at Morozov twenty-five years before, but the assaults following release of the 1929 logging figures were more caustic and more focused on Orlov's personal thoughts than on the suitability of one practice or another. "Professor Orlov considers himself the protector of proper forest management," Zdorik wrote in late 1929, "but we have a right to demand a more serious attitude to the question of exploiting forest massifs."[99] Orlov's insufficient seriousness, according to his enemies, lay in his adherence to psychological or exchange theories of value, revealed when he opined in his forestry textbook that "man is the measure of all things," that "not only timber, but also gold is valuable only insofar as man desires to have it."[100] This comment, it was argued, betrayed his "captivity to the bourgeois school of psychology," which equated use value with exchange value; because Marxist economics were predicated on the labor theory of value, the Marxist and exchange-theory schools were incompatible. When critics argued that Orlov's point of view threatened to bring about the "negation of the study of Marx and a transition to bourgeois economics," Orlov found himself on shaky footing indeed.[101] Also suspicious, in an age when tsarist-era experts found themselves under increasing attack, were Orlov's activities as the head of Narkomzem's Forestry Scholar Committee (LUK), a body "so covered with the mysterious darkness of scholarly high authority that it is frightening to touch it or even say anything bad about it," and far too similar to the old tsarist Special Study Committee for comfort.[102] At about the time of these assaults, Orlov's personal suffering began, as his grandson recollected: "More and more often after dinner grandfather would not lie down with a book, but instead sat, deep in thought, at his desk. His eyes glazed over, and when grandmother asked him what was the matter, he answered, 'My heart hurts, hurts for our forests.'"[103]

Orlov's students then harassed him until his body broke. Beginning in early 1930, the campus newspaper of the Leningrad Forest-Technical Institute, Orlov's alma mater and lifetime employer, printed prominent condemnations of Orlov, the denunciations at first careful and timid, but later full-throated in their aggression.[104] The earliest critique focused on Orlov's final textbook, *Forest Organization,* and his claim that "the best way to provide forest management with the labor it needs is to create a certain combination of forested and agricultural lands, so as to encourage simple agricultural industry and smallholding land tenure."[105] One of Orlov's students cautiously pointed out in an opinion piece how impolitic these views, perfectly acceptable when published in 1927, had become by January 1930: "We will hope that our respected Professor Orlov will review the question about peasant labor in forest management, because . . . socialist construction in the village completely excludes the 'development of petty industry.' Orlov's path is harmful to us."[106] Later that year, the critiques turned into calls for Orlov's ouster: "The struggle on the ideological front has revealed the [existence of] those who keep silent, but at the correct time, under the banner of 'eternal scientific truth,' impose a system of views foreign to socialist construction. The student representatives to the Institute's Methodological Council juxtapose their theses to the scholarly program of Orlov and demand a reorganization of the faculty."[107] At the beginning of the 1932–33 academic year, Orlov was indeed removed from the faculty of forest organization, a department he had chaired for thirty years. But still the student newspaper continued to denounce Orlov as a "wrecker"; a "house dog [*dvorovyi pes*] of his capitalist masters"; "bourgeois rubbish"; and a vulgar, rude, rotten, Trotskyite liberal. The coup de grâce was landed on 25 December 1932 by S. V. Malyshev, a graduate student at the institute and a Komsomol leader, when he casually walked into Orlov's office without an appointment and announced, "I just don't know, Professor, when it will be better to take you away, today or next week? No, we must arrest you tomorrow—you are a deadly dangerous person for this country."[108] Later that day, Orlov died—officially of a brain hemorrhage, but in reality from fright and a broken heart.[109]

Before his death, however, Orlov suffered yet one more indignity: the publication of a book-length denunciation entitled *Against Reactionary Theories on the Forest Front,* which argued that Orlov and Morozov deserved scorn for approaching the forest in the same, overly Germanic way. The authors, two professors from Orlov's Leningrad Forest-Technical Institute, contended that "both the Morozov and the Orlov schools perpetuate the ideas of manorial forestry and, having borrowed their ideas from German forestry, transfer the social laws of the bourgeois social structures into Russian forest politics."[110] This critique was both untrue and unfair—Morozov's teachings explicitly turned away from Germany as a role model, and the methods of forest management then in ascendance, such as concentrated cuts and artificial regeneration, were effectively borrowed wholesale by Bogoslovskii from Germany—but nevertheless, proponents of expanded exploitation began to warn of an "Orlovist-Morozovist school" that sought to limit Soviet growth by urging obedience to foreign masters.[111] Industrial radicals thereby found a way around their inconvenient admiration for progressive German forestry by cloaking ideas and methods borrowed from the West in xenophobic rhetoric.

As baseless and self-contradictory as the industrializers' criticisms may have been, they succeeded in destroying Orlov's reputation. Shortly after Orlov's death, the Forest Institute abolished Orlov's faculty of forest organization, with forest organization, much like genetics in the 1940s, dismissed nationwide as a pseudoscience. Orlov's works, for thirty years the bedrock of Russian forestry, went out of print.

The Great Break of 1929–31 revolutionized not only industrial policy but agricultural policy as well, most significantly through introducing agricultural collectivization, whereby millions of smallholdings were combined, often at the point of a gun, into state-owned enterprises called collective farms. Peasant forest policy changed as well. Policies that encouraged an alliance between the peasants and the state in forest management were almost completely repudiated. Throughout the 1920s, Narkomzem had pursued three tactics so as to bridge the gap between urban ideals of forest management and traditional rural usage: the integration of the peasant into the everyday work of forest management; continuing education to teach peasants how to relate to forests; and support for "forests of local significance," those returned to peasant control by the Forest Codex of 1923. By 1931, the state had abandoned two of these three policies, and only the forests of local significance remained patent.

The Soviet effort to inculcate a conservationist spirit among the peasantry was the first to go. After 1924, Narkomzem had actively propagandized in favor of a loving attitude toward the forest, most concertedly with the springtime Forest Day holiday, but also through public lectures, guided excursions into the forest, and traveling museums dedicated to forest issues. The lectures, Narkomzem recommended, should take on the form of conversations so as to involve listeners, should "be brief so as to not exhaust attention, and should be accompanied by a reading from Russia's rich artistic literature about the forest."[112] Recommended topics for the conversations included "The Nature of the Forest and Its Imprint on the Life Patterns of the Russian People," "The Forest as a Social Organism," "The Forest as Protector of Water," "The Process of Respiration in Trees and Its Significance in Cleaning the Air," "The Forest as an Example of Nature's Beauty," and "The Forest as a Symbol of the Collective."[113] The programs appear to have been popular, with six hundred peasants in Vladimir province attending a lecture entitled "The Forest and Its Significance in the Life of Man" and communes complaining to central authorities that the local forester did not offer enough public events, leading at least one forester from Vladimir province to declare that "the belief that 'the forest is God's' or 'the forest belongs to no one' has been shaken from the minds of the people."[114] Narkomzem's efforts won enough converts in one town to transform the Orthodox holiday of Whitsunday, which followed soon after Forest Day in many regions of Russia, into an occasion for environmentalist action. Responding to Narkomzem's call to love the forest, a group of amateur foresters tried to stop believers from cutting down their newly planted willows and birches to decorate their churches, as a letter written to *Krest'ianskaia gazeta* (Peasant Gazette) explained: "On the twentieth of April, we planted around three hundred trees of different species. But the pealing of church bells called for the murder of the young forest, and thousands of trees were destroyed. I ran to the church with branches held to my chest and proclaimed, 'We know the proper use of the forest! And we hope that in the near future, those who have submitted to that windbag of a priest will spurn him, will stop destroying the forest for the sake of a religious opiate!'"[115] The celebration of Forest Day in the 1920s thus added an ethical component to Narkomzem's more practical aim of encouraging peasants to participate in forestry reclamation work and recommended that peasants see forests as analogous to human communities and deserving of moral standing.[116]

The political storms of 1929, however, brought immediate changes to the meaning and message of Forest Day and then its discontinuation. Foresters working with the peasantry were instructed to avoid "hackneyed phrases about 'love for the forest' and so on," an article from *Lesovod* reported, and to employ instead unromantic slogans such as, "The development of socialist construction demands the strengthening of the exploitation of the forests of the Soviet Union!"[117] On 21 May 1929, Forest Day became, by decree of Sovnarkom, a "formal, recognized legislative affair, regulated by special instructions," and henceforth the spirit of the holiday turned cold and mechanical, less about love and more about quotas.[118] By 1930, the last year that Forest Day was celebrated until after the war, the holiday had lost nearly all of its original meaning. "Forest Day in 1930," an editorial in *Lesnoi spetsialist* (Forest Specialist) instructed, "should be celebrated by reviewing the fulfillment of the Five-Year Plan and should proceed under the slogan of the strengthening of the struggle with the kulak. This year a special campaign of firewood logging will be organized in the spring and summer to be conducted as part of Forest Day. We must rebuff the opinion that timber cannot be felled in summer, as some forest workers think."[119] Forest Day thus became a time for peasants to cut trees down rather than plant them with their own hands, to amplify social differences rather than reflect on the power of the forest collective to protect itself, and to disregard natural rhythms instead of joining in kinship.

By 1931, a second revolution in the forest had been completed, and this time the fires of revolution burned much more completely than they had the first time. Unlike the blaze of 1917, which dispatched Georgii Morozov but left his ideas intact and able to sprout up again, the Great Break destroyed the intellectual old growth from the tsarist era (in the person of Mikhail Orlov) and also burned down to the soil, changing the possibilities for regrowth in the future. The second fire, set by a zealous group of self-described "young scientific workers, well-schooled in Marxist-Leninist methodology," committed to "purging forest economic theory of bourgeois rubbish and all forms of Trotskyite contraband," succeeded in destroying all the elements of the ideological ecosystem that had previously constrained unchecked exploitation. Sustainable yield as a guiding principle was discredited, conservation was dismissed as so much superstition, and forest organization as a concept was placed in doubt. Furthermore, popular education encouraging affection toward the forest was terminated. Interestingly, those who kindled the second fire were not members of the Party apparatus, but rather industrialists and student activists who felt that the first revolution had failed; the Party leadership did its best to prevent the fire from spreading. Put another way, the effort to remake the Russian forest was not devised by members of the upper reaches of the government and imposed on the country, but rather represented a reluctant co-optation of a long-standing lobbying effort generated from below. The second revolution in the forest represented an improvisation, an alliance of convenience, more than a premeditated move, but its destructive effects altered the Russian forest, as well as Russian forestry, permanently.

FIGURE 1.
Dmitrii Nikiforovich
Kaigorodov, Morozov's colleague
at the St. Petersburg Forest
Institute, tutor to the tsar's
children, and author of the
popular book *Conversations
about the Russian Forest*

FIGURE 2. Georgii Fedorovich Morozov with his wife, Lidia
Nikolaevna, and their first child, Olga

FIGURE 3.
Georgii Fedorovich
Morozov

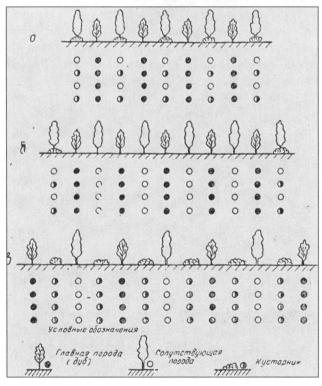

FIGURE 4. A chart showing the prescribed method to establish
artificial oak forests in the Russian south

FIGURE 5. The two individuals behind the effort to establish
Soviet forest preserves: Narkomzem chief A. I. Shul'ts and
Morozov's student Mikhail Elevfer'evich Tkachenko

FIGURE 6. A picture advertising Forest Day in 1928

FIGURE 7.
Mikhail Mikhailovich
Orlov

FIGURE 8. "According to Stalin's Plan, We Will Transform Nature!"

FIGURE 9. "In The Name of Communism"

FIGURE 10. "And We Shall Conquer Drought"

FIGURE 11. A statue of Stalin near Grutas, Lithuania

FIGURE 12. A poster illustrating the preferred method of forest management in the first years of the Soviet Union: complete clear-cutting and artificial regeneration

FIGURE 13. A poster illustrating the Great Stalin Plan, entitled "Two Worlds—Two Plans." The captions read: "We are planting life! They are sowing death!"

FIGURE 14. The catastrophic flood that struck Moscow in 1908. Such floods prompted the Moscow City Soviet to create forest preserves.

FIGURE 15. A poster illustrating the Great Stalin Plan. The caption reads: "We are transforming deserts into flowering regions. They turn cities and villages into deserts."

FIGURE 16. A poster representing a map of the Great Stalin Plan

5 REGENERATION

Forest Conservationism Returns to
the Soviet Union

Dictators like trees. Perhaps the appeal lies in the fact that forests vibrate with a kind of cultural resonance most helpful to authoritarian political actors, tying a dictatorship to the nation's distant poetic past and creating an impression of stability for the future. The Nazi regime famously endorsed green politics in general and *Dauerwald* in particular, mouthing the rhetoric of forest conservation even after war demands made *Dauerwald*'s tenets impractical.[1] Benito Mussolini created a "National Forest Militia," a black-shirted paramilitary group under the direction of the General Command of the Voluntary Militia for Natural Security, to assist in "technical work, reforestation . . . and propaganda in the field of silviculture."[2] Communist China placed considerable emphasis on afforestation in the early years of its existence and, after a hiatus during Mao's Cultural Revolution, rededicated itself to forestry projects in 1978 with the Three North Shelterbelt Development Program, the "Green Great Wall," which increased the forest cover of China's northern regions from 5 percent to 9 percent. The Three North program was followed by nine other programs to increase forest cover throughout China, and efforts have extended into the twenty-first century.[3] In short, although environmental preservation has frequently been linked with quality of life in liberal democracies, environmentalism, and forest conservationism especially, can produce benefits that redound to the collective just as much as to the individual. Hitler, Mussolini, and the heirs of Mao all enacted policies designed to expand forest cover, not for the enjoyment of individuals but to increase the power of the state.[4]

Stalin also actively promoted forest environmentalism for the benefit of the state, establishing levels of protection unparalleled anywhere in the world, but in a unique form, strongly influenced by prerevolutionary ideas about the Russian forest. Stalin's environmental policies codified into law an assumption that healthy land was forested land and that deforestation represented serious environmental dangers to the state's larger project of modernization, in the form of droughts, floods, hydrological disturbances, and crop failures. Accepting an argument made by forest ecologists struggling to recover from the setbacks dealt to conservationism in 1929 and 1930, Stalin's government reversed course and in the 1930s and 1940s set aside ever larger tracts of Russia's most valuable forests as preserves, off-limits to industrial exploitation. Forest protection ultimately rose to such prominence during the last six years of Stalin's rule that the Politburo took control of the Soviet forest away from the Ministry of Heavy Industry and elevated the nation's forest conservation bureau to the dominant position in implementing policy. The results of this struggle for supremacy in the forest, which pitted the Party leadership against those very bureaucratic interests assigned to carry out the Party's industrial ambitions, provides another example of a rapidly industrializing, authoritarian regime endorsing environmental protection, if provided with a suitably collectivist rationale.

Indeed, forest protection had long enjoyed sustained institutional support in the Soviet Union, but it found a secure place in Stalin's system only after conservationists began to stress the practical significance of the forests in rapid industrialization. In the 1920s, conservationists promoted the concept of sustainable yield for its own sake, and the Soviet government tended to support this view. However, industrialists and student activists, acting in concert with the industrializing push of the first Five-Year Plan, were able to label such concepts as bourgeois. In response, advocates of conservationism regained the upper hand in the 1930s by citing the theories of the prerevolutionary soil scientist V. V. Dokuchaev, who linked the hydrological stability of Russia to the maintenance of permanent forest cover.[5] By arguing that deforestation would increase the silt load of the rivers, and thus decrease the life span of the regime's hydroelectric dams, conservationists provided an argument that industrialists never successfully rebutted, thereby enabling the institutionalization of environmentalism.[6] After 1931, hydrological concerns became the justification for the creation of a vast forest preserve in the center of European Russia, at the time the largest in the world.

The decision to create an enormous forest preserve represented a compromise, advanced by Stalin himself, to settle the long-standing dispute between conservationists and industrialists about what form socialism would take in the forest. As previously described, the Soviet leadership attempted to pursue the ideals of both forest conservation and aggressive industrialization in the 1920s and early 1930s, but despite repeated signals sent by the Party leadership indicating that the forest cultivation agencies and the forest exploitation bureaus should work together toward shared goals, the logging trusts only attacked conservationism as a bankrupt concept. With cooperation and compromise proving unworkable, the Party leadership abandoned hopes of a single socialized forest and divided the forest into three classes: the first dedicated to preservation, the second to conservation, and the third to unchecked exploitation. During Stalin's years in power, the Politburo steadily and dramatically increased the authority of the agencies administering the protected groups, in a pattern so uniform that mere bureaucratic counterbalancing as a determining factor seems unlikely. The result was a unique and remarkably strong system of environmental protection, one that allowed Morozov's romantic, ecological ideas, so popular among forest professionals, to survive and even thrive. After Stalin's death, the conservation bureaus fell from their prominent position, but the dictator's forest laws remained in force, and Morozov's ideas, newly applicable to the problem of improving hydrological function, emerged from the shadows and never again came under attack.

Judging by its actions, the Soviet leadership almost instantly regretted the laws passed in 1930 and 1931 that gave the forests over to the industrially oriented Supreme Soviet of the Economy (VSNKh). And with good reason: VSNKh used its new authority to embark upon a program of forest exploitation inspired by Bogoslovskii's dismissal of sustainable yield, but so exaggerated that even Bogoslovskii himself came under fire for insufficient revolutionary enthusiasm.[7] "Logging under the Five-Year Plan," the union of timber workers declared, "is logging of a military order. The fetishization of forest organization based on individual parcels should be brought to an end. Harvests based on chance should be replaced with firm plans of cuts."[8] Traditional patterns of forest use based on regularity and order were abandoned because they did not allow the necessary mechanization of forest work, as one engineer explained: "We have tried to implement mechanization using the old forms of forest management. . . . It turned out that [the prescribed] cuts were scattered all about, in narrow belts. And in actuality, it was impossible to tap these scattered areas using heavy machinery."[9]

In order to overcome such inconvenient aspects of forest management, plans for concentrated logging were drawn up. Instead of isolated belts of mature forest, enormous swathes of densely forested territory in the far north and east would be bulldozed, areas measured in square kilometers felled all at once.[10] Regeneration, it was promised, would be accomplished through replanting, although VSNKh's true intentions were betrayed by its successful effort in 1930 to repeal the laws mandating timely replanting.[11] Plans for shifting large-scale forestry to the hinterlands, however, belonged to the future, after remote regions had received the necessary investment and capitalization. Until then, the ballooning quotas of the Five-Year Plan were to be filled by conducting concentrated cutting in the most accessible timber in the country, those areas located near the railroads and rivers of European Russia, at rates far exceeding annual growth.[12] Dramatic overlogging of the most accessible stands ensued. The 1930 take of timber exceeded annual growth in Leningrad province by 47 percent, in Western province by 125 percent, in Moscow province by 129 percent, and in Ivanovo-Voznesensk province by 104 percent.[13] In 1930, VSNKh felled plots in Riazan district scheduled for harvest in 1976.[14]

Protest in the forestry press appeared at once, although the general hostility to the concept of sustainable yield precluded a frontal assault on VSNKh. Instead, advocates of conservation began to emphasize the hydrological influence of forests and warned of the danger to the state's canal and dam projects if deforestation continued apace. Narkomzem's chief A. I. Shul'ts first sounded the alarm in 1929, when he warned Gosplan that "the main water artery in the Ukraine is the Dniepr, and if suddenly the Administration of Forests decided in a fit of revolutionary enthusiasm to cut the forest along the basin of the Dniepr—this would lead, perhaps, even to the breakdown of Dnieprstroi. After all, the forest regulates the water regime there."[15] Morozov's most devoted surviving acolyte, Mikhail Elevfer'evich Tkachenko, also pointed to the hydrological dangers posed by the new forestry when he recommended that "on steep slopes, where forests have a protective character, clear-cuts should be replaced with selective cuts, as well as along the banks of reservoirs, where forests act as the protector of water."[16]

The appeals for careful logging near bodies of water found a friendly reception at various levels of the government remarkably quickly, first at the local level and then at the national level. In the summer of 1930, the Moscow City Soviet published a decree replacing clear-cuts with selective cuts in the forests located in the basins of the rivers Moscow, Istra, and Ruza.[17] The Moscow City Soviet, presuming a link between deforestation and the periodic floods that had caused twenty million rubles' worth of damage in 1908 and five million rubles' worth in 1926, sought to prevent further catastrophes by enacting legislation, at that time applicable only in the immediate area (see table 5.1).[18]

TABLE 5.1.
Disastrous Flooding of the Moscow River, 1806–1926

Year	Depth of Floodwaters in Central Moscow
1788	7.53 m (24.70 ft)
1806	7.72 m (25.32 ft)
1828	7.87 m (25.82 ft)
1856	8.34 m (27.36 ft)
1879	8.39 m (27.53 ft)
1908	9.15 m (30.02 ft)
1926	7.79 m (25.55 ft)

Source: Reproduced from RGAE f. 9449, op. 1, d. 2069, l. 18. The floodwaters were measured at Danilov monastery. The first flood was recorded in 1396.

For the editors of the journal *Lesnoi spetsialist,* however, the actions of the Moscow City Soviet, while a remarkable achievement given the forest trends of the previous two years, only highlighted a problem that demanded a larger response: "Although the decree applied only to the forests of the Moscow River, do we not need analogous instructions for the Volga as well? Did we not read today in the newspaper that 'navigation on the Volga from Tver to Rybinsk has been halted due to low water levels'? The Mariinskaia system has been shut down. Navigation from Kolomna up the Oka has been closed for many years, and the Dniepr and Don are unnavigable for almost a third of their extent, as a consequence of the destruction of the forests."[19] The solution to the problem, the editors asserted, was to turn to Morozov's teachings: "the soil near rivers should be constantly covered in forest . . . and [because] the cut and the regeneration are synonyms . . . the prescribed cut for forests near rivers should be significantly more complex than pure clear-cuts."[20]

Stalin himself agreed with this assessment. On 30 May 1931, he raised a topic for discussion, "On the order of cutting of timber," instructing Sovnarkom to prepare, "in a month's term, a draft law about the absolute forbiddance of cutting timber in certain regions so as to conserve the water in other regions."[21] On 15 July, Sovnarkom returned its draft law to the Politburo, and by the end of July 1931, decree number 519, dividing all the forests of the country into two zones, became law. Forests inside a new "forest industrial zone" remained in VSNKh's control, but a portion of the forests in a new "forest cultivation zone," including the forests along banks of the Volga, Dniepr, and Don, were transferred back to Narkomzem. Most of the forests in the forest cultivation zone remained in the control of VSNKh, but these were to be managed according to a "special, rigorous regime of cutting these forests, providing for their reestablishment," devised by Narkomzem.[22] Regardless of which bureau administered the forest, any cutting in a one-kilometer belt along both banks of the Volga, Dniepr, Don, and Ural rivers was forbidden.[23] Hence, less than one year after uniting the forests under one management system, Sovnarkom again divided them into two. This time the division possessed historical resonance, because Peter I, centuries before, had also forbidden logging along major rivers.[24]

Morozov's followers played a key role in Stalin's push for increased forest protection, since they first publicized the risk posed to the nation's hydrology caused by wanton logging, and the 1931 law undoubtedly helped them by providing them with ideological breathing room. Subsequent legislation authorized new forest management institutes, in order to determine the best way to meet the needs of the forest cultivation zones. They were founded in Moscow and Kharkov, creating new academic posts for scholars such as Tkachenko, who was named to head the forest regeneration department at the Moscow Institute. These schools' general approach can be discerned from the claims of the Moscow Institute's first annual report, which asserted that "the lower productivity of the forests of the lower Povol'zhe is explained not so much by the unfavorable climate, as by the incorrect conduct of forest management in these forests."[25] These words, almost certainly penned by Tkachenko, show that the state had perhaps unwittingly created a space where Morozov's dictum "the cut of the forest and its regeneration are synonyms" regained direct and undeniable relevance.

The new legislation also helped the conservationists by blunting the drive toward maximalism in forest politics, weakening the position of the activists who had pushed for a second revolution in the forest, and the enraged activists knew it. Seeking to repeat the successes of 1929 and 1930, promoters of forest industrialism agitated for an end to the protection regime. "The construction of a classless, socialist society," an article in *Lesnaia pravda* declared, "demands the subjection of the forest industry to the interests of the present day. Either we can relate to the forest carefully and give power to the capitalists, or we can provide for stormy tempos of industrialization and make our country better able to protect itself." The Party, the author of the article dared to suggest, had made the wrong choice and thus taken a step away from the construction of socialism: "Unfortunately, the seventeenth Party conference on the forest industry . . . supports measures conducted in the forest cultivation zone that are based on principles of sustainability. Such Orlovesque planning subverts the spirit of Marx and Engels and subjugates the forest industry to nature itself rather than to planning. The forest is not for man, it would seem, but man for the forest."[26] The revolutionaries at the Leningrad Forest-Technical Institute recognized that they had suffered a serious setback. They had fought to repudiate all older standards for forest management and apparently won, but less than two years later, the Party suddenly reversed course and backed conservationism. The campaign to radicalize forest management never again regained its prior momentum.

Just as important for the conservationists, the decision to divide the forests into zones of exploitation and zones of protection created forest refuges for the specialists who adhered to older ideas about forest use, especially those who loved Morozov. Even during the most dangerous years of 1929 and 1930, many followers of Morozov, though under attack in the forestry press, continued to work in their ranger districts, clinging to their principles and demonstrating flashes of remarkable courage when they found their forests threatened. A forester from the Middle Volga *leskhoz* named Belov, for instance, reported that by July 1930 almost half of the management staff had been cashiered by VSNKh and placed under arrest. Nonetheless, he and his colleagues, concerned that "the tragic and senseless industrial tendency of forest management [would] threaten, if not the destruction of the pine forest, then its technical possibilities and its regeneration," decided as a group to "go their own way and continue the selective cuts proposed for the forest and insisted upon by the late professor Morozov, rather than clear-cuts."[27] In other places, foresters simply refused to follow direct instructions, as happened in Northern *krai* in 1930, when the timber factory in Mekhrenskii district asked the foreman of the ranger district to mark trees suitable for felling, and the foresters refused. After three weeks of squabbling, the foresters gave in, but chose to mark a far lower percentage of timber than the factory had requested. The actual logging of this parcel never reached the levels prescribed by VSNKh.[28]

After the promulgation of the July 1931 law, true believers such as the foresters in Mekhrenskii district could choose to transfer to a station in the forest cultivation zone and apply Morozov's ideas there, and records from Moscow-area forests indicate that many did precisely that. In the Shaturskii forest district, for instance, a grove near Moscow was converted by the 1931 law from a *lespromkhoz* (a forest industry unit) into a *leskhoz* (a forest cultivation unit), the old organizational plan drafted in 1930 did not use Morozov's terminology at all, instead accepting uniform clear-cuts with no measures taken to improve the quality of the forest. According to the 1930 plan, devised by VSNKh, cuts designed to improve the stand were rejected, "since they forced the forest manager to devote special attention to them instead of producing wood" and as a result turned out to be "completely unprofitable."[29] However, the organizational plan written in 1931 was entirely different, with Morozov's forest types explicitly recommended as management tools. A box for forest type was placed on the worksheet that surveyors carried with them, and special mention was made of Morozov's *bor-iagodnik* (pine forest with a ground cover of berries).[30] Furthermore, the managers foresaw that the use of Morozov's ideas would only grow: "The question of stand types in the Shaturskii *leskhoz* has, as of yet, not been studied," the 1931 report noted, but "forest organization parties will soon begin that research."[31] Likewise, in the Lebiazhinskii experimental forest near Moscow, one stated goal of the foresters working there was to "research natural regeneration in connection with stand types" and to revive "the *sukhie bory* [dry pine forests] destroyed as a consequence of the formulaic application of clear-cuts."[32]

The industrial bureaus found themselves obliged to protest the revival of conservationism, a situation that, from their perspective, made no sense. The bureaus were closely allied with state interests and in possession of every ideological and rhetorical advantage, yet they were unable to defeat their enemies conclusively or eliminate conservationism as an ideal. In May 1932, Narkomles (the People's Commissariat of Forestry, the new name for VSNKh's logging bureau after VSNKh's reorganization in 1931) invited 478 functionaries to Moscow to discuss the reconstruction of the forest industry, with nearly all participants employees of national or regional planning commissions, Narkomles, or another industrial bureau. The speakers did their best, without going too far, to link the repudiated concept of sustainable yield to the ideals behind the forest cultivation zone and to equate the newly protected forests with the discredited theories of Orlov and Morozov. A Narkomles employee named Kalinin contended that "it is necessary with all decisiveness to unmask the Trotskyite, right-opportunist wrecking position in forest management and forest organization. We must strike a blow at the reactionary theories attempting to counterbalance and undermine forest exploitation based on mechanization and increased labor productivity, identified with the well-known slogan of the old forestry, 'the cut and the regeneration of the forest are synonyms.' The principle of permanence . . . is not compatible with our plan of moving toward socialism."[33] Kalinin's speech, which aptly reflected the mood of the conference, shows that for the workers of the industrial bureaus, the issue was not only free access to exploitable resources, but whether communist society would be characterized by fearless change or by caution and conservatism.

The Party's puzzling insistence upon finding a place for conservation was evidenced further when Sovnarkom rejected numerous petitions VSNKh filed in the wake of the May conference, designed to roll back the clock to 1929–30. For example, in the summer of 1932, Narkomles (the forest arm of VSNKh) requested control of the forests of Ukraine, but on 5 August 1932, Sovnarkom directly repudiated the attempt, citing the "exceptional significance of forest management in the Ukraine for the development of agriculture and the water regime of its rivers and . . . the fragmentation of mature forests into small parcels."[34] Narkomles did not always receive rejections, but even in forests that it succeeded in regaining, Narkomles found its freedom of action restricted. On 17 September 1932, Sovnarkom transferred the forests of Western Siberia province to Narkomles, but stipulated that the forests in that region that had been protected should remain so and further instructed Narkomles to harvest the forests of Kalininskii region as though they were forests of "water-protective significance."[35] In a few cases, especially powerful local governments were able to dilute the authority of Narkomles by winning the right to insert their own oversight. On 5 December 1932 Sovnarkom ordered that the forests of the Leningrad suburbs should be retained by Narkomles (contrary to the wishes of the Leningrad executive committee), but managed in agreement with the Leningrad provincial government.[36] The Moscow City Soviet won an even more decisive victory when Sovnarkom approved its petition to establish forest cultivation zones in fifty-five *raions* of Moscow province, a significant expansion beyond the three named in the 1931 law.[37] On 27 March 1933 this edict was augmented by a decree "forbidding all cuts in the green zone of the city of Moscow."[38]

Although the Party and the state did not waver in their defense of forest cultivation zones in the years after the 1931 law, the results of the experiment were rather disappointing, regardless of which bureau formally administered them. After being gutted in 1929 and 1930, Narkomzem lacked the resources and infrastructure to regenerate the exhausted forests it had inherited from VSNKh, and as a result it repeatedly failed to meet its quotas. A 1936 report found that "from 1932 to 1935, Narkomzem's Main Administration of Forest Management conducted forest amelioration plantings on an area of 32,421 thousand hectares, equal to 16 percent of the government plan."[39] The protected forests under the control of VSNKh (or the People's Commissariat for Heavy Industry—Narkomtiazhprom, as it was called after January 1932) fared even worse, since its bureaus had logging quotas to fill, and reafforestation largely represented a distraction from its main objectives. In Konstaninovskii *leskhoz* near Moscow, for example, where Narkomzem prescribed the modest task of sowing pine seeds on five hectares, planting pine seedlings on twenty hectares, and sowing spruce seeds on five hectares, "factually the work was not conducted . . . due to a shortage of labor."[40] A scientific commission organized in 1937 to assess how Narkomtiazhprom had managed its protected forests in the Donets province of Ukraine found that loggers had taken 150 percent of the annual growth, that 28 percent of pine forest plots had failed to regenerate at all, that logging was conducted in sections where it should have been forbidden, and that the managers had used a system so abstruse that "what exactly their categories mean remains a secret of the organizers."[41] The 1931 forest reorganization, the passage of time made clear, had failed, since the state had chosen to divide its protected forests among two organizations, neither of which was well-disposed to defend them properly. Narkomzem lacked the power, and Narkomtiazhprom the will, to fulfill the leadership's wishes.

The state solved this dilemma not by abandoning the experiment, but instead by creating on 2 July 1936 a powerful new administration, the Main Administration of Forest Protection and Afforestation (commonly referred to as Glavlesookhrana, or GLO), to look after lands henceforth called "water-protective forests."[42] Unlike Narkomzem and Narkomtiazhprom, organizations that balanced forest protection with other, sometimes incompatible responsibilities, GLO was charged with only four tasks:

1. To conduct all forest planting measures in the water-protective zones;
2. To organize forest management in the bounds of the water-protective zones;
3. To protect the forests of the water-protective zones from illegal felling and violations of the rules of conduct of forest management; and
4. To combat forest pests and forest fires.[43]

There would be no intervening layers of bureaucracy. The head of the GLO and his two deputies were to be designated by Sovnarkom and would answer to that body alone, and only Sovnarkom could allow exceptions to the logging restrictions.[44] The GLO was granted control of "all the forest massifs located in the basins of the rivers Volga, Don, Dniepr, Ural, the upper courses of the Western Dvina . . . and the forest massifs of Vinnitsia and Odessa provinces of the Ukrainian Republic." Forbidden under threat of criminal responsibility was any cutting of the forest (aside from sanitary cutting) in the following areas:

A. In a twenty-kilometer belt along the Dniepr and two of its tributaries, the Don and three of its tributaries, the Volga and ten of its tributaries, the Ural, and the Western Dvina;

B. In a six-kilometer belt along two tributaries of the Dniepr, four tributaries of the Don, five tributaries of the Volga, two tributaries of the Ural, and two tributaries of the Oka; and

C. In a four-kilometer belt along five tributaries of the Don, eleven of the Volga, one of the Bel', and one of the Oka.[45]

In the areas that lay outside these belts but still inside the basins of the rivers named above, logging was allowed, but this would be conducted by GLO, and the harvest could not exceed the annual growth of the forests in question. The transferred area totaled 51,737,000 hectares (roughly 200,000 square miles)—not only a significant percentage (roughly a third) of the forests of European Russia, but more important, the very best forests of European Russia—the most accessible, the cheapest for transport to population centers, the best watered, and the most productive.[46]

Like the 1931 law, the striking decision to sequester the nation's richest forests came from the very top of the Party apparatus. As the deputy head of Narkomzem's forest protection arm, V. M. Solov'ev, reported to a convention of foresters, "This unusual law, comrades—a turning point in forest management—was developed under the direct guidance and with the direct participation of Stalin himself."[47] At a different conference, Stalin was referred to as the "initiator and inspiration of this great idea."[48]

The "limitlessly happy" foresters who convened at GLO's first conference in November 1936 expressed the obligatory thanks to Stalin, but they also shared reports illustrating that employees of Narkomtiazhprom were rather less pleased with the new law. Loggers, it was said, thought of the law as a "handicap," as "reactionary legislation written under the influence of Morozov and Orlov," and made the transfer of lands and personnel to GLO as difficult as possible.[49] In the Russian republic's Western province, Narkomtiazhprom's logging representatives "unconditionally refused to transfer the primary expert foresters," and at the meetings called to discuss the new boundaries, "the director categorically forbade the discussion of 'takeovers' and 'surrenders'" and refused to call any conference of forest guards. Then the logging director told the GLO representatives to leave.[50] In the Middle Volga region, the local logging agency, Sredles, steadfastly refused to give up any worker housing, automobiles, or horses. In Gor'kovkii province, representatives offered the GLO, which was charged with overseeing almost six million hectares of local forests, office space in their *bania*.[51] The logging bureaus also played cynical jokes on GLO. In the Ukraine, the regional administrator recalled, "the logging bureau UkrLes promised us a large staff of workers. Then one day an old man shows up and asks to receive his prize—a year and a half earlier he had been awarded a prize but he had never received it. They told him to come to us for his prize.

Then ten days later our 'director' arrived, all wrapped up and barely breathing. I asked—what exactly are you? He says he is tubercular, straight from the sanatorium, but they've named him the director of our *leskhoz*."[52] In other cases, the directors of the logging trusts agreed to surrender the land, but then acted as though nothing had changed, their actions amounting, in the opinion of the Perm GLO director, to an Italian strike: "The logging plots had not even been divided yet, but the director of the *lespromkhoz* dropped by and, pointing at a map, stated, 'Here we will cut.'"[53]

Once Narkomtiazhprom's land and materiel had finally been transferred—a process that was not complete until the middle of 1937—GLO could fully assess the damage to the forests it had inherited. The flagrant disregard for the state's instructions displayed by the logging trusts surprised at least one GLO representative from the central apparatus: "I expected to hear that Narkomles's system would be poor, since their organization thought only about fulfilling the program in cubic meters and never about proper forest management as we understand it. . . . But when I heard about the dismal condition of forest management in the water-protective zone, I was nevertheless astonished."[54] Research conducted in 1937 found that 28 percent of the forests planted by VSNKh/ Narkomtiazhprom in the Ukraine had died, 34 percent in the Upper Don region, 42 percent in the Middle Volga, and 51 percent in the Lower Volga.[55] On average, 31 percent of the artificial forests were dead, and the reason was simple: "Until 1930, the forest plots designated for replanting were carefully cleared of brush and rubbish . . . but after 1930 the attention paid to forest planting work weakened, and crops were sown directly on rubbish."[56] In the Western province, no care for the forest had been rendered at all. In the Tatar republic, concentrated cuts along rivers had taken 2.5 times the annual growth. In the Kirov region, 20 percent of the transferred forests were completely dead, and the local population had taken to calling the water-protective forests "birch graveyards."[57] In 1935, Narkomtiazhprom had budgeted 67,000 rubles to care for the twenty-seven million hectares of water-protective forests under its supervision, or less than one-fifth of a kopeck per hectare—but in many places, even this small sum had not been spent.[58] The inattention brought consequences. Thirty-nine percent of the forests in Ukraine's forbidden zone were factually denuded of tree cover, and in the Lower Volga region, 58 percent of such forests had no trees.[59]

To repair the damage done, GLO reversed almost all of the practices that Narkomtiazhprom had employed since 1929 and replaced them with ideas borrowed from Morozov. In the Timiriazevskii *leskhoz* in Ukraine, forests were again divided into parcels, test plots laid anew, and calculations linking logging to annual growth were made once more. The logging plans that Narkomtiazhprom had left for 1936 were revised dramatically downward, from 17,583 cubic meters to 6,180 cubic meters, a reduction of 63 percent.[60] In determining where and how to cut, organizers across the country thought in Morozov's language. The national instructions issued by GLO in 1938 divided the forests according to forest type, recognizing both the "root type" and the "second-order type" formed after various disturbances, because forest type was "helpful in determining the best management measures for each *leskhoz* in each independent case."[61] The author of the instructions, GLO's senior engineer Aleksandr Vasil'evich Malinovskii, explicitly recommended using Morozov's nomenclature, terms such as "pine forest with a second layer of linden trees" (*bor lipniak*), "pine forest with a ground layer of berries" (*bor iagodnikovyi*), and "pine forest with long mosses" (*bor dolgomoshnik*).[62] Managers working in the forests followed his lead. In Taldomskii *leskhoz* in Moscow province, the forest was divided using Morozov's system, and management was tailored to each type: on *sukhye bory* (dry pine forests), foresters would plant pine and yellow acacia; on *chernichnye el'niki* (whortleberry spruce forests), they would plant spruce, larch, and associated shrubs.[63] The Taldomskii foresters showed most clearly that they had been reading their copies of *Uchenie o lese* when they explained in their plan that "in the plots logged thirty years ago, spruce is beginning to catch up and crowd out the deciduous species that currently dominate these plots, corroborating the idea that spruce should be a dominant species here and might predominate now, if the proper cuts were conducted. In any case, our research shows that spruce is the maternal type here on these loamy soils, although they are now occupied by birch and aspen forests."[64]

The rediscovery of Morozov was no accident. Although his passing had been lamented or trumpeted many times since 1920, and although his theories, inspired as they were by emotion, religion, and vitalism, could scarcely have been more out of step with state-sanctioned ideology, Morozov's memory had never faded among his acolytes, and indeed his influence had only grown. By the 1930s, hydrological institutes were studying the implications of his forest stand concept, and workers in the water-protective forests were using his classification system. It would have cheered Morozov, no doubt, to know that although his books were out of print for nearly all of the 1930s and 1940s, his *bory belomoshniki* and *el'niki brusichniki* retained their importance after his death. Well-placed forest experts still believed that the cut and the regeneration were synonyms, and many still thought it best to divine the true nature of a forest before making their recommendations. The very first research papers composed in 1936, written soon after the founding of GLO and used to direct its policies, proclaimed that "Ukrainian regions will be divided into ecotopes and forest types; for other regions, stand types have been accepted according to Professor Morozov (for Voronezh and Kursk provinces) and Professor Sukachev (for Kuibyshev, Orenburg, and part of Saratov provinces)."[65]

But this is not to say that the Morozov carried by foresters in the water-protective zones was the same Morozov who had written and lectured until 1920: his teachings had been domesticated by the events of subsequent years.[66] Soviet forest types were but pale imitations of the originals, drained of much of their radical color and only tangentially related to Morozov's teachings. Moreover, they did nothing to save most Russian forests from remorseless exploitation. Morozov had endeavored to revolutionize the entire Russian forest, not just a protected fraction, by giving natural considerations pride of place in economic decisions and by asking loggers to follow the contours of the landscape when drawing up their plans. This certainly is not what took place in the Soviet Union. Morozov's ideas survived in the water-protective zones, but in a sense were incarcerated there, since forests beyond the boundaries of the water-protective zones were felled at astounding rates and in the least mindful ways possible.[67] From 1928 to 1940, the amount of timber logged in the Soviet Union increased almost tenfold, from 28 million cubic meters to 246 million cubic meters, almost all taken unsustainably in European Russia.[68] Looking back upon the era of Soviet forestry that began in 1929, Russia's most accomplished forester of the late twentieth century, Ivan Stepanovich Melekhov, regretted that "in no other country of the world did forest management suffer from such predation as did the Soviet Union, and Russia most of all."[69] Morozov had never advocated strict preservation of forests in one region so as to balance hyperexploitation in another, since he was a conservationist, not a preservationist. Yet the Soviet system accorded him relevance only in the management of forests left largely untouched.

Even in the water-protective zones, stand types were used in a way that Morozov would have found peculiar. They were not used to determine the methods and placement of forest cuts, but instead to determine how a particular area, damaged by the abuses of the period between 1929 and 1936, might be most easily reforested. The engineers of GLO did not create logging plans after walking among the trees, consulting their Morozov, and intuiting the essence of the landscape. Instead they took soil samples, pored over logging records, and searched for relic pieces of nearby woody cover in order to determine the stand type and thus how to best proceed with reafforestation. Once a forest near a body of water had been successfully regenerated, Morozov's teachings fell from importance, for the law required that water-protective forests could only be thinned, not logged. (In practice, these sanitary cuts were made but rarely. The result was the rise of a "disproportionate share of mature and overmature timber in these forests," an age structure more susceptible to disease and insects than young forests.)[70] With Morozov's theories diverted from their true purpose of determining which practices might engender healthy forests, and toward the creation of permanent, never-changing hydrological machines, a method for mediating ecological change was discarded.

Nevertheless, Morozov's influence on GLO policy was clear. GLO explicitly mandated the creation of complex, mixed-species, multistoried forests, the kind of forests prized by Morozov, although not by industrial forestry, and the exact composition differed for each individual forest type.[71] The wide implementation of forestry theories and practices so recently left for dead, at a time when the concept of sustainable yield was still openly condemned as a bourgeois deviation, placed GLO in a very precarious position and created a strange institutional schizophrenia, most clearly manifested in the organization's journal, *Za zashchitu lesa* (In Defense of the Forest).[72] While simultaneously publishing articles encouraging foresters to approach their protection work enthusiastically, the editors also issued warnings about overenthusiasm. When Molotov issued a threat to Narkomtiazhprom at the February–March plenum of the Central Committee of the Communist Party ("It goes without saying that in the forest industry . . . it is time for the unmasking of the wrecking-spying activities of the Japanese-German-Trotskyite agents"), the editors of *In Defense of the Forest* made sure to point out to their readers that Molotov was talking about GLO as well: "The lack of political vigilance has allowed the penetration of enemies of the people into the water-protective zone. [These people] have created difficulties for important industrial firms and have chosen for their cadres a number of Trotskyites and wreckers."[73] Workers inside GLO, the editorial claimed, "had deliberately seized forests useful for mining and placed them in the protected zone; in so doing, these Trotskyite-Bukharinite monsters hoped to impede the extraction of phosphorus, . . . but these enemies were not successful."[74]

Accusations of wrecking, though implausible, carried real menace, for the Great Terror struck the GLO with the same violence and unpredictability it did all Soviet economic managers. The first head of GLO, Ivan Konstantinovich Iakimovich, for instance, was dismissed in 1937, after only a few months on the job, as were the first head of cadres and the heads of the Moscow and Upper Volga administrations.[75] The articles in *Za zashchitu lesa* written by Iakimovich's replacement, German Petrovich Motovilov, make clear he understood the precariousness of his position, consistently balancing a properly vigilant tone with passion for GLO's mission: "Amid honorable, dedicated, loving forest management specialists," he wrote in 1938, "there undoubtedly exist criminals and impostors who work to halt the fulfillment of tasks in the water-protective zones, kulak elements who hide behind the name of honorable forest management workers."[76]

The ambiguity of GLO's mission was only amplified by the articles that *In Defense of the Forest* published, written by long-standing enemies of forest protection, openly attacking the very basis of GLO's project, interspersed among technical plans for carrying out that same project. S. A. Bogoslovskii, lamenting that the Soviet Union had not yet "rid itself of its attachment to 'old village ways' and antimechanist moods," urged GLO to accept clear-cuts for the water-protective zones, just as Narkomtiazhprom had for the Soviet Union's other forests.[77] Otherwise, Bogoslovskii asserted in a different article, "GLO's instructions fully reproduce Narkomzem's instructions of 1926, wholly built on the unmasked bourgeois forest organization theories of Mikhail Mikhailovich Orlov," treasonous principles that "contradicted the basic principles of socialist management."[78] The journal provided space for M. G. Zdorik (Narkomzem's central forest administrator in the 1920s and by 1937 a Gosplan administrator) to tell GLO employees that their work was not actually inspired by Morozov, despite the fact that the founding documents of the bureau were shot through with Morozov's concepts: "It might be thought that by dividing the forests into natural-historical zones, we are hoping to subjugate the activity of the forester to nature, to bring to life the ideas of Georgii Fedorovich Morozov. Such an opinion would be mistaken. The division of the forests into zones is proposed . . . so as not to be subordinated to them, but to use them to the fullest extent for the benefit of socialist management."[79] Later, Zdorik had to correct himself. "The influence of Morozov in the sphere of forest planting work," he admitted the next year, "at the present time still continues to be felt," but this was nothing to celebrate, because each forester "should build his forestry world outlook not on Morozov's idealistic studies, but on the basis of the material dialectic of Marx-Engels-Lenin-Stalin." Echoing Marx, Zdorik reminded foresters that their task, after all, was "to study the nature of the forest, but not in order to passively receive it, but to change it.[80] Orlov's ghost, too, continued to haunt Soviet forest management, according to Zdorik: "GLO has brought nothing new to forest organization, and it seems as though nothing new is even planned; in 1938, at least, all remains as before. In a word, Professor Orlov is dead, but his spirit looms over GLO."[81]

These lines of attack, seemingly tailor-made to influence the regime, completely failed, and the state only strengthened the provisions of the 1936 law as time went by. Despite a less-than-perfect performance record during GLO's first year of existence, or perhaps because of it, the state expanded GLO's reach and funding in 1938.[82] At the explicit request of republic-level governments, GLO's fourteen administrations were divided into twenty-three so that inspectors could observe conditions on the ground more closely.[83] At the same time, GLO's funding was greatly enlarged, from 465,440,988 rubles in 1937 to 843,883,442 rubles in 1938, an increase of 81 percent, with the money allocated for capital investment almost quadrupled.[84] In 1939, GLO's authority was increased further when the Tula-Orël office was divided into two and a Kazakh office was opened, thereby increasing the number of regional administrations by two.[85] Sovnarkom's decree of 9 April 1939 gave GLO the responsibility to oversee the forest activities of every other state agency in order to verify that hydrological function would not be impaired, even in non-water-protective forests.[86] Finally, in 1940, a large percentage of the forests obtained in the Molotov-Ribbentrop Pact was granted to GLO, raising its holdings from fifty-eight million hectares to seventy-four million.[87] Narkomtiazhprom stemmed the tide successfully only once, when in 1941 it persuaded Sovnarkom to reduce the four-kilometer-wide "forbidden zones" near rivers to three kilometers, although the six-kilometer and twenty-kilometer belts were left intact.[88] More sweeping measures, however, such as Gosplan's proposed legislation to "fun-

damentally rework" GLO's logging rules, or Narkomlesprom's efforts to eliminate GLO entirely, were rather easily foiled by Motovilov.[89]

These expansions of GLO's authority carried real weight, as evidenced by
the frequent complaints filed by the state's main logging bureau, the People's
Commissariat of Forestry (Narkomles). For instance, in August 1940, Narkomles's head of forest management grew so frustrated with GLO's interference in the forests of Krasnodar province and the Crimean peninsula that he
asked Gosplan and Sovnarkom to convene a conference to settle the matter.
The Krasnodar provincial executive committee and GLO wanted the forests
near Krasnodar reclassified as protected forests, since they "had been greatly
disturbed by irrational cuts and are now found in an unsanitary condition,"
while Narkomles hoped to retain the right to exploit Krasnodar's forests freely
so as to meet its quotas.[90] To Narkomles's annoyance, however, both Sovnarkom and Gosplan sided with GLO, and the forests were removed from the
forest-industrial zone.[91] Such conferences, unsurprisingly, were called less often afterward, but GLO was still cited as the source of Narkomles's administrative shortcomings. In 1942, after the People's Commissariat of Finance issued
a report indicating that Narkomles had failed to fulfill its responsibilities and
that apparently "Narkomles had conducted its work without a plan," the deputy head of the logging branch could only offer in his defense that "GLO allots
the forest plots slowly, and in the overwhelming majority of cases, they give
only negative responses to our requests for increased allotments."[92] Soon, such
excuses would result in the complete elimination of Narkomles.

Soviet forest organization achieved its final form—a shape it would retain
until the end of the Putin era—on 23 April 1943, when Sovnarkom reversed the
temporary wartime legislation allowing unsustainable logging and issued decree number 430, dividing the nation's forests into three groups, two of which
were subject to protective measures.[93] Into Group I would go "the forests of
the state zapovedniki, soil-protective, field-protective, and resort forests, forests of green zones around industrial firms and towns, and also the lentoch-
nye bory of Western Siberia and the woods of the steppes."[94] In these forests,
only "sanitary cuts and selective cuts of overmature timber" were allowed, and
clear-cuts of all kinds were forbidden.[95] Into Group II went all the "forests located in the Kazakh, Uzbek, Tadzhik, and Turkmen republics; the Mordovskii,
Chuvash, Bashkir, Tatar and Mari autonomous republics; and the forests located on the left bank of the River Volga in Ivanovsk, Yaroslavl, Cheliabinsk,
Kurgansk, and Chkalovsk provinces." There, only cuts less than or equal to the
annual growth, as ratified by Sovnarkom, were allowed. Group I and II forests
remained under the control of GLO. In Group III were grouped all other forests, on which no restrictions whatsoever were imposed.

The 1943 law in some ways amounted to a refinement of the 1936 law, with
Group I forests representing the forests along major and minor rivers (but with
resort forests and forests planted to protect agricultural fields added), Group II

TABLE 5.2.
Growth of the Group I Forests, 1956–73

1956	62.9 million hectares
1961	170.1 million hectares
1966	161.3 million hectares
1973	194.3 million hectares

Source: Compiled from Blandon, *Soviet Forest Industries*, 238.
See also Backman and Waggener, *Soviet Timber Resources and Utilization*.

forests representing water-protective forests not immediately abutting bodies of water, and "Group III" forests representing the new designation for the forest-industrial zone. However, the new classification protected much more territory than did the 1936 law. The forests of entire provinces, among them Moscow, Tula, Voronezh, Kursk, Orlov, Briansk, Kaluzhskii, Smolensk, Vladimir, Tambov, Penza, Riazan', Ul'ianovsk, Kuibyshev, Saratov, Rostov, and Stalingrad, were placed in groups I and II, effectively protecting them from widescale exploitation.[96] Additionally, the grouping structure would prove to be an immensely popular and powerful tool for forest protection in the Soviet Union, because over time, the size of Group I forests grew tremendously, until they represented by far the world's largest area that was so protected (see table 5.2).

The 1943 law, issued just weeks after the Battle of Stalingrad, when victory was by no means certain, signified a strengthened dedication to the protection of the nation's most ecologically sensitive forests, even at an uncertain time. It is true that concerns about the hydrological function of forests, rather than fears about overuse, continued to underlie Soviet forest protection, and the 1930s ethos that held that sustainable yield was a bourgeois superstition had not been repudiated. But forest protection driven by different motivations than those that animate conservationism in other countries is forest protection nonetheless, and Stalin invested ever more power in the apparatus charged with making it real.

Stalin's environmental policies reached their zenith in 1947 with the creation of a new Ministry of Forest Management, charged with the management of all Soviet forests and assigned the task of fundamentally reforming forestry throughout the country. Throughout the 1940s, Soviet governments at both the union and the republic levels had repeatedly expressed frustration with the chronic underperformance of the forest industry sector. In 1945, the logging firms of the Russian republic met only 75 percent of their logging targets, with a financial loss of seventy-seven million rubles.[97] As a result, the Council of Ministers issued stern warnings to Narkomles in July 1945 and May 1946 urging decisive action.[98] In the spring of 1947, after yet another disappointing year, Sovnarkom carried through on its threats and eliminated Minlesprom as an independent entity, folding its duties into the new Ministry of Forest Management (Minleskhoz). According to a decree signed by Stalin, Minleskhoz was given total control of all the nation's forests, including the duty to "define the size and placement of all logging plans, to allot the parcels to various logging bureaus," and to ensure that the logging rules were observed.[99]

Gross industrial output, however, was only one factor in the decision to liquidate Minlesprom, and likely not the predominant one, for if output were the guiding concern, the state could have relaxed or eliminated the restrictions regarding Group I and Group II forests. Instead, conservation issues were the primary consideration. In its decree creating the new agency, Sovnarkom cited the confusing welter of logging agencies (at least twenty-four ministries contracted with Minlesprom for logging rights, and countless more, including NKVD's GULag, conducted their own felling[100]) as a cause of serious mismanagement and environmental degradation: "The forest fund is distributed among many ministries of bureaus, which leads to the incorrect exploitation of the forest, a predatory logging of immature and middle-aged stands, and the use of construction timber as firewood. As a result of unsystematic and destructive cuts, the water-protective and soil-protective role of the forests is violated, and the logging of stands along the banks of rivers leads to the deterioration of the water regime."[101] Sovnarkom also expressed worry that the "restoration of forests lags far behind their rate of harvest, and the planting and sowing of new forests is performed poorly, leading to their death and the formation of large forest barrens." Minlesprom, in the central government's estimation, had proved itself unable to protect the forest from overlogging, fires, insects, disease, or logging errors hindering regeneration and thus was abolished.

The elimination of Minlesprom might have amounted to a simple reorganization without practical significance, like the many reshufflings that Soviet forest management later underwent in the 1960s and 1970s, if not for the fact that the leadership of Minleskhoz was drawn from the old protection agency, GLO. For the six years of its existence, Minleskhoz was dominated by GLO's former employees and their priorities. In his first report to Sovnarkom, written in the fall of 1947, the head of Minleskhoz, G. P. Motovilov, immediately set out the objectives of the new ministry: to bring forest management in line with the conservationist aspects of Soviet law and to undo many of the industrialists' reforms from the early 1930s. At the top of Motovilov's agenda was strengthened enforcement of the 1943 law, since GLO had never been able to implement it fully. "In 1946," he wrote, "fifty-four million cubic meters of timber were taken from the Group II forests, when the calculated yield from these regions was 40.8 million cubic meters, . . . while the Group III forests were underutilized, providing only thirty-one million cubic meters against a projected harvest of ninety-two million cubic meters."[102] Because "this systematic overcutting brings about the exhaustion of mature and young stands and leads to

TABLE 5.3.
Forest Harvests under the Direction of the Ministry of Forest Management

	1948	1949	1950
Group I + II forests	114.9	103.2	96.7
Group III forests	147.0	168.5	180.5
Total	261.9	271.7	277.2

Source: Reproduced from RGAE f. 9466, op. 5, d. 273. l. 11.

the formation of large barrens and blowing sands," Motovilov vowed to bring harvests from Group II forests in line with sustainable yields by 1950 and to shift more activity to the Group III forests to make up the difference.[103]

Motovilov sought to effect this reform by using economic forces to encourage conservation. By reintroducing mandatory logging fees, not paid since VSNKh eliminated them in 1929, and by charging more for Group II plots and less for remote Group III tracts, Motovilov hoped to eliminate a situation in which "the free delivery of wooded plots encourages loggers to develop unsystematic and wasteful practices."[104] In three years' time, these efforts began to bear fruit. While harvests were basically constant, logging in Group I and Group II forests was down throughout the Soviet Union, and logging in Group III forests was up (see table 5.3, which gives all figures in millions of cubic meters).

Leningrad province saw the most dramatic shift away from protected forests to unprotected, albeit with a moderate increase in overall harvest (see table 5.4, which gives all figures in thousands of cubic meters). As these readjustments took effect, they sometimes occasioned protest from local governments, but the central authorities remained resolute. When the premier of the Russian republic, B. N. Chernousov, passed along a petition from the Gor'kii provincial executive committee requesting that the allowable take from Group II forests, revised downward by 40 percent for 1951, be restored to 1950 levels, the request was denied, for the stated reason that the USSR's Council of Ministers had "redefined the yield."[105]

TABLE 5.4.
Forest Harvests for Leningrad Province, 1948–49

	1948	1949
Group I	369	233
Group II	1,224	1,005
Groups I + II	1,593	1,238
Group III	3,089	3,703
Total	4,682	4,941

Source: Compiled from RGAE f. 9466, op. 5, d. 207, l. 25; RGAE f. 9466, op. 5, d. 259, l. 1.

Minleskhoz also carried forward the work of GLO, and advanced the cause of Stalin-era environmentalism, by steadily expanding the size of protected forests throughout the country. During its six years of existence, Minleskhoz submitted seventy-six petitions to Sovnarkom requesting that forested land be designated as deserving Group I protection, and all were approved. Many of these transfers were quite small, such as the transfer from 15 May 1950, when one hectare in Voronezh province was classified as a Group I forest, but other transfers were very large, in nine instances exceeding one hundred thousand hectares.[106] The total area granted Group I protection during the years of Minleskhoz's existence amounted to millions of hectares, and in 1950 alone, according to Minleskhoz's 1950 annual report, "there was transferred from Group II and III forests to Group I forests 3,540,000 hectares," an area larger than all of the forests of the United Kingdom.[107] In addition to creating new Group I forests, Minleskhoz was able to expand those already existing by reversing the wartime legislation narrowing the protective belts alongside rivers. On 29 September 1949 the Council of Ministers (RSFSR) restored the twenty-, six-, and four-kilometer forbidden zones throughout the Russian republic.[108] Group II forests grew as well. In April 1948, Minleskhoz transferred 2.8 million hectares of forest, more than half a million in Leningrad province alone, from Group III to Group II.[109] The power of the ministry to increase protection was so extensive that at times Minleskhoz succeeded in reversing decrees even from the Council of Ministers. On 27 September 1951, for instance, after the Council of Ministers issued a law "obligating Minleskhoz SSSR to grant logging plots in Tula province in order to eliminate damaged and overmature stands," Minleskhoz responded that, "given the exhaustion of the mature stands in Tula province and also the special significance of those forests, [the Ministry] does not find it possible to give permission to cut these stands of overmature timber."[110]

The forest again became a friend to the Soviet people under the tutelage of Minleskhoz. The government began to encourage Soviet citizens and scientists alike to cherish and dote on their forests as it had in the 1920s. Beginning in 1948, the ministry reintroduced the celebration of forest holidays, this time called "Forest Weeks," to encourage an adoring attitude toward green spaces, and circulated booklets asserting that "to be a friend of the forest means to love the forest, to love every plant, to protectively relate to the trees, to protect and guard the trees from fires and grazing cattle, not to break or ruin the trees and so on."[111] Morozov, too, returned from exile. In 1948, Morozov's books were printed for the first time since 1930, although reedited and now including "corrections, insistent marginal notes, incantations, and even a direct command to the reader redefining the thoughts of [Morozov] so as to conform to the thoughts of the editor," as one of Morozov's students put it.[112] Henceforth a condemnation of Morozov's ideas had to be articulated rather than silently assumed—a step forward, of sorts; never again would Morozov's books be un-available in the Soviet Union.

The Ministry of Forest Management's swelling authority wrought one additional, highly controversial change in Soviet environmental policy: the evisceration of the *zapovednik* system. On 29 August 1951, Sovnarkom passed a decree reducing the area of the *zapovedniki* from 12.6 million hectares to 1.38 million, thereby decimating the Soviet Union's most famous environmental achievement, its network of nature preserves dedicated not to tourism or game management, but to the scientific study of how ecosystems function. Historians of Russian environmental history, among them Felix Robertovich Shtil'mark, M. V. Geptner, Vladimir Boreiko, and Douglas Weiner, have castigated Minleskhoz for its role in the gutting of the *zapovednik* system, claiming that Minleskhoz, impelled by warnings that Stalin directed toward the Ministry of Forest and Paper Industry (the logging arm of the Ministry of Heavy Industry) in 1950, sought to open the *zapovednik* forests to economic exploitation.[113] Such an explanation, however, ignores the long-standing antagonism between Minleskhoz and the logging trusts and, more important, misconstrues the function of the Ministry of Forest Management. Minleskhoz did not covet the timber found inside the borders of the *zapovedniki,* because the ministry's stated mission was to check environmental degradation, not increase production, and indeed, the harvesting trend under Minleskhoz's supervision, as described above, was basically flat.[114] Minleskhoz did support the transfer of *zapovednik* forests to its control, but only because its leaders believed that the *zapovednik* forests required more active measures to ensure the forests' health. At issue was not whether to chop the *zapovednik* forests down—nearly all of the *zapovednik* forests were transferred to Group I—but whether measures should be taken to prevent *zapovednik* forests from becoming hotbeds of disease, insects, and wildfires, unable to fulfill their hydrological role. The conflict did not pit industrialists against environmentalists, but instead set two different kinds of environmentalists against one another: the preservationists of the *zapovedniki* versus the conservationists of Minleskhoz.

The clash over the *zapovedniki* sprang from a fundamental disagreement between the foresters of Minleskhoz and the ecologists of the *zapovedniki* about what constituted a healthy forest. While the ecologists considered completely untouched forests to define the very concept of well-being and believed that disease and death were part of the natural condition, the foresters felt that the principle of absolute inviolability (*zapovednost'*) brought about undesirable results for no good purpose. Minleskhoz's annual report for 1950 clearly stated the problems, as the foresters perceived them: "In 1950, the Ministry of Forest Management conducted research into the quality of forest management on the state *zapovedniki* on an area of 961,100 hectares, and the research noted no improvement versus 1949. Forest restoration measures are conducted in extremely small volumes . . . and forest protection is organized weakly. The anti-fire measures do not protect the forest from fires, and as a result the Il'menskii and Chitinskii *zapovedniki* have suffered greatly from fires. Aerial patrol, the best measure for the protection of the forests from fires, is conducted not at all or in restricted amounts."[115] Elsewhere, *zapovednost'* had produced "valuable forest massifs with extremely unsatisfactory sanitary conditions . . . stands in-fested with diseases and forest pests such as the *shelkoriad,* the oak *listovertka,* the rye *pilil'shchik,* and the May Beetle."[116] To remedy these ills, Minleskhoz proposed for the *zapovedniki* "a special, strict regime of forest management, including the removal of part of the standing timber, . . . for the enrichment of the forest growing conditions and the protective properties of the forest," the removal of insects by hand and via aerial bombardment, and the construction of fire breaks.[117] However, none of these interventions satisfied the *zapovednik* administration, dedicated as it was to the ideal of absolute inviolability. Even worse, the punctilious observation of *zapovednost'* sometimes led to undesir-able, or at least unforeseen, consequences. In the Buzulukskii *zapovednik,* for instance, the mills and dams that had dotted the river since time immemo-rial were removed in 1930, and as a result the groundwater level dropped ap-proximately five meters, killing large swathes of riverside forest. The foresters wanted to restore this forest, but the rules of the *zapovednik* forbade this.[118] The foresters' standpoint was summed up accurately by A. I. Bovin, Motovi-lov's successor at Minleskhoz,[119] when he claimed that "*zapovednost',* applied without exception, interferes with the tasks presented to forest *zapovedniki,* where the protection and restoration of valuable and rare woody species are possible only with active interference in the life of the forest."[120] The interven-tions that Bovin had in mind, including thinning cuts and the application of pesticides, were scarcely transformational in spirit, but they were wholly out of step with the *zapovednik* ethos. Given the emphasis that the environmentalism advocated in Stalin's policies placed upon a very specific kind of protected for-est—an eternally young, stable forest, one that was managed to secure the soil and the water and thereby to protect the nation—it is not surprising that the *zapovednik* ethos lost out.

Stalin's Council of Ministers gave the Ministry of Forest Management one additional task: to bring order to the collective farm forests, by the late 1940s in harrowing disarray. Created in 1924 as "forests of local significance" in a conciliatory move, peasant-managed forests never represented a satisfactory solution to the countryside's forest problems, least of all for the peasants them-selves. According to official estimates, peasants in the RSFSR succeeded in ob-taining only 47 percent of their overall forest needs, 21 percent from their own forests and 26 percent allocated from the state's general fund.[121] During the "Great Break," a number of different visions of peasant forest management were advanced. Perhaps the new collective farms would be supplied exclusively by state timber,[122] or perhaps the state would create forest *kolkhozy,* offering a "life entirely different from that in the grain *kolkhozy*," where "*kolkhozniki* will breathe forest air," where "a truly healthy generation, like oaks," would be cultivated.[123] But ultimately, the state reduced its ambitions, and forests of local significance simply became collective farm forests, with no meaningful changes in policy.[124]

Perhaps unwilling to provoke the collective farmers more than was absolutely necessary, the state largely withdrew from the *kolkhoz* forests during the 1930s and 1940s, allowing local authorities, usually *kolkhoz* directors or regional executive committees, to do as they saw fit. In 1947, soon after receiving the orders to introduce order to the *kolkhoz* forests, Minleskhoz surveyed its new holdings and found that "regardless of the considerable forest income from the forests of local significance—which goes entirely into the local budget—forest management is conducted to an extremely insignificant degree and does not correspond to the needs of these forests."[125] As a result of this neglect, the *kolkhoz* forests resembled prerevolutionary peasant forests, disorganized and managed for multiple uses, rather than for large timber yields or optimal hydrological function. "The condition of the *kolkhoz* forests," a 1949 Minleskhoz report stated, "is unsatisfactory. The forests remain unorganized, they are managed unsystematically, and reports are not filed."[126] Inspectors found that *kolkhoz* forests were most often used as woodlots and pastures, despite their official designation as water-protective forests, and that "the majority of *kolkhoz* forests," as another analysis noted, "are young forests of age class I and II [i.e., forests that were not allowed to grow to economic maturity], trampled by cattle and thinned by unauthorized cuts."[127]

Worse still, from the perspective of the foresters, by the late 1940s the collective farmers had come to think of the *kolkhoz* forests as their private property and resented efforts to impose order on them, while local governments were loath to insinuate themselves. "The forest is ours," one collective farmer told a Minleskhoz surveyor, "and we pay for it with our grain. Go away, for there is nothing for you to do here."[128] In Novgorod province, the president of the Path to Communism collective farm asked permission from the regional government to log one hundred cubic meters of timber above the prescribed amount "in order to escape from personal financial difficulties." He was told that he could so long as he kept the *raion* executive committee apprised of the sale.[129] Provincial governments tried to crack down on these kinds of abuses, but the chain of authority broke down at the local level. "*Raion*-level executive committees," Minleskhoz investigators reported, "follow up only with extreme reluctance, and as a result of the indifferent attitude of the *raion* governments, the local governments make no account of the allotment of timber; the forest is cut without the issuance of permits . . . exceeding several times over the volumes allowed by the provincial governments."[130] Some reports suggested that the *raion* governments simply wanted to avoid antagonizing the collective farmers: "Usually the *raion* executive committee, regardless of the repeated reminders of Minleskhoz and the local foresters about the need to bring forest violators to account, do not bring the guilty to account, explaining that the *kolkhozy* are the managers of their own forests, and therefore they may do in them what they like."[131]

Minleskhoz was charged with remedying this situation, but for all of its success in implementing conservationist forest policy in the state's ranger districts, Minleskhoz had almost no success in changing *kolkhozy* forests. The reports filed with the Moscow office in 1952, the last full year of the ministry's existence, describe conditions almost identical to those noted in 1948. "The *raion* soviets are completely uninterested in the *kolkhoz* forests," an inspector in Mari Republic lamented, "and the majority of the *kolkhozy* in the republic do not conduct any kind of forest management work, do not observe the rules of sanitary cutting, and allow logging according to whim without any documentation whatsoever."[132] In the end, the state simply threw up its hands and allowed the *kolkhoz* forests to function free of government oversight, much as it had capitulated to peasant demands about private agricultural plots.[133] In 1953, soon after the elimination of Minleskhoz, the deputy minister of agriculture wrote to the Council of Ministers that "the forest organization of *kolkhoz* forests proceeds in a very unsatisfactory manner . . . [and] 1.5 million hectares are under serious threat. But considering that the organization of the *kolkhoz* forests is not a pressing issue, and also that the *kolkhozy* do not have sufficient resources, . . . the Ministry of Agriculture requests that you cancel plans for forest organization in the *kolkhoz* forests for two to three years."[134] The request was approved.

Although its shape was nothing that Morozov or any other reformer would have recognized as desirable, the Soviet Union did fashion a distinct and uniquely Russian approach to forest management, one that aimed to serve the state rather than individuals or wild nature. The environmentalism of Stalin's regime resulted more from accommodation and negotiation than from design, but it was a structure nonetheless built around ideas about ecosystemic function and the best way to integrate the environment and economic activity. The most unusual and distinctly Russian part of the Soviet system was its collection of Group I forests, lands protected on the assumptions that healthy land was forested land and that deforestation represented a serious environmental danger to the Soviet economy, engendering droughts, floods, and crop failures. No other country has protected so much of its territory, and specifically so much of its best forestland, from commercial logging for hydrological reasons. The environmentalist aspect of Stalin's forest policy was sufficiently strong that space was made even for Morozov's teachings in the protected forests, albeit in a neutered version.

This is not to say that Stalin's forest policy pursued forest protection uniformly. Stalin fragmented the forest so as to give mutually exclusive priorities, including industrial expansion, ecological conservation, and peasant participation, their own spaces in which to predominate. In the 1920s, Soviet forest policy sought to encourage all three principles simultaneously in all the nation's forests, but in the 1930s this hope was abandoned, and the forests were divided into different zones with drastically differing levels of environmental oversight. The majority of the forests, the Group III forests in Siberia and the far north, were subject to no environmental control whatsoever and were logged at rates that Russian foresters still lament today. In addition to these industrial forests, Soviet forest policy also created, although unintentionally, peasant forests, spaces where traditional usage prevailed and where scientific ideas about forest health played no role at all. These various kinds of forests—peasant forests, water-protective forests, and industrial forests—existed in their own isolated spheres, with little or no impact upon each other. This was a dictator's solution to the problem of conflicting interests: rather than blend priorities, Stalin created separate spheres where smaller dictators could rule.

Yet the existence of zones dedicated to priorities other than forest protection does not vitiate the accomplishments of Stalin's environmental initiatives. A forest preserve the size of France, which grew over time to an area the size of Mexico, was created and defended against bureaucratic opponents. Beginning in 1931, and consistently thereafter for the remainder of Stalin's rule, the state endorsed meanings for the forest aside from that of a simple source of timber, with hydrological (and hence environmental) concerns occupying a prominent position. As was the case in Nazi Germany, Fascist Italy, and Communist China, dictatorship in Russia brought with it environmentalist legislation focused on forest health, designed not to promote beauty or relaxation, but rather to increase the power of the state.

6 TRANSFORMATION

The Great Stalin Plan for the Transformation of Nature

The story of the Great Stalin Plan for the Transformation of Nature, the world's first explicit attempt to reverse human-induced climate change, replicates in miniature the larger story of Stalinist environmentalism, which emerged in 1931 with the creation of the forest cultivation zones and developed steadily through the 1930s and 1940s. Both the Stalin Plan, which aimed at creating nearly six million hectares of new forest in southern Russia so as to cool and moisten the climate, and Stalinist environmentalism, which reorganized Soviet forests for hydrological reasons, were motivated by the beliefs that landscapes without forests are fundamentally unstable and that the integration of forests into the landscape is a prerequisite for successful economic modernization. The implementation of both initiatives provided Morozov's followers with opportunities to revive his romantic and vitalist concepts about forest ecology. Both initiatives faced furious criticism from well-positioned opponents, who argued that ecological ideas yielded too much authority to nature and entrusted humans with too little control over outcomes. And in both cases, the supporters of an ecological approach won the debate, despite apparently overwhelming political advantages, when actors at the upper levels of the government ultimately chose to endorse the ecological viewpoint. In a final similarity, the death of Stalin ended the ascendance of technocratic ecology in both enterprises and led to the shuttering of both the Great Stalin Plan and the conservation-oriented Ministry of Forest Management.

Put another way, the story of the Great Stalin Plan for the Transformation of Nature recapitulated the story of Stalinist environmentalism because both became battlegrounds for a struggle between two powerful aspects of Bolshevik ideology: technocracy and prometheanism. Over the course of the 1930s and 1940s, with respect to the Soviet forest as a whole, and then again from 1948 to 1953, with respect to the Great Stalin Plan, epistemologically conservative technocrats squared off against prometheans, those who believed that the arrival of the Communist era had invalidated all natural limitations of human action.[1] The technocrats, inspired by Morozov's teachings, promoted an approach to forestry that acknowledged local variation, natural limits, and the importance of experimental results, with special scientific training required to determine the best outcome, while the prometheans advanced the notion that forests could be made to conform to the human will and relied upon ideological claims to back up their beliefs. The technocrats and the prometheans first clashed in the 1920s, over the concept of sustainable yield, when prometheans such as Sergei Bogoslovskii argued that sustainable yield was one of many "outmoded methods of work" that "act as a brake on the progressive development of forest organization," while technocrats tried to prove that forests follow their own rhythms independent of human intentions. In the 1930s, the prometheans succeeded in discrediting sustainable yield, but technocrats pushed back by stressing the hydrological role of forests, which led to the creation of vast water-protective forests, overseen by scientists. The conflict was replicated again in the late 1940s, when technocrats tried to expand the reach of the hydrological forests by proposing the Great Stalin Plan, grounding it in considerations of natural conditions, while prometheans responded by advancing the theory that forests could be instructed to act purposively for human goals. Although the individuals promoting prometheanism during these debates changed, they shared a common faith in the primacy of human will over matter.

This conflict between prometheanism and technocracy could play itself out three times in closely related fields largely because the field of biological sciences in Soviet Russia remained an outpost of radicalism long after Stalin had curtailed revolutionary experimentation in most other fields. In a process described as a "Great Retreat" by Nikolai Timasheff, Stalin's Soviet Union departed from the avant-garde of the early revolutionary era in the 1930s and moved toward conservatism in art, literature, family policy, education, and a host of other fields, focusing more on stability than on the radical restructuring of social norms.[2] The move away from radicalism extended to science as well, with the prerevolutionary physiologist Ivan Pavlov "knighted as a Soviet hero," Stalin personally deleting references to "class-based science" in scientific papers and the Party leadership "gradually [coming] to accept scientists' authority to ascertain laws that were beyond human ability create or control."[3] The general trend away from radicalism also helps to explain Stalin's reorganization of the Soviet forests into protected and exploited zones, with its implied

rejection of the claims about the irrelevance of forest ecology and its acceptance of prerevolutionary ideas about the role of wild forests in the landscape.
But the biological sciences, as a whole, stood somewhat apart from this phenomenon, in large part because of the influence of the infamous agronomist
Trofim Denisovich Lysenko.[4]

Lysenko helped keep prometheanism alive in Soviet biological science by
using his post as the president of the Lenin All-Union Academy of Agricultural Sciences, a position he held from 1938 to 1956, to champion the position
that agricultural crops could be changed according to need, thereby rescu-
ing Soviet agriculture from its chronically low productivity. The primary re-
searcher in this endeavor was Lysenko himself, who promoted a long string of
agricultural nostrums whose ineffectiveness was obscured by phony evidence,
as well as by Lysenko's uncanny ability to remain one step ahead of his critics. Before the announcement of the Great Stalin Plan, Lysenko's main contribution to agronomy was the practice of "vernalization," a process of treating
seeds in a way that purportedly created new species.[5] The appeal of Lysenko's
promise to remake agricultural crops to order, his unassuming peasant affect
and humble background, and his Russian chauvinism, plus a willingness to attack opponents aggressively, allowed him to rule over Soviet science for a generation while never producing a single prescription of enduring value.[6]

Lysenko thus had the opportunity and the inclination to bring prometheanism into conflict with technocracy in forest management for a third time,
and the primary casualty of this contest was the plan itself. The Great Stalin
Plan was, especially during its earliest stages, a conservative and conservationist enterprise, dedicated to restoring the Russian countryside to perhaps
an idealized, but more diverse earlier state. Only later did it draw the attention of Lysenko and his allies, who hijacked it and transformed it into high-
modernist fancy.[7] As the plan unfolded, the technocrats who first devised the
plan slowly undermined the position of the prometheans and succeeded in
convincing Party functionaries that Lysenko's ideas wrought poor results. But
just as their arguments began to persuade those at the top of the Party hierarchy, Stalin died, and his successors chose to tackle other problems. The Great
Stalin Plan cast a spotlight on the same troubling, perhaps hidden tension between technocracy and prometheanism that had played out with respect to the
water-protective forests, and although technocrats were poised to win the debate for a third time, the death of Stalin allowed his successors to avoid the tension, rather than resolve it, by ending the program.

Although the Great Stalin Plan evolved into perhaps the most ambitious example of Soviet modernism, at its core lay an exceedingly old Russian
dream: to make the southern steppe more like old Muscovy. The first efforts to
afforest the steppe date to the mid-nineteenth century, when the agronomist
Viktor Yegorovich von Graf investigated which woody species were best suited
to colonize the dry prairies of southern Russia.[8] The trend developed further

after the drought and famine of 1891, when Tsar Alexander III appointed the influential soil scientist V. V. Dokuchaev to determine the causes of the catastrophic crop failure. Dokuchaev, hypothesizing that the steppes of Russia had been forested in the distant past, published a report urging the construction of reservoirs and forest belts throughout the south, so as to reverse the damage caused by desultory deforestation. Dokuchaev hoped to roll back the clock to a distant past when southern and central Russia were united under one canopy of trees, with science—soil science, hydrology, geology, and dendrology—providing the tools needed to conduct the restoration work.[9]

For reasons that extend beyond purely scientific calculations and more strongly resemble cultural and imperial prerogatives, Dokuchaev's suggestions gained near immediate acceptance. A diverse but influential set of groups in art and politics, and the common people, had over the course of the late nineteenth century cast the steppe as "a land of fertile soil, opportunity, prosperity, freedom, beauty, and Russianness" in the popular imagination and thus had freighted the environmental condition of the steppe with deep meaning.[10] Perhaps the most famous exponents of this view were the playwright Anton Chekhov, who gave voice to the meaning of the forest in his play *Uncle Vanya*, and the historian V. O. Kliuchevskii, who claimed that the history of Russia *was* the history of the struggle between the Russian forest and the Asiatic steppe.[11] In his lectures, Kliuchevskii described how "the forest played a crucial role in our [Russian] history, [how] it was for many centuries the basis of Russian life," and how "the steppe intruded into this life only during harmful episodes, Tatar incursions, and Kazakh raids."[12] For those adopting this perspective, as David Moon puts it, "the hot, dry winds from Asia were the new Mongols," and any forests that the Russians established on the steppe would become outposts in a cultural war against Asiatic influence. Despite the fact that meteorological records extant at the time did not appear to bear out the assertion that the steppe was in fact growing drier over time, the tsarist government nevertheless financed Dokuchaev's proposals, albeit on a limited scale, by establishing experimental forests in the steppe and promising ever more.[13] Mikhail Orlov enthusiastically predicted soon after the publication of Dokuchaev's report that in the future, all of Russia aside from cropland would be occupied with forests and that in the south of Russia the fields would be "crisscrossed with a network of protective forests and highways lined with fruit-bearing trees."[14] Traveling to the semiarid south and learning how to cultivate forests in inhospitable conditions became a part of the forest cadet's training; it was during a stint at an experimental forest in the steppe that Morozov first encountered Dokuchaev's writings, and it was for steppe afforestation that Morozov received his promotion to forester, first-class.

After the revolution of 1917 swept more ambitious leaders into power and more ambitious ideologies into currency, steppe afforestation projects only grew in importance, scope, and scientific rigor. Both Lenin and Stalin called for aggressive afforestation at Party conferences in the 1920s, and as time went by, Stalin-era legislation creating protective areas and government agencies to oversee them encouraged ever more concerted, empirically based efforts.[15] Between 1918 and 1923, forest-ameliorative work all but came to a halt, but in 1924, in response to another crop failure in the southern and southeastern stretches of the Russian republic, the People's Commissariat of Agriculture (Narkomzem) financed and organized the afforestation of forty thousand *desiatiny*, with an even larger area converted to nurseries.[16]

The Great Turn of 1929–30 and the transfer of the nation's forests to VSNKh again interrupted afforestation work, but the 1931 law setting aside forest-cultivation zones also instructed Narkomzem to "battle drought by creating protective belt stands on the territory of the state and collective farms," forty thousand hectares in 1932 and 350,000 hectares for the second Five-Year Plan in its entirety.[17] Sovnarkom also decreed the opening of forest-amelioration schools in the southern cities of Novocherkassk, Saratov, and Samara, as well as one in Central Asia, and in 1931 requested a report about the usefulness of a "screen of forest belts between the Ural and Caspian seas to defend against winds originating in the eastern deserts."[18] The schools became havens for scholars driven from older schools like the Leningrad Forest-Technical Institute (see chapter 5), and scholars in the new institutes took seriously the best methods and benefits of changing the steppe into woodland, concluding in a 1935 report that "narrow, wind-permeable belts give the most protection from the wind and retain the most snow, reduce the amplitude of temperature variation more than wider belts, . . . and with optimal placement of the belts, doubled the yields of rye and winter wheat yields while increasing chickpea and lentil harvests by 40 percent."[19] The institutes also developed detailed plans for different planting patterns in different forest types, prescribing elaborate grids of pine, yellow acacia, and other species, depending on climatic conditions.

The earliest Soviet efforts foundered, however, because the plans were implemented by the Commissariat of Agriculture, overwhelmed at the time by the chaos of agricultural collectivization and therefore unable to guarantee the assistance of collective farmers. Most of Narkomzem's foresters were lost as part of the 1929–30 reorganization, and as a result the work largely fell to the *kolkhozniki*. As a 15 May 1936 report to Sovnarkom made clear, the rural population wanted no part of the efforts and offered no help: "No kind of forest-amelioration work in the collective farms or machine-tractor stations has been organized, and as for the creation of wide social movements to fulfill the state's plans for forest planting—there are none now. The directors of the machine-tractor stations have strictly refused to participate."[20] An internal review of afforestation work conducted by Narkomzem in April of 1936 found more encouraging signs, but expressed similar doubts about popular support for the state's ambitions: "At the Seventeenth Party Congress, Stalin pointed to forest planting as one way to combat drought and the *sukhovei* [drying winds from Central Asia]. But this work has not been developed as it should. Without the help of the collective farmers, this work will not succeed."[21]

Even when Narkomzem planted the forests with its hired professionals, success was far from guaranteed. "Absent a permanent forest-tending brigade," concluded a study issued just before Narkomzem's afforestation bureau was shuttered, "the forest belts become 'orphans' without systematic attention and care from the collective farms and therefore mainly die."[22] A 1937 report analyzing Narkomzem's performance found that their forest belts perished on average almost one-third of the time and attributed that failure to the facts that "the cadres lacked even the most elementary knowledge of forest planting tasks" and that workers "were often unable to carry out even relatively simple tasks although provided with instructions and forms."[23] Although Narkomzem established 301,373 hectares of field-protective forest belts between 1931 and 1936, a number that compares favorably to Canada's 16,000 hectares in the first thirty years of the twentieth century,[24] the poor survival rate of the belts, and the state's intention to establish 3.5 times more forest in 1937 than it had in 1932 (and 460,000 hectares per annum by 1942), prompted the state to seek another solution. The Main Administration of Forest Protection and Afforestation (Glavnoe upravlenie lesookhrany i lesonasazhdenii, or GLO), created by Stalin's order in 1936 to manage the water-protective forests, also oversaw the reafforestation efforts.[25]

The establishment of a state bureau dedicated solely to afforestation and forest preservation, provided with the opportunity to publish new research in the journal *Za zashchitu lesa* and protected from outside interference by its proximity to Sovnarkom, produced an efflorescence of thought about the possibilities of afforestation and how best to build a field-protective forest. GLO employees soon began to prod their superiors to set their sights higher than merely securing riverbanks: on 13 October 1937, in a letter that likely represents the direct precursor to the Great Stalin Plan, an engineer from GLO's Ukrainian branch named Mikhail Vasil'evich Lokot' sent a letter to the Moscow office (and a copy to Molotov) calling for the "construction of two to four parallel forest belts of a width of one hundred to two hundred meters around all agricultural fields" near the water-protective zones.[26] It was "completely clear," wrote Lokot', "that the 1,500,000 hectares of protected forests scattered about the enormous territory of the Dniepr basin [were] insufficient to fulfill the water-protective function" the state had assigned to them, and he recommended requisitioning 10 percent of the collective farm area, planting trees there rather than grain crops.[27] In responding to Molotov's request for an expert opinion, the head of GLO, G. P. Motovilov, expressed interest but recommended caution, because the hydrological role of such belts lacked "sufficient research and exploration in scientific literature" and because a "special conference with representatives from Narkomzem and the state farms" would first be needed.[28]

In the meantime, GLO produced in the pages of *In Defense of the Forest* a series of articles exploring the geological, botanical, and hydrological aspects of afforestation, tightly linking the potential success of any effort to the peculiarities of the landscape under consideration. Although ecological approaches that imbued the forest with agency were still considered suspicious in mainline forestry, contributors to *In Defense of the Forest* were free, if talking about field-protective afforestation, to analyze forests as though their biological properties mattered. A characteristic article published in 1937, for example, highlighted the importance of ecological principles by asking whether conifers, deciduous, or mixed stands provided the greatest advantage in their ability to restore the hydrological balance and then concluded that deciduous stands performed best, because they allow more precipitation to reach the ground than do conifers.[29] Chemical analyses of fallen leaves, soil acidity during different times of the year, the water-retaining properties of soils found under different species—all these factors were considered and collated to compose charts depicting optimal species composition for any given soil, such as one for "dark gray forest soils in which the process of podsolization [the leaching of organic matter from the A horizon to the E horizon] is not strongly developed" (see table 6.1).[30] The articles tended to avoid citing Morozov or Orlov directly, but authors found it possible to make distinctly Morozovesque claims, such as "the system of management [in newly planted forests] must be established in correspondence with the basic physical conditions of the forest massifs including climate, relief, and so on," or to condemn work showing "full ignorance of the local forest growing conditions."[31] The planting schemes offered in the pages of *In Defense of the Forest* may or may not have represented the best possible arrangement of seedlings, but the journal nevertheless illustrates that GLO adopted, especially in light of what came later, a decidedly technocratic approach to afforestation work, one based on empirical results rather than ideological prescriptions.[32]

GLO's internal documentation reveals that the agency was able to achieve considerable success in its assigned tasks. By 1942, the administration was establishing twice as much new forest per annum as Narkomzem did in 1935, despite the constraints imposed by the war.[33] The survival rate of planted forests, GLO claimed, was steadily climbing, assisted by the graduation of fourteen hundred students from its educational programs each year: the mortality rate declined from 31 percent in 1936 to 25 percent in 1939, then to 17 percent in

TABLE 6.1.
Pattern Developed by the GLO for Creation of New Forests

#	^	#	°	#	^	#	*	#	^	#	°
#	+	#	°	#	+	#	*	#	+	#	°
#	^	#	°	#	^	#	*	#	^	#	°
#	+	#	°	#	+	#	*	#	+	#	°

The code is as follows: # = oak, ^ = bird cherry, ° = linden, * = sharp-leaved maple, and + = any suitable shrub
Source: Reproduced from Stepanov, "Tipy lesnykh kul'tur," 31.

1940.[34] GLO attributed its successes to increasingly educated cadres, but also to improved, ecologically based central planning. The country was divided into fourteen regions, with each region given its own list of suitable trees and shrubs. In zone A, for instance, a strip of territory linking Vinnitsia, Kiev, Zhitomir, and Chernigov regions, workers were allowed to plant Siberian larch, pine, and birch. But in zone B, a region just to the south, stretching from Dnieprpetrovsk to Moldavia, they were not; conversely, currant and white mulberry were sanctioned in zone B and not in zone A.[35] Significantly, the work was carried out not by collective farmers, but by the employees of GLO.

World War II halted afforestation work entirely, but soon after the war's conclusion, the state renewed its dedication to protective afforestation with a rapid sequence of new legislation.[36] In April 1947, when GLO became the much more powerful Ministry of Forest Management (Minleskhoz)—its creation "the most radical of all reforms in the history of Soviet forestry," according to its deputy minister, Vasilii Iakovlevich Koldanov—a special bureau dedicated solely to steppe afforestation was formed, with Koldanov, an avowed follower of Morozov, at the head of the effort.[37] On 11 October 1947, the Council of Ministers approved an ambitious plan, drafted by Minleskhoz, to establish new forests on the collective farms in Kursk, Orël, Tambov, and Voronezh provinces (see table 6.2). Six months later, on 24 April 1948, a nearly identical but smaller version for the Ukraine received approval. Based on the modest premise that "field-protective belts decrease the speed of the wind across agricultural fields, which in turn decreases the moisture transpired by crops and hence their desiccation," the April 1948 law decreed 391,000 hectares of forests around Ukrainian collective farms be established by 1955.[38] Together, these two plans foresaw the establishment of more than 1.5 million hectares of new forest, but the grandiosity of the plans was offset by an unhurried pace, a limited scope, and a sober methodological approach. The work would start slowly, with only one-sixth of the plantings conducted during the first three years while the nurseries were being established, and the planting instructions, featuring the species lists and charts developed during the 1930s, were to be provided by Minleskhoz. The planting of the belts was to be performed only

TABLE 6.2.
Projected Increase of Forest Cover in Central Russia, 1947–55

Forested Province	Forest Area in 1947	Forested Area Projected for 1947 (%)	Forest Area by 1955	Forested Area Projected for 1955 (%)
Kursk	342,000	6.7	660,000	12.9
Tambov	298,000	8.7	464,000	13.5
Voronezh	488,000	7.1	723,000	10.5
Orël	151,000	4.8	404,000	12.8

Source: Reproduced from RGAE f. 9466, op. 1, d. 23, l. 4.

"on freshly cleared ground, plowed to a depth of twenty-five to twenty-seven centimeters just after the spring harrowing of the field stubble and concluded in six to seven days," and planting was forbidden on snow-covered or lightly plowed soil.[39] Both plans, ambitious though they were, shared relatively modest and scientifically grounded objectives: to make landscapes more stable by making them more diverse, which would change the microclimates and the hydrology of relatively small spaces. Never mentioned was changing the climate of the country as a whole.

As sweeping as the plans of 1947 and early 1948 were, the Soviet government soon decided that more aggressive action was merited. A drought in 1946 brought the worst grain harvest in over a century and in its wake Ukrainian famine, ugly rumors of cannibalism in the countryside, and forced rationing of basic foodstuffs in the cities. The grain harvests of 1947 and 1948, while improvements over the disaster of 1946, nonetheless failed to match prerevolutionary levels.[40] Furthermore, the nascent Cold War and the competition with the West made any agricultural failure all the more embarrassing. In order to fashion a response, a national conference of foresters and agricultural experts—but also, crucially, Party leaders—convened in Saratov in February, and when that meeting failed to produce suitable proposals, a second conference in the southern city of Velikii Anadol' was called for the summer.[41] Transcripts of this conference have not been preserved, but Koldanov later wrote in a private letter that the Velikii Anadol' conference of foresters marked "the eve of a new era in steppe afforestation" and that "the materials of the conference were one of the basic sources in the preparation of the decree of 20 October 1948"—the Great Stalin Plan for the Transformation of Nature.[42] A comparison of the afforestation plans published before the meeting with those that came after makes clear that the participants at the conference desired something much grander than the technocratic formulations that the Ministry of Forest Management had been producing on its own—something that demonstrated the superiority of communist ideology and its power to compensate for nature's shortcomings.

The caution that marked Soviet afforestation proposals from the 1930s until the summer of 1948 had little place in the resulting decree of 20 October 1948, heralding the Great Stalin Plan for the Transformation of Nature, theretofore the world's largest ecological engineering project.[43] The programs of October 1947 and April 1948 were expanded tremendously, embracing not 1.5 million hectares but 5.7 million and repurposed to join a larger effort: to change the climate of the country as a whole. The centerpiece of the Stalin Plan would be the construction of eight enormous shelterbelts, their walls of foliage screening dry winds (the *sukhovei*) that rushed in from Central Asia, thereby rendering southern Russia as cool and moist as Moscow. The belts were to be established at the following locations: a 900-kilometer belt from Saratov to Astrakhan along the Volga River; a 600-kilometer belt from Penza to Kamensk along the northern Donets River; a 170-kilometer belt from Kamyshin to Stalingrad; a 580-kilometer belt from Chapaevsk to Vladimirovka; a 570-kilometer belt from Stalingrad to Cherkessk; a 1,080-kilometer belt from Vishnevaia to the Caspian Sea along the banks of the Ural River; a 920-kilometer belt from Voronezh to Rostov-on-Don paralleling the Don River; and a 400-kilometer belt from Belgorod to the River Don.[44] The new forests would extend across sixteen provinces and 204 regions, over an area equal to that of Britain, France, Italy, Belgium, and the Netherlands combined, and if arranged in a belt thirty meters across, would circle the earth fifty times.[45] In an effort to generate support for the project at a time of worrying agricultural shortages, the Soviet government disseminated newsreels and booklets showing children eating fruits and berries growing in the belts and strolling through desert landscapes turned into oases.

International politics also played a key role in transforming the Ministry of Forest Management proposals into the Great Stalin Plan. As Nikolai Krementsov has argued, the Cold War exerted a distorting influence on Soviet science, and the path that Soviet afforestation followed before and after World War II supports this view.[46] Soviet foresters made comparisons to afforestation efforts in Western countries throughout the 1930s, but after 1948 these comparisons grew sharper. Only a country as progressive and rational as the Soviet Union, articles in the scientific and popular press claimed, with its proven ability to harness collective human action in the service of scientific reason, could address environmental problems in such a coherent manner; certainly bourgeois countries could never accomplish such a feat.[47] At a 1949 conference dedicated to the eight major shelterbelts, the head of Ministry of Forest Management expounded on this theme: "Which of the capitalist countries could take on a task of such a grandiose scale? None are able to cope with such a task. They are not interested in the people, but in the bags of money they protect. The robbery of their own and other people—this lies at the base of the programs of bourgeois countries."[48] While capitalism sought to spread destruction, plan propagandists asserted, communists spread gardens; or, as one poster from the time had it, communists planted life, while capitalists sowed death. Thus, as a result of both internal and external political pressures, prometheanism took center stage for the first time in the Soviet afforestation effort, although at the heart of the plan still remained the dream of restoring the Russian landscape to an earlier state.

Beneath the surface of the fantastic claims about transformation of the climate and the Cold War rhetoric, the influence of the technocrats working in Minleskhoz still predominated. Newsreels and newspaper articles emphasized the symbolic power of the mighty oak, but afforestation workers were ordered to use the old lists of species suited to each region prepared by the afforestation institutes in the 1930s. Oak, birch, and ash were recommended for the western half of the Saratov-Astrakhan belt on the right bank of the Volga River, while oak, poplar, and ash were suggested for the strips on the left bank. In addition, the decree included recommendations for suitable secondary trees and bushes, and foresters were instructed to observe the soil type when choosing species.[49] Minleskhoz won the right to manage the new forests as water-protective zones and to designate nearby areas as off-limits to logging.[50]

In general, the technical aspects of the October decree conformed to practices established by GLO up to 1947, with one critical exception: a heavy and ill-fated reliance on collective farm labor. Despite the fact that the state had largely withdrawn from the peasant forests, a decision described in earlier chapters, curtailing its initiatives to involve the peasantry in the daily work of forest management and canceling educational programs about the importance of healthy forests, the sheer scope of the project required the conscription of the rural population to do the bulk of the work. This decision was made despite the additional fact that the record of afforestation conducted by peasants up to that time was extremely poor. Collective farmers had been asked to create field-protective belts on a limited basis in the 1930s, and these belts had died more than half of the time.[51] The efforts of the farmers in the 1940s were no better. In the year before the announcement of the Stalin Plan, Minleskhoz had planted 12,800 hectares, or 82 percent of its quota, whereas the collective farms had planted only 2,700 hectares, or 26 percent of its planned quota.[52] And these numbers would have been worse still had Minleskhoz not picked up some of the slack left by collective farmers, as it did in Kursk province, where Minleskhoz overfulfilled by 85 percent its quota for collective farms.[53] The Council of Ministers for the Russian Republic tended to blame the failure on poor publicity work in the countryside: "There has not been developed," one report stated, "explanatory work for the collective farm worker, to explain the government's decision," while another noted that "as of yet there has not been printed a single newspaper or magazine article on the [afforestation] question in the countryside."[54] Officials assumed that if collective farm workers knew that they would receive 100 rubles or credit for fifteen workdays, provided that the trees they planted survived at an 80 percent clip, and 150 rubles or twenty-two days if 85 percent survived, they would want to cooperate.[55] However, the problem stretched beyond mere poor public relations. A report to Malenkov from 12 December 1948 noted that the Ministry of Agriculture and many provincial governments were apparently uninterested in the new campaign and had established only twelve of the fifty-eight new forest-protection stations needed to perform the work. Sites for fewer than half of the stations had been selected.[56] Only a few months after the plan's announcement, signs were emerging that interest in forest matters among the peasantry was simply too weak to ensure its participation.

The October announcement contained within it one additional component whose significance was perhaps not recognized at the time, but that ultimately served to undermine the Great Stalin Plan: the creation of an independent Main Administration for Field-Protective Afforestation (Glavnoe upravlenie polezashchitnogo lesorazvedeniia, or GUPL) directly under the Council of Ministers. It was GUPL's duty to oversee the implementation of the Great Stalin Plan, to provide technical guidance, and to coordinate the efforts of Minleskhoz and the Ministry of Agriculture. Appointed to GUPL's advisory Scientific-Technical Council were a wide array of specialists of varying ideological orientations, among them followers of Morozov, including the illustrious ecologist Vladimir Nikolaevich Sukachëv, as well as Koldanov and the Ukrainian forest typologist P. S. Pogrebniak.[57] In the first months of its existence, the Scientific-Technical Council favored traditional ecological approaches, and one of its first actions in December 1948 was to authorize the republication of Morozov's *The Theory of the Forest* and *Essays on the Cultivation of Forests,* both out of print for nearly twenty years. But soon the council, and GUPL in general, came under the influence of Lysenko.[58]

Lysenko's appearance on the council, to say nothing of his eventual domination, was something of a coup. Just six months before the unveiling of the Stalin Plan, Iurii Zhdanov (the son of Politburo member Andrei Zhdanov and Stalin's son-in-law) had criticized Lysenko at a Moscow Party meeting for his numerous failures, as well as his habit of accusing any detractors of anti-Sovietism.[59] Lysenko appeared decisively beaten, his innovations exposed as useless and he himself singled out for abusing his authority, but after he sent Stalin a series of letters and an example of his latest miraculous discovery, a stalk of branched wheat, the tide turned again in Lysenko's favor.[60] Zhdanov was forced to recant, and at the historic August 1948 meeting of the Lenin All-Union Academy of Agricultural Sciences, Lysenko achieved his greatest victory when genetics was officially renounced as bourgeois idealism.[61] Lysenko's influence subsequently reached unprecedented heights. On 30 September, the Ministry of Forest Management was forced to organize a series of lectures for its workers popularizing the ideas of Lysenko and to review the curricula of their schools so as to "incorporate the principles and methods of Lysenko in the operation of forest management."[62] Lysenko was named to GUPL's Scientific-Technical Council, and one of his most ardent supporters at the August 1948 meeting, Evgenii Mikhailovich Chekmenev, then became head of GUPL.[63] After developing a completely new, made-to-order theory of natural selection, Lysenko used his spot on the council to steer the Great Stalin Plan in a doomed but politically charmed direction: toward an expansion of the plan's prometheanism.

Lysenko and his allies maneuvered skillfully to take control of the GUPL, despite obvious shortcomings in Lysenko's resume. Although Lysenko's assistant I. I. Prezent claimed it was Lysenko who had "proposed to defend the grain fields with squadrons of trees," Lysenko played no role whatsoever in the development of field-protective afforestation in the 1930s and 1940s (see above) and had published nothing before 1948 about tree biology.[64] However, the state's sudden interest in the practice drew his attention and prompted the articulation of a fantastic new theory of forestry: that trees could become collectivists. At the time of the Stalin Plan's announcement, Lysenko told a reporter that he was then giving "considerable thought to the planting of forests in nests," but just a few months later, before experimental trials of this theory had even been properly started, Lysenko began to declare his new scheme, the "nest method," a complete success.[65] Lysenko's work with a dandelion-like steppe plant called *Kok-saghyz* (*Taraxacum kok-saghyz*) had suggested to him that Darwin's theory of competition deserved revision: Darwin had been correct when he asserted that members of different species did indeed compete for resources, but members of the same species, Lysenko had learned, actually helped one another. By way of proof, Lysenko demonstrated that when *Kok-saghyz* was planted in high densities, its survival rate increased. From this Lysenko deduced that all plants possessed a quality called "self-thinning" (*samoizrezhivanie*), which allowed them to work together in fighting against weeds during their early years and then to pool their energy for the benefit of one shoot in the nest, the other shoots sacrificing themselves for the main plant, when the appropriate time came.[66] Thus, in Lysenko's scheme, plants could become soldiers in the fight for the survival of collectivism, if organized properly.

To encourage oaks to act selflessly, Lysenko made two recommendations. First, he suggested that acorns be planted in nests, spaced five meters apart. Around each central hole, four auxiliary holes were to be dug, creating a nest in the shape of a plus sign.[67] Lysenko claimed that this formation would allow the oak seedlings to defend one another from weeds most effectively, although he never provided any explanation as to why this might be so. Second, Lysenko posited that any favorably inclined domesticated plant, not merely other plants of the same species, could help each other struggle against undomesticated interlopers. Accordingly, Lysenko recommended that agriculturally useful crops, including "winter wheat, oats, barley, sunflowers, flax, potatoes, and alfalfa," should be sowed alongside the acorns, so that these useful plants could do battle with weeds.[68] Lysenko's ideas inspired the head of GUPL to reimagine the entire landscape in terms of Kliuchevskii's historical theories and Cold War rhetoric:

> I want to say a few words about the struggle of the steppe with the forest and the forest with the steppe. Until now, in the majority of cases the steppe has defeated the forest. This happened because the forest is not always in a position to fight the steppe, and because the interference of man under conditions of anarchic capitalism always enabled the victory of the steppe. . . . But can't we, workers of science, bring together forest plants and agricultural crops against their common enemy and then win? I think that this is possible. Leaving biological theory aside, it is possible to recognize, purely on a practical level, that two may be joined, although temporarily, against a common enemy.[69]

Even if traditional biological theory had to be set aside, Lysenko wanted nothing less than to harness the internal drive of domesticated crops to conquer Russia's historical enemies.

Many have stressed the absurdity of Lysenko's ideas regarding self-selection and its implications of plant consciousness, but the main import of the nest method, practically speaking, was that it saved labor. Lysenko himself made this very clear in his 1950 booklet *Posev polezashchitnykh lesnykh polos gnezdovym sposobom* (The Planting of Field-Protective Forest Belts with the Nest Method): "Until now, the widely accepted method of planting forests in the steppe . . . has required working the soil frequently to remove the wild steppe vegetation. But planting oaks with crops to protect them makes this unnecessary. Only three man-days are needed for the hand-planting of one hectare of oak forest using the nest-method. . . . For the planting of seeds of bushes, the expenditure of labor is scarcely needed at all, as the planting is conducted simultaneously with the planting of rye."[70] Elsewhere, Lysenko claimed that "the nest method of planting forest trees, it seems to me, is a promising approach. . . . In a relatively short order there will be a forest created without a single treatment."[71] The real motivation behind the nest method, then, was not to test a new theory of competition, but to allow workers to accomplish in one year what ordinarily would require a decade or more. If the acorns were planted in nests and agricultural crops were sown to provide cover, Lysenko argued, the belts would mature on their own with a minimum of additional effort. Yet this aspect of the nest method was its most serious drawback. The recommendation to plant acorns in nests was relatively harmless, aside from the fact that planting so densely is wasteful. The young oaks could be expected to grow normally, the smaller shoots dying off as the competition for resources sharpened. Indeed, planting more acorns than necessary might provide some short-term benefits, in that more acorns were likely to germinate, and thus the total number of oak seedlings in the early years of a plantation would be higher than the number of seedlings on a normally seeded plot. But Lysenko's recommendation that the belts could be seeded once with acorns and agricultural crops, and then left to develop on their own, could and did occasion harm. Establishing new forests, as the administrators who worked in GLO and Minleskhoz knew, requires a great deal of effort beyond the initial sowing of seeds. Young forests must be weeded, thinned of underbrush and dead seedlings, and replanted if necessary, if they are to reach maturity quickly. Whereas Lysenko claimed that a hectare of forest could be established with the application of three worker-days, Minleskhoz calculated that the true number was closer to eighty-five.[72] Three worker-days per hectare were just enough to sow forests that would die within a year or two.

Nonetheless, hundreds of young people, most without any prior experience in afforestation, dutifully left their homes and schools in the spring of 1949 to establish new forests in the southern steppe. Among them was a recent graduate of Rostov Forest Institute, Anna Podchenko, whose story illustrates both the power of Lysenko's promises and the failures of his methods when applied in the field. When Podchenko arrived at the steppe, she recounted at a 1951 conference about field-protective afforestation, she was dumbfounded by what she saw. She had read about the great treeless plain and its blasting sandstorms while studying at a forestry institute, but seeing it for the first time terrified her. "The Rostov steppe did not welcome me kindly," she remembered, "and I looked with horror at the view, thinking 'Better the sand bars of Briansk than this.' I sat at the train station and, seeing not a single tree, was burned by the sun. I admit openly that the steppe scared me." All that unimaginable open space, stretching in every direction, and no shelter. But her coworkers took her aside and assuaged her doubts about making oaks grow in the semidesert. They told her about how this terrible emptiness could be filled in, how the great new forests would block the parching winds and the awful black dust storms. They calmed her down, reminded her of the larger task at hand, and put her in a romantic frame of mind—for the creation of forests, they convinced her, was a profoundly beautiful, creative task. "And who could resist?" she asked her listeners.[73]

She went to work, though her forest-protection station had not been built. There were no dormitories, no tractors, no machines, no tools. The material privation could only be partially overcome with rousing talk; even the older specialists acknowledged that the bare steppe and the enormous volume of work frightened them as well. The nearest nursery was fifty kilometers from the train depot. Five directors came and went in rapid succession. Soon, Podchenko herself became the director.

She followed Lysenko's method as she was told, but the results disappointed. The shape of Lysenko's nests prevented working the belts with machines, and without the soil around the saplings being worked, she soon found, the saplings stood no chance. First she rotated the nests forty-five degrees, so that they were no longer in the shape of a plus sign, but in an X. That way, the tongues of the cultivators could pass between the trees, freeing the workers from the back-breaking labor of removing weeds by hand. Lysenko had promised that the sowing of grain around the oaks would stave off weeds, but she found that this turned out not to be so. Not only were the crops of no assistance, but they robbed the seedlings of water: "The barley shoots appeared just after the sowing of the acorns, removing the moisture from the upper layers of the soil, and left the oaks only a meager ration. Sunflowers and millet were not as bad, but the best was no cover at all." Deviating freely from the prescribed instructions, she claimed, allowed for excellent results, in her case an 86 percent survival rate. She had proven to herself and to any who doubted that for Soviet people there are no insurmountable obstacles and that even oaks can grow in the steppe. She finished her plantings in three years rather than six and moved on without a second thought, sure that her little oaks would survive. She knew that one day she would return and find an oak forest "in all its beauty, where flowers bloomed and birds weaved little nests."

But Anna Podchenko's seedlings almost certainly died. According to a letter Koldanov sent to Malenkov, more than half of the belts sown on both collective farms and state shelterbelts between 1949 and 1953 had died by 1954.[74] Koldanov's figures, though, referred to efforts for Russia as a whole, including the northern areas near Riazan, where conditions were mild and seedlings survived more often. Podchenko planted her little seedlings near Rostov-on-Don, on the border between steppe and semidesert, where rates of survival were much worse. A survey of plantations in Rostov province made in late 1952 showed that "in 1950, 100 percent of oak forests—and in 1951, 73 percent—were created with the nest method, with agricultural crops applied instead of care, and of such plantings, only 5.5 percent were retained."[75]

Such negative results had not yet been collected in 1949, however, and Lysenko was able to use his position on the GUPL Scientific-Technical Council, as well as the widespread confusion about the best way to carry out the Great Stalin Plan, to transform his nest method from a labor-saving suggestion into the only legally prescribed way to establish forests in the Soviet Union. Although Minleskhoz's considerable expertise in field-protective afforestation allowed its workers to acquit themselves well in the first year of the Stalin Plan, that bureau was responsible only for about a quarter of the Stalin Plan work.[76] The lion's share fell to the Ministry of Agriculture and its collective farms, and they, on the whole, had very little experience in the matter.[77] (Some collective farmers had created field-protective belts in the 1930s, but nowhere near the scale envisioned by the Stalin Plan, and their efforts had generally been unsuccessful.)[78] As a result, a state of bewilderment greatly helpful to Lysenko reigned at the local level. In February of 1949, GUPL held a conference of regional directors, who collectively reported the near-total lack of preparation for the upcoming planting campaign. The GUPL director of Ul'ianovsk province noted that "the collective farms still have not seen the state plan for afforestation work, and the provincial government does not even know what to tell the collective farms to do."[79] At best, collective farms would receive mystifying decrees instructing them, as a delegate from Kursk province recounted, to plant "five hectares of field-protective belts, four hectares of forests on gullies, create a 1.5-hectare forest nursery, build two ponds, grow 50,000 seedlings, and prepare ninety kilograms of acorns," but without an indication about how this should be done.[80] At worst, collective farmers would hear nothing about the plan at all, as in Tambov province, where the chain of command, from provincial executive committee to the local executive committee, and then to the rural soviet and finally the collective farm, collapsed so often that only one collective farm saw any sort of numerical breakdown of expected tasks.[81] The numbers that emerged from the 1949 spring planting season were accordingly disheartening. Against an established plan of 1,500 hectares, only 645, or 43 percent, were sown.[82] Worse yet, some local executive committees were issuing permits to graze cattle among the newly established seedlings.[83]

Lysenko recognized this situation as an ideal opportunity to advance his ideas, simplicity and ease being their main strengths, and went to work. Lysenko's ally and head of the GUPL, Chekmenev, personally lobbied Khrushchev (then the secretary of the Ukrainian Communist Party) as to the drawbacks of the existing instructions and the potential benefits of the nest method: "In many collective farms, the number of rows and the correct width of belts indicated in the instructions was not observed. . . . In Khar'kov province, only 3 percent of the plantings were made on newly plowed land. . . . Only 4.8 percent of the belts in the Ukrainian republic are found in good condition; 28.8 percent feature weeds, and 35 percent are strongly infested with weeds."[84] The answer to all these problems—the failure to observe the rather complicated instructions delivered by Minleskhoz, the inadequate care, the infestations of weeds— was the nest method, which offered an elegantly simple planting diagram and required no follow-up attention. Responding favorably to entreaties such as these, the Council of Ministers on 9 August 1949, citing "positive experimentation with the nest method," decreed that the "best way to construct long-lived, durable and economically viable forest stands with the least expenditure of work and resources" was the "universal application of the nest method, elaborated by Academician Lysenko."[85] Although only tested for fewer than twelve months on plants that live for hundreds of years, Lysenko's method was made the obligatory way to create not only oak forests throughout the Soviet Union, beginning in 1950, but pine forests as well.

Lysenko's capture of the GUPL and his victory on 9 August 1949 again reopened the persistent schism in Soviet forest management, with the prometheans of GUPL on one side and the technocratic Minleskhoz on the other. Although they at first made a show of endorsing the nest method, the leaders of Minleskhoz and the Academy of Sciences' Institute of Forests deeply resented Lysenko's intrusion into their affairs and his reckless attitude toward their hard-won achievements in ecological management, and soon they began to fight back. They proved resourceful and formidable critics of Lysenko, unafraid to appeal directly to Stalin or Georgii Malenkov and willing to interact directly with workers in the field to limit the influence of Lysenko's prometheanism. Ultimately, though, their protests led not to reform, but to the abandonment of the program.

Hints that Lysenko's dominance would be contested came early on and became more explicit as time passed. Even before Lysenko's prescriptions became official policy, at the first All-Union Conference on the Planting of the State Protective Forest Belts held in February 1949, foresters carefully inched toward casting doubt. The head of the forest-planting sector of the Institute of Forest Management told his audience, pace Lysenko's denial of competition between species, that "we foresters most often encounter antagonistic relationships in natural conditions" and that foresters "must provide for the victory of the forest over the steppe by working the soil and physically destroying the weeds."[86] This was a mild critique, noteworthy only because it came so soon after the announcement of the Stalin Plan and at a very dangerous period in Soviet history. But after the nest method was made obligatory, the critiques sharpened. In the autumn of 1949, Koldanov wrote directly to Stalin—a bold move, perhaps, but comprehensible in light of a face-to-face meeting in 1947 that conveyed to Koldanov Stalin's personal interest in forest issues[87]—to complain about the mandated application of Lysenko's scheme. He insisted that it would be "premature to assert that [Lysenko's] method of planting forests is irreproachable. . . . Minleskhoz would consider it proper to remove the words 'the universal transition to the nest method' from the latest decree about spring 1950 forest planting."[88] A letter that Koldanov sent to Malenkov stated his objections less cautiously:

> Regardless of the fact that Lysenko's proposal has already been ratified by GUPL and therefore my objections have no practical significance, I nevertheless consider it necessary to express my disagreement with his scheme. . . . What serves as the basis for Lysenko's ideas? Nothing in the relevant literature, nor any practice, has promoted such schemes. To support his claims, Lysenko cites plantings made near Odessa in the spring of 1949, but I visited these groves in September, and I expressed to Lysenko my negative opinion. Yet directly adjacent to his trees were protective belts lining the highway, fully satisfactory and healthy. It is incomprehensible to me why he would have ignored those indisputable experiments.[89]

Koldanov later described this encounter with Lysenko to Malenkov in more detail, complaining about Lysenko's "impatient and tendentious attitude, focused on discrediting me."[90]

Advocates of orthodox scientific methodology did not focus their attention solely on high Party functionaries. They also took their activism to the field. Undoubtedly, the most effective source of resistance was the Comprehensive Scientific Expedition for Problems of Field-Protective Silviculture, organized after the October decree to study local conditions and to give technical guidance to workers. The appointment of agronomists to a comprehensive study of the environment made little sense, and so trained geologists, hydrologists, and ecologists, rather than Lysenko's followers, were named to the expedition. The importance of expertise in the physical sciences, as well as the continuing influence of the Ministry of Forest Management and its allies in the Great Stalin Plan, was reflected in the choice of leadership for this expedition: the accomplished ecologist, botanist, and opponent of Lysenko academician Vladimir Nikolaevich Sukachëv.[91] Sukachëv unabashedly used his position as director to full advantage, populating the expedition with orthodox biologists in an effort to rescue them from persecution after the massive layoffs in the wake of the August 1948 meeting of VASKhNIL.[92] In 1952, Sukachëv's lieutenant S. V. Zonn published an account of the main expedition's work, illustrating Sukachëv's efforts to lessen the import of the August 1949 law: "After the first year of the application of the nest method, subsequently accepted as the single most important means of cultivating the stands, its shortcomings were observed, and [Sukachëv] issued a series of critical remarks, aimed at the improvement of this method. In subsequent years, the expedition made concrete proposals on its [the nest method's] alteration."[93] Zonn also noted that the expedition set for itself the goal of "enlightening" the public, especially partisans of the nest method, about the method's scientific baselessness. Because the expedition featured a great many ecologists who felt, as Zonn remembered, that the "creation of the forest shelterbelts in all geographic conditions by means of a single method—nest planting—ignored the constant interaction of the created stands with their complex environment," the leaders of the expedition almost certainly recommended that workers dispense with the method, at least in some cases.[94]

Sukachëv's actions appear to have had their desired effect. Even after the August 1949 law mandating the nest method for the establishment of new forest, government officials, such as the leader of afforestation in Chkalov province, felt comfortable deviating from prescribed norms, boasting that the "*komsomoltsy* and other young people of the Chkalov province . . . promised to complete by the fall of 1952 the work of planting one hundred kilometers of government forest shelterbelt, [and] hardships aside, they significantly overfulfilled their obligations. By the tenth of May, 148 hectares had been seeded and planted, rather than the 100 hectares specified in the plan, of which 12 hectares were planted with the method of Academician T. D. Lysenko."[95] The proud tone of this account shows that even for motivated supporters of the Stalin Plan, the state was speaking with two voices, and it was not clear which should be heeded. Official documentation promoted a simple recipe for planting acorns in the shape of a four-pointed star, but visitors from distant agricultural and forestry institutes talked about complex, Morozov-inflected plans that took local conditions into account and entailed years of follow-up work. Both schemes had their problems, and the confusion about proper methodology only aggravated them.

Koldanov and Sukachëv pitched their critiques of Lysenko at a theoretical level and did not need comprehensive experimental trials to know that the nest method was doomed to failure, but beginning in 1950, they received copious evidence nonetheless. Minleskhoz held two conferences in 1950 to gauge the success of its work, specifically the nest method, which had been employed for three years and could thus be evaluated. There was little use in denying that Lysenko's methods, if followed to the letter, did not produce stands that protected themselves, but instead belts that required additional work. At the first of these conferences, held in August, the director of the Stepnovskii forest planting station, not far from Anna Podchenko's nursery, contended that the experiments with the nest method

> prove that the official method must be changed. Across Rostov province, the trees under the cover of agricultural crops developed weakly and then died. Lysenko has said that the agricultural and forest crops will work together to attack weedy vegetation. But in fact the forest and age crops compete for water. Under the cover of wheat and barley, the oaks died completely, though under millet they survived, because millet sets seed later. The Rostov administration feels that in the future, we should not apply agricultural crops thickly—I, for example, violated the instructions this year by not sowing crops, when I saw that the oaks felt unwell [chuvstvuiut sebia nevazhno]. As a result, my crops survived 64 percent of the time, while those of the neighboring station survived 36 percent of the time.[96]

By the time of the second conference, held in December 1950, the survival rates looked even worse. The head of the Kursk administration reported that "95 percent of [his] belts were sown with agricultural crops—oats, vetch, millet, and buckwheat, but of the 1255 hectares he sowed, 47 hectares were found in good condition, 39 in satisfactory condition, and 1,169 [93 percent] in poor condition."[97] The head of Minleskhoz, Bovin, and a director named Masliannikov danced around the obvious fact that to survive, artificial forests required care, even if the scale of the Stalin Plan made such care difficult or impossible:

> Bovin: Planting 660 nests per hectare—this is hellish work. Can you handle ten thousand hectares?
> Masliannikov: When we began to see what was happening with the nest method, we saw the danger. We began to provide care for the stands; we cleared them of weeds—then we had to remove the agricultural crops.
> Bovin: Were the results better where there was no weeding?
> Masliannikov: We found that the nest method gives best results if the covering crops are removed and comprehensive care is given to the seedlings.[98]

In Stalingrad province, the director of the Stalingrad Agricultural Institute reported that the nested oaks were a total loss, with acorns sown under the cover of wheat, millet, and even pumpkins uniformly dying off; by the end of the summer, all of the seedlings had withered, and all of the plots were plowed under.[99] Sukachëv and Zonn wrote to Koldanov to tell him that as of September 1951, 100 percent of the nested forests in the Ural territorial administration had died.[100] By that time, two clear patterns had emerged: first, the nested forests died off as time went by for lack of care, and second, the farther south a forest was sown, the more likely it was to die.[101]

Greatly compounding the problems caused by the nest method was the complete indifference of the collective farmers toward the plan, made worse by the state's weak position in the countryside and hence its inability to compel the peasants to participate. By 1951, the collective farmers were planting field-protective belts in a haphazard manner at best and conducting almost no care at all. In the spring 1951 sowing season, for instance, collective farms filled 64.6 percent of their quota, and only 22 percent of the follow-up work.[102] According to a report prepared by Russian Republic's Ministry of Forest Management, "as of 1 July 1951, not a single province or autonomous republic is fulfilling its plan."[103] In Groznensk province, it was reported that "not a single collective farmer in over three years of activity has engaged in forest planting measures."[104] Distressingly often, the resistance went beyond merely ignoring requests and shaded into open defiance. According to Koldanov, the general plans composed by Minleskhoz were approved and ratified by the collective farms, but in many cases the collective farms refused to surrender the land and instead used the allotted territory to sow food crops, while the local governments and Party organs refused to apply firm measures to make the collective farms comply.[105] The local governments, Minleskhoz complained, were unwilling to expend political capital on the matter and sometimes actively opposed forestry initiatives. "For instance," one report claimed, "the people's court of Dubenskii region in Tula province refused to review a case when the head of the Kaganovich collective farm intentionally destroyed six hectares of forest belts"; in Tambov province in 1951, the regional executive committee forbade the local *leskhoz* from requisitioning labor to sow new forest belts.[106]

At least some foresters recognized that collective farmers were already burdened with tasks and that real error lay not in inadequate measures of compulsion, but in the original choice to rely upon collective farm labor so heavily. As one voice at the August 1950 Minleskhoz conference put it, "the collective farms are not guilty. . . . They say to us 'Yes, we know about the decision of the province executive committees, but you yourselves need to make a choice—either grain or care for the forest!'"[107] After collectivization, the collective farmers had been told in not so many words that their job was to provide grain for the state. When the state tried to renegotiate the terms of the contract unilaterally in order to complete the Great Stalin Plan, it found the rural population quite unwilling to comply. The local governments sided with the farmers.

By the summer of 1951, evidence of the nest method's drawbacks and of the problems inherent in relying on collective farmers to carry out the Great Stalin Plan gave Koldanov and Minleskhoz sufficient confidence to criticize both of these policies publicly (if indirectly), but the political situation prevented them, for the time being, from effecting meaningful change.[108] Although Stalin had given a famous speech in May 1950 denouncing "Arakcheevism," a term meant to describe the tendency of Soviet scientific leaders to monopolize their fields dogmatically, and widely interpreted in the forestry world as referring to Lysenko, Lysenko nonetheless maintained his control of GUPL, a dominance fully demonstrated at its March 1951 conference.[109] A few voices dared mention the poor results of the nest method in Russia's southern regions, but Lysenko had a ready defense: his basic theories about cooperation among plants were still correct, he maintained, but he had discovered that tilled crops, such as potatoes or melons, sometimes provided better cover for baby oaks than did grain crops.[110] If the instructions had produced occasionally poor results, Lysenko announced with the help of sympathetic interlocutors, it was due to an excessively legalistic interpretation of his prescriptions:

> Chekmenev: We have been talking about the ability of tilled crops to protect the seedlings. It is more difficult to cultivate tilled crops, but it is possible, and it must be done. And in the instructions this must be mentioned.
> Lysenko: But where in the instructions were tilled crops forbidden? In the instructions, it was said that *predominantly . . .*
> [Presidium]: That means that they were not forbidden![111]

Lysenko's instructions mentioned only rye, wheat, and similar plants and made no mention of tilled crops, so accordingly, he was not to blame if no one had thought to use them. Furthermore, Lysenko accused the collective farmers of failing in their duties by failing to weed and thin the belts, although Lysenko designed the nest method explicitly to obviate such work.[112] The presidium of the 1951 conference, convinced that the theoretical basis of the nest method was sound, resolved that the "nested sowing of oak elaborated by Academician Lysenko, with the corrections noted, fully justifies itself and should be recommended for future planting seasons, with some additions," rejecting six amendments that would have introduced variations in the instructions for soil and climatic conditions.[113]

Lysenko's temporizing bought him two more years of influence in forestry matters, challenged most seriously when the Ukrainian Ministry of Forest Management attempted to repudiate the nest method and allow its foresters to deviate from GUPL regulations. In June 1951, a forester from the Ukraine, I. S. Lototskii, widely disseminated through private channels an article entitled "About the Nest Method and Row Method of Planting Oak," in which he argued that "three years of practice with the nest method has demonstrated its bankruptcy," that "the growth and development of woody and shrub species is negatively influenced by the sowing of agricultural covering crops," and that the "nest method significantly increases the costs of care for new stands."[114] Like a good follower of Morozov, Lototskii also critiqued Lysenko's uniform recipe for afforestation in the all the wildly varying environments of southern and central Russia, proposing instead GLO's different plantation types. The Ukrainian Ministry of Forest Management took the daring step of decreeing that Lototskii's point of view was correct.[115] GUPL responded with pointed letters asking Koldanov and Bovin to consider their positions carefully,[116] after which Minleskhoz SSSR turned its back on both Lototskii and Minleskhoz Ukraine in a December 1951 decree: "I. S. Lototskii, in denying the theory elaborated by Lysenko about the lack of intraspecific struggle, travels on an incorrect path, toward the bourgeois-reactionary Malthusian theorem about overpopulation. . . . Therefore, it is resolved that the Collegium of Minleskhoz SSSR judges the proposals of Lototskii to be baseless and also notes that the Ukrainian Ministry of Forest Management erred in not uncovering Lototskii's harmful positions."[117] With Minleskhoz unwilling or unable to break with Lysenko definitively, the instructions for the 1952 planting season remained essentially unchanged.

It was only after the 1952 planting, and another year of dismal returns, that the nest method was finally nudged aside. GUPL's internal reports offered increasingly distressing statistics, such as a 1952 report about the survival of the nest method on the eight large state shelterbelts (see table 6.2).[118] Because plots supporting fewer than 2,500 seedlings per hectare were generally recognized by afforestation experts to be dead and in need of complete reconstruction, GUPL's own numbers indicated that fully half of the nested forests had died and that the first two belts were near-total losses.[119] Seventy-one percent of the forests planted on collective farm lands in the Tatar republic had died. In Kuibyshev province the number was 61.9 percent.[120] Worse still, GUPL received signs that the bright spots on their ledgers might be mirages, since the Kursk executive committee reported in May of 1952 that the peasants were not performing follow-up care 61 percent of the time, as the regional office had reported, but 26 percent of the time.[121]

Chekmenev, Lysenko's lieutenant and the chief of GUPL, never repudiated the nest method and refused to acknowledge these failures, but his reports were made available to Minleskhoz, who used them beginning in 1952 to openly assault Lysenko, the nest method, and GUPL as a whole. At a March 1952 conference, the head of the Saratov territorial administration held nothing back: "The reason for the high death rate of the forest plantations is not the planting of oaks in nests per se, but the covering agricultural crops. Yet

TABLE 6.3.
Survival Rates of Forest Seedlings on the State Shelterbelts

	seedlings/hectare		
Belt	> 5,000	2,500–5,000	< 2,500
Chapaevsk-Vladimirovka	10.6[a]	7.9	81.5
Vishnevaia-Caspian Sea	9.0	13.9	77.1
Saratov-Astrakhan	18.6	17.9	63.5
Kamyshin-Stalingrad	15.4	37.9	46.7
Voronezh-Rostov	51.0	15.1	33.9
Penza-Kamensk	53.3	28.4	18.3
Belgorod-River Don	72.3	16.4	11.3
Stalingrad-Cherkessk	77.0	11.8	11.2
Total	32.8	19.3	47.9

[a] All figures are given in percentages.
Source: Reproduced from RGAE f. 243, op. 1, d. 481, l. 2.

it is not so much we who are guilty, as those who defined the tasks. . . . We and the provincial organizations warned, requested, objected, but they would not listen to us."[122] Koldanov used GUPL reports, as well as his own data, to compose a letter to Malenkov in February 1952 condemning almost every aspect of GUPL's management. Only 2.2 percent of the new forests in Astrakhan *oblast'*, he reported, were in satisfactory condition, and Lysenko had "brushed aside all recommendations and advice given to him by foresters, denouncing these experts as reactionaries, denying accepted facts, and proposing unheard of ideas, such as the so-called friendship of grain crops with oaks."[123] Worst of all, Koldanov wrote, millions of rubles would be needed to repair the damage done. Innumerable plantations had died or soon would die, and because "the cost of restoring one hectare of damaged forests, including soil preparation, forest materials, and labor, is equal to approximately 550–600 rubles per hectare, . . . four hundred million rubles would be needed."[124] Koldanov accused Lysenko and Chekmenev of disregarding Russia's "rich and ancient experience of steppe afforestation," most specifically Morozov's instruction that "the sowing of seeds to form new forests is inadvisable for its low reliability and increased expense and excluded in all extreme conditions, including wet soils, dry soils, areas covered with weeds, and eroded areas."[125] The failure of the nest method was showing Morozov to be correct.

On 25 March 1952, Koldanov received the answer he had petitioned for. According to an official decree, the Council of Ministers "judged the application of a formulaic method of creating protective stands inexpedient" and accepted the necessity of a differential technique for the creation of new forests depending on local conditions, with the "mandatory use of accumulated local experience and the allowing of wide flexibility in the matter of protective afforestation."[126] Minleskhoz responded to the decree by rapidly revising its plans in preparation for the 1953 planting season. There arose, according to a pair of engineers working near Stalingrad and Astrakhan, a period of exuberance, of "creative initiative . . . in bringing to life the Stalinist plan for the transformation of nature."[127] On 5 March 1953, the deputy head of the Ministry of Forest Management proudly announced that "beginning in spring 1953, the sowing of oak without the simultaneous planting of appropriate secondary species will be forbidden" and that the plantation types devised by GLO but shelved since 1949 would be implemented. "The experience of the past four years, comrades, has taught us much," the head of the Saratov territorial administration proclaimed at the same conference, "but the gloomy days of the past are behind us."[128]

That night, Stalin died.

On 15 March, six days after Stalin's funeral, the Ministry of Forest Management was liquidated.[129] With the functions of Minleskhoz transferred to the Ministry of Agriculture, forest conservation fell into deep decline. The number of workers assigned to forest matters in Moscow fell from 927 to 342 in the space of six months, a drop of 62 percent, and then to 120 workers after a year. From the regional administrations, 701 workers out of 1,458 were let go.[130] The Council of Ministers shifted power away from the conservationists and back to the industrial bureaus by decreeing that, beginning in 1954, "Russia's exploitable forests will be allotted by the local organs of forest management according to economic plans established by ministries and agencies demanding timber," rather than by a central forest management agency. As a result, sixty-five different ministries and agencies shared control of the forests of the Russian republic, and once again forest management and forest exploitation were separated from one another.[131] Koldanov sent a series of alternatively angry and despairing letters to Khrushchëv asking why the state had chosen to forsake forest management: "Since the time that Minleskhoz SSSR was eliminated, the administration of forests has not improved, but continues to get worse. It becomes clearer and clearer that the unification of the forestry and agricultural administrations was a terrible error. I wish to know the true motives for such an incomprehensible reorganization, carried out rudely and spitefully by [the minister and deputy minister of agriculture], . . . and why the capital investment in forest management has fallen from 217 million rubles in 1952 to 40 million in 1955."[132] When pleas to Khrushchëv came to naught, Koldanov turned to Molotov: "Viacheslav Mikhailovich! Foresters highly value the support that you have always rendered to forest management and hope that you will turn attention to what is happening. The army of foresters is powerless, and there is growing alarm for the further fate of forest management."[133] Though the administration of the Russian forest was reorganized many times in the years to come, industrial interests never again lost control, and never again were forest cultivation and exploitation unified in one bureau as Koldanov wished.

The Field-Protective Afforestation (GUPL), the coordinating bureau for the Great Stalin Plan, was also eliminated soon after Stalin's death, at the initiative of Lavrentii Beria and Khrushchëv.[134] In isolated instances, the afforestation efforts continued; the Kamyshin-Stalingrad belt, the only shelterbelt fully built, was adopted by the Komsomol and the directors of the Stalingrad tractor factory, who took up the task after the near-total die-off of the belt in 1953. Guided by local foresters, they completed the belt in 1956, and its contours can be discerned today using satellite photos and Google Earth.[135] But this was an anomaly. In most places the plantings halted immediately. The Great Stalin Plan for the Transformation of Nature and Stalinist environmentalism were no more.

As a whole, the Great Stalin Plan met almost none of its stated goals. The eight great shelterbelts designed to stop Central Asian winds from blowing across Russia were only half completed (see table 6.4). Less than half of the area planned for sowing was afforested, but the actual results were worse still. According to a letter Koldanov sent to Malenkov, more than half of the seedlings sown between 1949 and 1953 had died by 1954.[136] As a result, the belts

TABLE 6.4.

Completion of the State Shelterbelts at the Time of the Plan's Cancellation

Name of Belt	Planned Size (hectares)	Planted (hectares)	Percentage Completed
Saratov-Astrakhan	13,200	6,400	49
Penza-Kamensk	13,700	9,700	71
Kamyshin-Stalingrad	4,800	4,800	100
Chapaevsk-Vladimirovka	17,400	5,400	31
Stalingrad-Cherkessk	18,500	6,200	34
Vishnevaia-Caspian Sea	27,900	8,000	29
Voronezh-Rostov-on-Don	11,500	6,800	59
Belgorod-River Don	3,100	3,000	97
Total	110,100	50,300	46

Source: Reproduced from RGAE 538, op. 1, d. 1, l. 361.

took on a patchy appearance. If massive forest belts could block Central Asian winds—and this was always a dubious proposition—then the great gaps made certain that the *sukhovei* blew right past. In the 1970s, a German geographer named Peter Rostankowski investigated satellite photos of the shelterbelts created during the Great Stalin Plan and could see quite clearly that the shelterbelt strips, jagged and zigzagging in the best of conditions, "stop[ped] at the boundary of the semidesert zone."[137] The plans for protective forests around the fields of the collective farms fared even worse. While 5.6 million hectares of new forests were originally planned, only 1 million were planted, of which only about four hundred thousand hectares survived.[138] As a whole, the collective farms and Minleskhoz completed only about 20 percent of the original quotas, at an expense never calculated.

Yet the Great Stalin Plan was not a complete failure, for the underlying rationale for the original decree, before it was twisted into a scheme to change the climate of Russia or the historical and ecological balance between forest and steppe, had real merit. Two hundred thousand hectares of field-protective forests were established—more in four years than in all the years before—and records from the Ministry of Agriculture indicate that mild but real improvements in agricultural yield from fields surrounded by forests were detected (see table 6.5). Koldanov received a scientific study corroborating these findings. When researchers investigated 573 fields that had been ringed with forest belts, they found respectable increases in yield (see table 6.6). The observed increases in yield, it was demonstrated, were best attributed to better snow retention and increased soil moisture, rather than to the forest's ability to block hostile winds from afar. One study from Novocherkassk indicated that winter wheat harvests equaled 28 centners per hectare near the forest belt, but only 20.5 centners at the center of the field, indicating that proximity to the forest itself wrought a salubrious influence.[139] If it was true, as Koldanov claimed, that

TABLE 6.5.

Increased Yields of Selected Agricultural Crops When Planted Near Forests

Province	Crop	Without Forest (centners/hectare)	With Forest (centners/hectare)
Vinnitsia	Spring wheat	8.55	9.75
	Winter wheat	10.8	14.5
	Barley	7.8	9.6
Dnepropetrovsk	Winter wheat	6.0	7.5
Odessa	Winter wheat	8.0	12.0
Nikolaevskii	Winter wheat	8.0	10.0
Stalingrad	Alfalfa	6.2	7.0
	Spring wheat	9.7	12.3

Source: Compiled from RGAE f. 538, op. 1, d. 1, l. 10.

TABLE 6.6.

Range of Increase of Agricultural Yields

Less than 1 centner/hectare	174 cases
1–2 centners/hectare	90 cases
2–3 centners/hectare	45 cases
3–4 centners/hectare	23 cases
4–5 centners/hectare	14 cases
More than 5 centners/hectare	30 cases

Source: Reproduced from RGAE f. 538, op. 1, d. 2, l. 277.

every hectare of forest protected thirty-three hectares of field, and the average increase per hectare was 2 centners, then the afforestation work conducted from 1949 to 1952 produced an annual benefit of 26 million centners of grain.[140]

If the modest improvements wrought by the plan, however, compare unfavorably to the original goals, this is because the Great Stalin Plan drew upon two impulses that were not entirely compatible or at least could not both predominate simultaneously. The Great Stalin Plan was born in the Ministry of Forest Management and thus grew out of the larger movement of Stalinist environmentalism, primarily a technocratic phenomenon founded on the proposition that scientific experts, rather than industrialists, should manage the most important Soviet forests. Yet Soviet afforestation stemmed more from a romantic, promethean desire to restore landscapes to a primeval state not yet damaged by human activity, even if scientists were needed to oversee the work. Until 1948, these motivations coexisted in a balance in which technocracy generally predominated, although always invigorated and sustained by promethean optimism. The result was steady progress in the science of afforestation. However, when prometheanism, in this case represented in a near-pure form by Lysenko, moved from a supporting to a dominant role, irreconcilable differences emerged. (Other episodes in Soviet science reflect the difficulty in serving two masters: the Soviet nuclear weapons program, famously, was shielded by Stalin from ideological interference, while in the Soviet social sciences, prometheanism generally held sway.) After Lysenko took control of the Main Administration for Afforestation, Soviet afforestation gained its second master, one no longer aimed at creating a landscape that accorded with nature's dictates, but rather at creating an improved nature.

CONCLUSION

Civilizations are like forests. They grow and change over time; they expand, and they contract. Neighbors invade them, and natural calamities alter their composition. Yet at the same time they are embodiments of continuity, and they create conditions that promote their own survival. They generate unique subcultures that defend the collective against incursion, and given favorable circumstances, they produce self-propagating entities capable of surviving for millennia. When they are knocked down, they grow back—but they do not grow back as they were before.

Anxiety that the Russian national culture was failing to regenerate itself drove a wide array of writers to express their worries in print at the end of the imperial period. Anton Chekhov famously worried in *The Cherry Orchard* that the aristocracy, so instrumental in molding the Russian cultural ecosystem into a phenomenon of world significance, was self-destructing. At almost the exact same time, Georgii Morozov made an essentially identical observation in reference to the forest itself and urged forest managers to embrace his new theory of the forest lest the Russian forest be transformed into something less valuable and less beautiful. Both Chekhov and Morozov lamented the fact that the venerable communities that surrounded them, that formed their identities and provided their lives with meaning, were fading from view, subject to the seemingly irresistible pressures of modern life. Morozov went one step beyond Chekhov, however; while Chekhov expressed concern that something vital to Russian civilization was being lost, Morozov sought to provide a solution to the problem. If Chekhov resigned himself to the inevitable advance of European concepts like capitalism, materialism, and egalitarianism, Morozov believed the battle for Russian cultural independence might still be won—that the European invader might be defeated or at least tamed. This belief lay at the heart of Morozov's theory of the forest, and it was his belief that Russia was capable of organizing itself according to different principles that ultimately made his theory so popular. Although it would be too simplistic to label Morozov's theory as purely Slavophile in inspiration, because of its debt to Western science and especially Darwinism, Morozov did offer a scientific system infused with Russian Orthodox piety and mysticism.

It was the Russianness of Morozov's theory that first brought it great acclaim, and it was also its Russianness that allowed it to endure in the Bolshevik cultural ecosystem, eventually a cornerstone for Soviet forest policy. Although Bolshevism was a self-consciously Westernizing political movement, one that revered the German ideology of Marxism and sought to install egalitarianism, rationalism, materialism, and industrialism, it was impossible for the Bolsheviks to disregard fundamental aspects of the Russian cultural heritage entirely, including the beliefs and concerns that inspired Morozov to formulate his theory, because self-propagating aspects of Russian culture continued to operate in the minds of Soviet policy makers.[1] Morozov's supporters were able to convince the party leadership to embrace a very Russian idea: that healthy landscapes included forests and thus that sustainable Soviet economic development could not proceed without forest protection. After a brief period of dominance from 1929 to 1931, the most radical and mechanistic Bolshevik ideas about forest management were relegated to the outlying "Type III" forests of Siberia and the far north, while Morozov's vitalistic concepts about forests as living entities gained dominance in the forests of the Russian heartland. In fact, Morozov's reputation grew to such size that in 1968, the Soviet Union created the Georgii Fedorovich Morozov Prize to recognize exceptional achievements in forestry. The surprising influence of romantic conceptions of forest management despite official and often fierce ideological hostility, and the eventual recognition of Morozov as a Soviet hero, demonstrates the power of cultural continuity to influence and even trump political considerations. The Russian cultural ecosystem continued to support ideas about the central role that forests play in healthy landscapes, regardless of ephemeral political shifts and even the upheaval of Stalin's Great Break.

The Soviet appropriation of Morozov's theories led to the creation of a unique, distinctly Soviet form of environmentalism, herein called Stalinist environmentalism. (Here the descriptor *Stalinist* is used, not because Soviet forest protection used coercion to achieve its ends, as is sometimes the implication of the word, but instead to echo Stephen Kotkin's use of the word *Stalinism* in *Magnetic Mountain*—Stalinism as a unique civilization with its own customs, mores, and values.)[2] Concerns about pollution, aesthetics, or public support played almost no role; instead, Stalinist environmentalism, like other Stalinist policies, was a top-down affair focused on rapid industrialization. Yet environmentalism it was. When the state decided to divide the nation's forests into three groups and assign the best forests in the country to a category protected from any economic exploitation whatsoever, real economic sacrifices were made in order to guarantee that the natural world retain its integrity. The Soviet timber industry was shifted from the country's center to its periphery so that the ecological function of forests would be preserved, thereby creating economic inefficiencies that plagued Soviet planners until the fall of the Soviet Union. One could argue, correctly, that the primary motivation behind protecting forests along the nation's waterways was to safeguard cities from floods and hydroelectric dams from silting up, not to defend the inherent worth of pristine natural landscapes. But not all environmental initiatives aim to preserve wild nature. Clean air and water laws, antinuclear protests, and global-warming treaties are all examples of environmentalist political action driven by anthropocentric concerns rather than romantic ideals about the value of untrammeled nature. Stalinist environmentalism differed from modern, Western environmentalism in its rejection of the idea that human interests should be subjugated to natural ones—yet its emphasis upon the protection of ecosystemic function and its co-optation of Morozov's theories to safeguard vast swathes of forestland qualifies it as a variety of environmentalism.

However, although the forests of the Russian heartland were protected by Stalinist environmentalism, the same cannot be said for Morozov's approach to forest management. Over time, the dissonance between Morozov's concepts and the deeper, materialist values of the Soviet project led first to the domestication and deradicalization of Morozov's stand types and then to their destruction as a viable field of scientific inquiry. By the time the Morozov Prize was created, Soviet foresters no longer studied stand types with an eye toward creating a more sustainable forest management; like the protected forests themselves, Morozov's theories had been cordoned off from the mainstream of Soviet economic life and incarcerated, although in a place of honor. Meanwhile, Stalin's policies of collectivization and rapid industrialization were driving people from the land, from the "idiocy of rural life," as Marx put it, and moving them into cities, where personal contact with the forest ceased to be a daily occurrence. In so doing, the Soviet Union succeeded in cutting down old Russian culture, and it did not grow back as it was before. The substrate from which the Russian cultural ecosystem grew was altered when a rural, agricultural, and pastoral civilization was changed into an industrial one. Support for Morozov persisted so long as the old cultural forms retained relevance— but the old forms were steadily fading. The Group I forests remained protected throughout the Soviet period, but represented more and more a dead relic rather than an active management priority, just as the very trees that populated the protected forests grew senescent. They were unceremoniously signed out of existence by Vladimir Putin on 1 January 2007, with scarcely a murmur of protest from society at large.

The dramatic arc of Morozov's theories reflects how concepts of Russian cultural identity persisted and changed during the twentieth century. Prerevolutionary ideas about forest protection were never solely about the ecology of woody plants; alternative visions of the Russian forest, such as Morozov's ideas and forest democratization, contained important encoded assertions about Russia, how it differed from other countries, and how economic policies should reflect that difference. (Environmental ideas, perhaps, are never solely about nature.) Morozov's blend of science and intuition, his claim that the Russian forest required a specially tailored approach, was not destroyed by Soviet rule, but it was stripped of its most radical implication—namely, that economic exploitation of the forest should be tied to its biological properties—and applied only on lands not intended for industrial use. Likewise, forest democratization found expression in Soviet forest policy, but in the form of collective farm forests, although these were more a concession to the rural population than an explicit confirmation of the peasant's ability to manage an important economic resource. In both cases, proposals that were complex combinations of conservatism and radicalism—conservative for their nationalism, radical for their economic ramifications—were tamed and then worked into the Soviet economic system. Katerina Clark critiques the trend in Western historiography that "has seen the evolution of Soviet culture in terms of a battle between the avant-garde, as the force committed to transforming culture, and traditionalists who sought to set the clock back rather than forward"; like Clark's analysis of avant-garde artists, the story of Soviet forest management suggests that such a bald opposition is too stark to be accurate.[3] Nationalism, cultural conservatism, and forest radicalism have been closely intertwined in Russian environmentalist thought, and the resurgence of the first two in Stalin's Russia allowed the third to live on.

Yet it must be recognized that Morozov's theories lived on only in a twilight existence. They were applied primarily in places where no management took place at all, and the heated discussion that they had once evoked faded to silence. The idea of reorganizing the country's forests so as to conform to their true nature lost its force. The relegation to irrelevance of Morozov's theories, which his opponents could not accomplish through direct argumentation between 1905 and 1953, was achieved by the social, cultural, and economic changes brought about by Soviet modernization. The question of how to live correctly with the forest simply became a dead letter. Morozov's radical contention that humans should converse with nature rather than dictate to it steadily faded in significance, a message from a world disappearing irretrievably. The axes began to fall on the forests protected by Stalin's fiat, and a lingering vestige of traditional Russian culture disappeared at the same time.

NOTES

Introduction

1. Shostakovich, *Pesn' o lesakh*. All translations by the author.

2. For a fuller discussion of the libretto, see Jack Weiner's "Destalinization."

3. See Josephson, *Industrialized Nature*, as well as his *Resources under Regimes* and *Totalitarian Science and Technology*.

4. Goldman, *Spoils of Progress*. Other works that explore and expand upon this theme include Pryde, *Conservation in the Soviet Union*; Singleton, *Environmental Misuse in the Soviet Union*; Komarov, *Destruction of Nature in the Soviet Union*; Feshbach and Friendly, *Ecocide in the USSR*; Massey-Stewart, *Soviet Environment*; Peterson *Troubled Lands*; Yanitsky, *Russian Environmentalism*; and Feshbach, *Ecological Disaster*. Among Russian scholars of environmental history, of special note are Vladimir Boreiko, an associate at the Kiev Ecological-Cultural Center's Center for the Protection of Wild Nature, who emphasizes the cultural implications of the natural degradation, and Victor Teplyakov, whose works on the history of Russian forestry focus on the leading figures in Soviet dendrology and silviculture. See Boreiko, *Belye piatna istorii prirodookrany*; and Teplyakov, *History of Russian Forestry*.

5. Ziegler, *Environmental Policy in the USSR*, 28.

6. The *zapovedniki* were not destroyed entirely, but reduced by 90 percent in the later 1940s. See Douglas Weiner, *Models of Nature* and *Little Corner of Freedom*. See also Shtil'mark, *History of the Russian Zapovedniks*.

7. Feshbach and Friendly, *Ecocide in the USSR*, 29.

8. Suny, *Soviet Experiment*, 238–39.

9. Husband, "'Correcting Nature's Mistakes,'" par. 2.

10. Ibid., par. 38.

11. Oldfield, *Russian Nature*, 1.

12. Douglas Weiner, "Demythologizing Environmentalism."

13. Billington, *Icon and the Axe*.

14. Leonov, *Russkii les,* 251. *The Russian Forest* was first published in 1955, but composed largely during the time of the Great Stalin Plan for the Transformation of Nature, from Jan. 1950 to Dec. 1953.

15. "Les i step' v russkoi istorii," 681.

16. The list of specialized words is longer if one considers local and regional terms. From the central *oblasti* and the Ukraine comes the word *gayok,* "a pure stand amid other species." In Voronezh *oblasti,* the word *griadina* referred to "a belt of oak, aspen, and cork oak along the edge of a floodplain in a wide valley." See Murzaev and Murzaeva, *Slovar' mestnykh geograficheskikh terminov;* and Grebenshchikov, *Geobotanicheskii slovar'.* The richness of the forest vocabulary led R. A. French to suggest that "only Finnish or some North American Indian languages . . . can match such subtlety of expression" ("Russians and the Forest," 24).

17. Kazantsev, "Poslovitsy o lese," 12–16.

18. Ivanits, *Russian Folk Belief.*

19. Chekhov, *Uncle Vanya,* 51–52.

20. Nilsson et al., *Forest Resources of the Former European USSR,* 6. The year 1696 was used as a baseline, for in that year, Peter I ascended to the throne, during his reign conducting surveys to determine the forest cover of his dominions.

21. Chekhov, *Uncle Vanya,* 26–27.

22. Ibid., 24.

23. Costlow, "Imaginations of Destruction," 92, 101.

24. Ibid., 101.

25. Costlow provides two more examples of famous Russian poems likening people to trees: Kol'tsov's "Les" (Forest) of 1837, which compares Pushkin to a forest; and Merzliakov's "Sredi doliny rovnye" (Within the Spreading Vale) of 1830 (ibid.).

26. Ibid., 113.

27. Costlow notes that "the linden is, according to Mikhail Epshtein, a symbol of Russia's past, of 'gentry culture,' and becomes identified by the late nineteenth century with cultural memory" (ibid., 113–14).

28. Ely, *Meager Nature,* 20.

29. Ibid., 187.

30. Ibid., 199.

31. Ibid., 204.

32. Ibid., 205.

33. The list of artists who sensed a special connection between the forest and the Russian people could be extended significantly: poems by Lermontov, Bunin, and Esenin; extracts from Gorki and Solov'ëv; and paintings by Nesterov, Klodt, and Levitan. See M. Egorov, "Iskusstvo na pomoshch lesnomu khoziaistvu," 22–24.

34. Damberg, "Tipy kak osnovanie klassikatstii lesov," 1214.

35. Morozov, "O biogeographicheskikh osnovaniiakh lesovodstva," 14.

36. Bramwell, *Ecology in the Twentieth Century,* 6.

37. "Natsionalizatsiia lesov i provedenie," 10–11; RGAE f. 243, op. 1, d. 41, l. 63.

38. Chekhov, *Uncle Vanya,* 25.

Chapter 1. Old Growth: The Origins of Russian Forest Management

1. Mikul'skii, "Zhizn' maiskago zhuka," 1–2.

2. Kirpakh, "Lesokhoziaistvennye zametki," 37–38.

3. "Pis'mo v redaktsiiu," 1211–13.

4. The word *forst* (or its variants *voorst* and *foresta*) originally merely referred to any property belonging to the king, rather than wooded lands per se. *Inforested* lands were lands where the king reserved the right of the chase, and *foresterii* were those officials who guarded the king's hunting grounds.

5. Fernow, *Brief History of Forestry*, 215, 235.

6. Lowood, "Calculating Forester," 321.

7. James C. Scott cited the German trend toward abstraction and rationalization in his articulation of the concept of "high modernism" in his influential work *Seeing Like a State*.

8. Tol'skii, "Iz praktiki zapadno-evropeiskogo lesovodstva," 23. Here Tol'skii, rather than presenting a caricature of German forestry, was in fact summarizing the opinions of the German forest historian Ernest Wiedeman.

9. Lowood, "Calculating Forester," 334.

10. During certain periods, even private landowners were forbidden from cutting trees on their land without special permission.

11. For a discussion of the content of these laws, see Teplyakov, *History of Russian Forestry*, 3–4.

12. Red'ko and Red'ko, *Istoriia*, 45.

13. Ibid., 122.

14. Arnol'd, *Istoriia lesovodstva*, 213.

15. Red'ko and Red'ko, *Istoriia*, 144–45. This was just one of the many forest initiatives of Paul I, whose assassination did not prevent his policy choices from influencing later developments.

16. Gershman, "Ocherk istorii lesovladeniia," 804.

17. Red'ko i Red'ko, *Istoriia*, 147.

18. Shelgunov, *Istoriia russkago lesnogo zakonodatel'stva*, 95.

19. Tiurin, "Professor M. M. Orlov," 8–9.

20. Morozov, "Pamiati Alekseia Nikolaevicha Soboleva," 35.

21. Arkhangel'skii, "Istoricheskii ocherk," 7.

22. Vitkovskii, "XXV let zavedovaniia Vyshenskim lesnichestvom," 12. Labor turnover in some remote posts exceeded 60 percent; see Lagarinskii, "Iz byta lesnykh konduktorov," 26.

23. Red'ko and Red'ko, *Lesnoe khoziaistvo*, 175.

24. Ibid., 208.

25. Iatsenko, "Esteticheskaia okhrana lesov i lesoustroistvo," 376.

26. One representative evaluation of the law declared that "the forest-protective law is toothless, since the forest-protective committees are inactive and the local oversight over the forests is lacking; the law does not reach its goal, since the application of it is not the same for different people, completely arbitrary and associated even with abuse; the law brings no use, because the forest-protective committees are far from life and their decisions are completely random" (Speranskii, "Iz literatury," 1078).

27. Red'ko and Red'ko, in *Istoriia*, provide the *soslovie* (official class designation) of most of the 123 foresters discussed in their work. The correlation is not perfect, but many reformers came from humbler families, and many conservatives were of noble provenance.

28. Of the 225 individuals who graduated from an apparently typical lower forest school between 1888 and 1913, 112 were from the peasant *soslovie*, 12 from the noble *soslovie*, and 69 from the *meshchanin* or petit bourgeois *soslovie* (Arkhangel'skii, "Istoricheskii ocherk," 7).

29. "O polozhenii lesnykh konduktorov," 630.

30. "K prestoiashchemu XXV-letiiu nizshikh lesnykh shkol," 1360.

31. Because crown (or appanage) forests were managed essentially like state forests, and because monastery forests were relatively small and have left little in the way of written documentation, the first three types of forest—private forest, state forest, and peasant forest—will be described here.

32. Red'ko and Red'ko, *Istoriia*, 338. The share of privately held land in the more productive and accessible forests of European Russia was much higher than in Siberia, where settlement was sparser. European Russia held 32.8 percent of Russian forests, Asiatic Russia 62.9 percent, and the Caucasus the remaining 1.3 percent.

33. For a full discussion of the 1888 law, see Bonhomme, *Forests, Peasants, and Revolutionaries.*

34. *Protokoly vneocherednogo*, 30. The speaker was M. S. Eremeev.

35. Gershman, "Ocherk istorii lesovladeniia," 516. Noble ownership of forests plummeted in the last quarter of the nineteenth century; in 1877, the nobility owned 48.2 percent of the forests of St. Petersburg *guberniia*, but by 1905 this number had dropped to 33.4 percent. These numbers for Moscow *guberniia* are 27.8 percent and 17.4 percent; for Kostroma, 38.9 percent and 18.7 percent; for Smolensk, 44.5 percent and 21.0 percent; for Tver, 23.7 percent and 13 percent; for Novgorod, 37.6 percent and 18.5 percent.

36. Rudzskii concluded that peasants needed to be given more respect (he advised that landowners treat peasants "lovingly") and more influence over forest policy, since any failure to satisfy their demands would eventually be satisfied in some other, less pleasant way. For a full discussion, see Rudzskii, *Lesnye besedy dlia russkikh.*

37. I. Ts., "Ocherk lesokhoziaistvennykh uslovii Vilenskoi guberniia," 78. The *desiatina*, a traditional Russian unit of measure, is equal to roughly 2.75 acres; there are approximately 680 *desiatinas* in a square kilometer.

38. *O Vserossiiskom s"ezde lesovodov*, 3.

39. Morozov, "Doklad vserossiiskomu s"ezdu soiuza lesovodov," 612.

40. Ibid., 12.

41. Orlov, *Ob osnovakh*, 93. This book, published in 1918, was completed on 18 Nov. 1917 and thus ostensibly was composed before the October Revolution.

42. Ibid., 93.

43. Ibid., 67.

44. Kaluzhnyi, *Zhizn' G. F. Morozova*, 189. Here, as Kaluzhnyi notes, one can see reflected the influence of Solovëv and his discussion of the Time of Troubles in his popular history of Russia.

45. *Protokoly vneocherednogo s"ezda*, 29. These words were spoken by A. P. Meshcherskii.

46. As Brian Bonhomme points out, "Terms such as 'nationalization,' 'popular' and 'state' could imply either central or local, planned or spontaneous use" (*Forests, Peasants, and Revolutionaries*, 50).

47. "Vserossiskii s"ezd lesovodov i lesnykh tekhnikov," 149.

48. The Department of Ship Forests was closed in 1859, and all those forests transferred to the Forest Department, which was already in the process of organizing its forests. The progress of organizing the forests into management units—*lesnichestva*—only accelerated as time passed; between 1908 and 1915, the number of *lesnichestva* grew from 1261 to 1549, an increase of 23 percent. See Nekhoroshev, "Lesnoe delo," 21.

49. Ibid., 33. The figures were as follows: 1909, 126,575 rubles; 1910, 138,205; 1911,

142,368; 1912, 153,380; 1913, 164,930; 1914, 102,000. The outbreak of the war accounts for the interruption of the steady upward trend, since Germany was the primary market for Russian exports.

50. Kliuchnikov, "Instruktsiia dlia lesoustroistva," 562. This system replaced another wherein forests were categorized according to predominating species.

51. The *sazhen* is an old unit of Russian measurement equal to seven feet.

52. Bogarevich, "O sokhranenii pamiatnikov prirody," 27. In 1900, 3,303,070 cubic *sazhens* were procured by clear-cutting, while 4,914,854 were obtained from selective cutting; in 1910 these numbers were 3,878,762 and 1,648,234 respectively.

53. V. A. Bugaev, "Vklad G. F. Morozova v razvitie lesnogo khoziaistva i nauki o lese," in *Lesovodstvo, lesnye kultury i pochvovedenie,* 6.

54. Pokaliuka, "K voprosu o reorganizatsii," 74.

55. Kliuchnikov, "Lesoustroistvo ili lesnoe khoziaistvo?" 211.

56. Sazhen, "Prodazha lesa bez torgov," 1450–51.

57. Red'ko and Red'ko, *Istoriia,* 338.

58. "Lesoustroistvo v krest'ianskikh lesakh," 145. As negative as this picture is, the peasant forest described here might have been a bit more orderly than others; there is mention here, after all, of forests being cut in rows.

59. "O pol'zovanii v krest'ianskikh lesakh," 404.

60. "Okhrana lesa v Rossii i zakon," 38.

61. Ispolatov, "Samovol'nye porubki," 39. This exchange occurred in the far north of Russia, and one imagines that the peasants, surrounded on all sides by hundreds of miles of forest, must have been chagrined by the stranger's attempt to claim the boundless expanse as protected.

62. Naumov, "Melkaia-razdrobitel'naia prodazha lesa krest'ianam," 33.

63. Ibid., 33. Peasants and merchants alike in the prerevolutionary and NEP periods were allowed to conduct logging in state forests if they first obtained a logging ticket, which indicated where, when, how, and which trees could be cut.

64. Tisenhausen, "Lesnye porubki," 206.

65. Ibid., 207.

66. Ibid., 208.

67. Sazhen, "Vol'nye i nevol'nye samovol'nye porubki," 1464.

68. Tisenhausen, "Lesnye porubki," 206.

69. Damberg, "O lesnoi tekushchei statistike," 867; "Krest'ianskaia lesnaia sobstven-nost'," 256. Since a *sazhen* equals seven feet, Novgorod peasants would have needed a pile of wood seven feet wide, seven feet high, and twenty-one feet long for their annual heating needs. A cubic *sazhen* is equal to 347 cubic feet, or 2.71 cords.

70. One discovery of French and German forestry in the seventeenth century was the concept of "biological maturity," the age at which the ratio of wood produced on a given plot to the number of years it has grown reaches its optimum. (The related concept of economic maturity specifies the age at which the ratio of sale value to years of growth is maximized.) The age of biological maturity varies according to species and growing conditions, but typically occurs at around eighty years for pine and one hundred for oak.

71. Modern observers of the forest have argued that scrubby forests, like those that peasant management tended to favor, feature humid soils, more conducive to the genera-tion of mushrooms—a result that peasants may or may not have been recognized.

72. Nikulin, "K voprosu o roli lipy v lesu i khoziaistvo," 708.

73. Linden (or basswood), in addition to providing the raw material for bast, provided

the best and most beautiful wood for the construction of food-storage boxes. Pine boxes impart a disagreeable smell to food stored in them, oak was too expensive, and other woods were generally not durable enough or suitable for box making. Linden was also a favorite wood for the fashioning of small tools and eating utensils, because of its softness and plasticity; whereas pine is liable to split, and oak requires expert handling, linden is more forgiving of amateur woodworking technique (ibid., 718).

74. Gershman, "Ocherk istorii lesovladeniia," 506.

75. Ibid., 510.

76. Ibid., 510. Not all peasants had belonged to the noble landowners. The state owned peasants, as did the church.

Chapter 2. Seeds: New Visions of the Russian Forest

1. Kaluzhnyi, *Zhizn' G. F. Morozova*, 20.

2. Beilin, *Georgii Fedorovich Morozov*, 9.

3. Morozov, "Neskol'ko slov priveta Petrovskoi akademii," 1–3.

4. Kaluzhnyi, *Zhizn' G.F. Morozova*, 69. Soviet-era biographies of Morozov attribute his decision to leave for the capital to revolutionary fervor inspired by his new friend Olga Zandrok. Morozov's subsequent activities do not lend much credence to this hypothesis. While Morozov supported the nationalization of the forests, he spurned any political activity beyond public education.

5. Georgii moved into the household of Olga Zandrok, where he met his future wife, Lidiia. Olga died of diphtheria soon after Georgii's arrival. Georgii and his father eventually reconciled, but Georgii never lived with his family again.

6. It is revealing of Prussia's continued prominence in Russian forestry circles to note that in 1900, Tsar Nicholas II awarded three German foresters imperial decorations: Schwappach received St. Stanislav, second class; Geyer St. Anna, second class; and Mayr St. Anna, third class.

7. Morozov wrote a letter to a friend upon his arrival in the Baltics that reveals his tendency to believe in German cultural superiority: "I have visited a few villages. Well, brother, the poverty was such that I've never seen before, except for in Kurland *guberniia*. Even our people in Belorussia are better off. And this from our culture bearers [*kul'turtregery*]—the Germans!" (quoted in Kaluzhnyi, *Zhizn' G. F. Morozova*, 129).

8. Morozov, "Pis'mo po povodu izbraniia," 1.

9. David Moon describes Dokuchaev's scientific approach, as well as Dokuchaev's contribution to Russian national politics, in "Environmental History of the Russian Steppes."

10. Dokuchaev, *Gorizontal'nye i vertical'nye pochvennye zony*, 51.

11. Quoted in Teplyakov, *History of Russian Forestry and Its Leaders*, 29.

12. Turskii, *Lesovodstvo*, 34.

13. Morozov, *Uchenie o tipakh nasazhdenii*, 147.

14. Morozov's attraction to peasant terminology echoes a similar predilection in the work of Vasilii Dokuchaev, for Dokuchaev also borrowed the terms he used for soil types from peasant usage.

15. Morozov, *Izbrannye trudy*, 14.

16. Kravchinskii, "Po povodu khoziaistvennogo," 314.

17. Chernogubov, "Iz zapisok taksatora," 15. The reason why the spruce forest made such a dismal impression upon the appraisers, and the pine the opposite, has to do with the form (or habit) of pine and spruce: spruce retains its lower branches as it grows,

which blocks the light and creates a dark understory, whereas pine drops its branches as it grows, leaving behind an open, light, airy space.

18. Sukachëv, "Tipy lesa i ikh znachenie," 2.

19. Morozov pointed out this linkage explicitly at the 1909 Forester's Congress in Tula. See Kaluzhnyi, *Zhizn' G. F. Morozova*, 350–58.

20. Lesnik, "Neskol'ko slov," 639. This quote, and the others cited in this paragraph, might be dismissed as fanciful speculation on "Lesnik's" behalf, were not this article published in *Lesnoi zhurnal*, the journal that Morozov himself edited. While Lesnik's identity cannot be known, one can assume that Morozov agreed with Lesnik's interpretation of the implications of stand types. In Russian, *lesnik* refers to a forester without academic training, or a forest ranger.

21. One could argue that Lesnik misconstrues Solovëv, since Solovëv's essay highlights the importance of subjugating the flesh (or the material world) to the will (or the spirit). However, Solovëv also notably advanced the concept that in beauty lay the salvation of the world, so perhaps Lesnik's interpretation, which placed great emphasis on aesthetics in forest management, is not without merit. See Solovëv, "Krasota v prirode," 1. However, even if Solovëv's philosophy had nothing particular in common with environmental ethics, it is noteworthy that Lesnik tried to use Solovëv's ideas, and that Morozov approved of this.

22. Lesnik, "Neskol'ko slov," 640 (emphasis in original).

23. Kaluzhnyi, *Zhizn' G. F. Morozova*, 101.

24. Jane Costlow analyzes the work and impact of Kaigorodov in "Dmitrii Kaigorodov and the Ethics of Attentiveness."

25. For a discussion of Kaigorodov's younger days, see Tkachenko, *D. N. Kaigorodov*, 6. On Kaigorodov's ideas about the importance of nature for spiritual health, see Bobrov, *Dom u zolotogo pruda*, 19, 154.

26. Bobrov, *Dom u zolotogo pruda*, 180.

27. For discussions of Silver Age modernism, see Hutchings, *Russian Modernism;* and Gasparov, Hughes, and Paperno, *Cultural Mythologies of Russian Modernism.*

28. Perekhod, *Modernizm v lesovodstve i demokratizatsiia*, 1.

29. Ibid., 1.

30. Ibid., 4. Perekhod, unlike Orlov, did not reject stand types outright. In fact, he came to champion them in the years directly after the revolution. He merely recommended that stand types be used jointly with Orlov's more conservative *bonitets*, for stand types, no matter their cogency, were simply too unusual ("modern") to be applied alone.

31. Figes, *Natasha's Dance*, xxvii.

32. Maes, *History of Russian Music*, 83–87.

33. Ely, *This Meager Nature*, 228.

34. Smith, *Recipes for Russia.*

35. Palimpsestov, "Vstupitel'naia beseda."

36. Moon, "Environmental History of the Russian Steppes," 157–58. For more discussion of the cultural implications of different geographic interpretations, see Moon, "Agriculture and the Environment."

37. "Literatura po tipam nasazhdenii."

38. Kravchinskii, "Po povodu khoziaistvennago," 313.

39. Anonymous, "Neskol'ko slov k voprosu o tipakh lesonasazhdenii," 273.

40. Quoted in Damberg, "Tipy kak osnovanie klassifikatsii lesov," 1214.

41. Uglitskikh, "Printsipy klassifikatskii sosnovykh nasazhdenii," 1157.

42. Morozov, "K voprosu o tipakh nasazhdeniia," 407.

43. Pedanov, "K voprosu o tipakh lesonasazhdenii," 318.

44. Kravchinskii, "Po povodu khoziaistvennago," 313–14.

45. *Protokoly XI Vserossiiskago s"ezda*, 15.

46. Rodd, "Uchenie o tipakh nasazhdenii," 94–96.

47. One enthusiast went so far as to say that "it was hard for the Slavic spirit to come to terms with the purely formal signs" associated with German forest management and that this created "a strong tendency to use an active system of classification—that is, to create stand types." See Botsianovskii, "O ratsional'nom i udobnom sposobe," 1496.

48. Iunitskii, "Neskol'ko slov k voprosu o tipakh nasazhdenii," 13.

49. Iakovlev, "G. F. Morozov," 78–79.

50. Korsh, "Neskol'ko slov o vydele nasazhdenii," 234.

51. Speranskii, "Iz literature," 948.

52. Orlov, "Sud'ba," 555.

53. Kliuchnikov, "Znachenie tipov v lesoustroistve," 407.

54. Orlov, "Sud'ba," 555. This very question—whether the stand type follows directly and inexorably from the local conditions of growth—was the main point of contention between Orlov and Morozov. This dispute remains unresolved today. While modern ecologists generally discredit the concept of a telos in nature and focus on instability and change in landscapes, this belief does not undermine the possibility of managing a piece of land for a given desired use.

55. Morozov hotly denied this and claimed that a properly defined stand type existed in a one-to-one correlation with growing conditions.

56. A modern ecologist might fault Morozov for assuming the existence of climax communities, the "highest" or "most developed" vegetation associations a piece of land can support. The concept of climax communities was pioneered by the American ecologist Frederick Clements, who noted that after a disturbance such as fire or storm, landscapes underwent a predictable progression: grasses appear first, then low shrubs and quick-growing, shade-intolerant trees. Slow-growing, shade-tolerant trees eventually crowd out the pioneer species, and finally a stable climax community results. Clements posited that all landscapes strive toward a telos, but by the end of the twentieth century most ecologists had rejected such a notion, instead arguing that landscapes are constantly undergoing change and do not "aim" toward any end. Morozov apparently did not know about the work of his contemporary Clements. Although Morozov's ideas resemble those of Clements in some respects, it could be argued that Morozov recognized, as do ecologists of the early twentieth century, that landscapes are shaped by perturbation and that he worked to understand the nature of those perturbations so as to maintain the most useful (or profitable) vegetation association.

57. Donskov, "O smene porod v lesnom khoziaistve," 30.

58. Perekhod, "Staryia i novyia idei v lesovodstve," 36. It is odd how quickly Morozov's ideas changed from cutting-edge to "old school." The same ideas considered revolutionary in 1905 and controversial in 1911 were described as "old school" by 1916. They would be criticized precisely the same way—as emblematic of a hoary, rejected past—in the upheavals of 1929–31.

59. Orlov, "Napravleniie sovremennago lesoustroistva," 30.

60. Morozov, *Izbrannye trudy*, 34.

61. Sazhen, "Lesoustroistvo i smety otpuskam lesa," 566. The area-mass method is a plan whereby a forest is divided not into equal areas, but into areas containing an equal amount of wood volume.

62. Grekov, "Neskol'ko slov," 1487.

63. "Protokoly zasedanii S-Peterburgskago Lesnogo Obshchestva," 817–18.

64. Ibid., 819.

65. The amount spent by the state on forest organization had dropped from 416,000 rubles in 1875 to 122,000 in 1905. See Kuznetsov, "Instruktsiia," 445.

66. Ibid., 446. As of 1908, 32.6 million *desiatins* of Russian forest had been organized.

67. Shabak, "Tipy i bonitety," 1422. *Vereschatniki* were mentioned as a subgroup of forests belonging to *bonitet* II, *belomoshniki* to *bonitet* IV.

68. *Instruktsiia dlia ustroistva*, 82; Kuznetsov, "Instruktsiia," 447.

69. Orlov, *Ob osnovakh*, 39.

70. *Protokoly XI Vserossiisogo S'ezda lesokhoziaiev v Tule*, i.

71. "Zhurnal 10-go ocherednogo zasedaniia Lesnogo Obshchestva," 616.

72. Orlov, *Lesoustroistvo*, 2: 140.

73. Morozov steadily increased the scope of his concept of stand type throughout his life. Early on, the stand type referred largely to vegetation. By 1920 it had evolved to encompass the sum total of all possible influences on a plot of forestland. The period when Orlov disseminated the reports coincided with the composition of Morozov's *Uchenie o lese*, when Morozov was modifying his core concepts.

74. Tsarist-era journals offer no information about the opinions of government officials, but Soviet-era discussions often note that the tsarist forest department was not well disposed to stand types. V. Savich, e.g., writes in a 1924 issue of *Lesovod* that "Professor Morozov advanced the study of stand types, but his research, although it found many adherents, met with strong opposition at the heights of the former state forest organization" ("Obsledovanie lesov na novykh nachalakh," 34).

75. Grekov, "Neskol'ko slov," 1490.

76. *Instruktsiia dlia ustroistva*, 2, 18, 55.

77. Orlov, "Sud'ba," 556.

78. *Postanovleniia*, 11.

79. Mikul'skii, "O maiskom zhuke," 3–4.

80. Nesmianov, "Po povodu unichtozheniia khrushcha," 646; Andreev, "O bor'be s maiskim zhukom," 1039.

81. Vorontsov-Dashkov, "Dva dnia v lesakh pri s. Novo-Tomnikove," 10; the price is drawn from Kviatkovskii, "S"ezdu g.g. lesnykh chinov 4 raiona Tambovskoi gub.," 14.

82. Gladilin, "Maiskii zhuk," 569.

83. Shal'vinskii, "Otpusk," 14. Peasants could borrow up to three hundred rubles. At first these loans were unsecured, but by 1912, borrowers had to pledge all their property, moveable and immoveable, and provide the names of cosigners to the loan.

84. Naumov, "Znachenie," 1.

85. A. P., "Na raznykh temakh," 3; Sazhen, "O kazennoi prodazha," 92. Sazhen also mentioned the influence of the forest on Russia's climate and the importance of the fish and game trade.

86. Shturm, "Les i zemleustroistvo," 12.

87. A review of Krivoshein's activity, published on his retirement in 1916, counted among his accomplishments "the implementation of a series of measures, including the 1909 instruction to the local administrations of agriculture to increase the sale of timber to the rural population without bargaining," the 1914 decision to further ease "the conditions of sale directly from the state to the rural population," and various decrees decentralizing forestry related decision making by investing greater authority in local actors." See Nekhoroshev, "Lesnoe delo pri A. V. Krivosheine," 18, 40.

88. Shal'vinskii, "Otpusk," 14. Shal'vinskii knew of only one case of outright default, and this was due to the peasant forgetting about the terms of the agreement, rather than intentional avoidance of payment.

89. Zhitkov, "O sokhrashchenii sroka operatsii," 20.

90. Ibid., 21.

91. Skliadnev, "K kharakteristike sbyta lesnykh materialov," 22–23.

92. Naumov, "Znachenie," 5.

93. Egorov, "O budushchnosti lesov Arkhangel'skoi guberniia," 1012–13.

94. The forester Shal'vinskii, quoted above, argued that "a new contingent of small buyers competing with each other, in turn increasing the marketing of timber, will elevate prices and lead to the delivery of wood to new places and new methods of wood use" ("Otpusk," 16).

95. Vysotskii, "O putevodnoi ideinosti," 22 (emphasis in the original).

96. Speranskii, "Iz literatury," 950.

Chapter 3. Ground Fire: The Russian Forest and the Bolshevik Revolution

1. "Natsionalizatsiia lesov i provedenie," 7.

2. P. Morozov, "Chto delat'?" 5; Sperber, *European Revolutions*, 118.

3. One reporter lamented the phenomenon this way: "Such ugly occurrences are the result, first of all, of mistrust toward the forest workers, as well as the simple desire to seize nearby forests for personal use. In all of these abnormal instances the attitude of the rural population to the forest is: 'Whoever needs it.'" See L. Iashnov, "Beregite lesa!" 343.

4. G. F. Morozov, "K voprosu o Vserossisskom," iii.

5. The burgeoning numbers of the Russian peasant were a powerful force of social change in this era and had important ramifications for almost all national problems, including the growth of revolutionary sentiment. According to Geroid Tanquary Robinson, the population of the Russian peasantry increased from fifty-five million to seventy-nine million between 1860 and 1897, and it grew even more in the last twenty years of tsarist rule. See Robinson, *Rural Russia under the Old Regime*, 94.

6. Iannovskii, "Udovletvorenie," 222.

7. Kaluzhnyi, *Zhizn' G. F. Morozova*, 407.

8. See G. F. Morozov, "Zamechaniia na proekt."

9. Given his nervous condition and the strain of the times, his death has never been discussed by his students or scholars of his life as anything other than an accident.

10. Matreninskii, "Vospominaniia o G. F. Morozove," 37.

11. Red'ko and Red'ko, *Lesnoe khoziaistvo*, 245. Red'ko and Red'ko aver that Kriudener assumed Morozov's position as the leader of Russian forestry after Morozov grew ill and left Petrograd in late 1917.

12. Kriudener, *Beskrainie prostory*, 7.

13. Migunova, "Lesovodstvo i pochvovedenie," 150. Alternatively, it was hypothesized at the time that Russian types did not catch on in Germany because German geology and geography differed so strongly from Russian. See K. Iashnov, "Lesnye tipy i lesnoe khoziaistvo," 167.

14. Iannovskii, "Udovletvorenie," 221.

15. Professor V. V. Guman, looking back in 1924 upon the previous decade of forest management in Russia, lamented the "breach in conservationism of forest management" brought about by the war and the fact that forestry work "was done by soldiers, urban

workers and even craftsmen . . . hoping to avoid war duties, including Kirghiz, Kalmyks, and Sarts, many of whom had never even seen a forest." Not only was too much timber taken with clear-cuts and high-grading, but inexperienced workers tended to make their cuts three to five feet above the ground, such that the remaining stumps could and did hamper regeneration. See Guman, *Rubki poslednogo desiatiletiia*, 5–6.

16. P. Morozov, "Chto delat'?" 5.

17. "Vserossisskii s"ezd lesovodov i lesnykh tekhnikov," 146.

18. *O Vserossiiskom s"ezde lesovodov*, 9.

19. "Vserossisskii Soiuz Lesovodov i Lesnykh Tekhnikov (Konduktorov)," 129.

20. Kuznetsov, "Gosudarstvennye lesa," 669.

21. "Natsionalizatsiia lesov i provedenie," 8.

22. Bonhomme, *Forests, Peasants, and Revolutionaries*.

23. The Council of People's Deputies, or Sovnarkom, was only nominally the supreme power in the Soviet Union; real power was invested in the highest reaches of the Communist Party, which made political decisions and in most cases then left them to the government to implement.

24. Bonhomme, *Forests, Peasants, and Revolutionaries*, 125.

25. Quoted in ibid., 128.

26. Voit, "O sud'be Lesnogo zhurnala," 11.

27. Red'ko and Red'ko, *Istoriia*, 386. *Lesa respubliki* itself ceased publication in May of 1921, leaving a void unfilled until the end of 1921, when VSNKh and Narkomzem both began to publish their own journals. See Taranovich, "Obzor periodicheskii pechati," 120.

28. RGAE f. 478, op. 9, d. 48, l. 6.22. (In this *delo*, *list* 6 consists of twenty-two sheets of paper.)

29. RGAE f. 478, op. 9, d. 48, l. 2.

30. From *Kratkoe tekhnicheskoe rukovodstvo dlia lesnykh smotritelei, instruktorov i nabliudatelei*, RGAE f. 478, op. 9, d. 83, l. 2.

31. The word translated here as "ranger district" is, in Russian, *lesnichestvo*.

32. RGAE f. 478, op. 9, d. 200, l. 121; RGAE f. 478, op. 9, d. 201, l. 32. In 1920, TsULR (then called TsLO) admitted as much, writing in a year-end report that "the number of *lesnichestva* is completely insufficient for the correct establishment of forest management affairs." See RGAE f. 478, op. 9, d. 1057, l. 4.

33. RGAE f. 478, op. 9, d. 513, l. 32.

34. RGAE f. 478, op. 9, d. 48, ll. 6.5, 6.9. The areas of "surplus growth" were located in the far north and beyond the Urals.

35. RGAE f. 478, op. 9, d. 83, l. 3.

36. RGAE f. 478, op. 9, d. 200, l. 124. One hundred *desiatinas* is equal to one square kilometer. Given that the nearby state forests ranged from 28,000 to 172,000 *desiatinas* in size, one hundred *desiatinas* would have rendered a large amount of timber for a small village, but scarcely have altered the management plan of a state forest.

37. The system of appeal seems to have been designed to frustrate the petitioner; after December 1917, those seeking special permission to obtain timber were required to send their requests to the local (*uezd*) land committee, which would then in turn either deny the appeal or send it to the next level for review. Every petition required approval from the TsULR. See RGAE f. 478, op. 9, d. 311, l. 6.

38. "The organization of [VSNKh's] Main Forest Committee," noted the regional forest newspaper *Lesnoi nabat* in 1920, "is complex. Below it at the *guberniia* level are the Guberniia Forest Committees, which have regional deputies in each *uezd*. Furthermore,

the Main Forest Committee has a railroad department, Zheleskom; there is a *zheleskom* for the northern railroad, for Nikolaevskii railroad, and so on. In turn the *zheleskoms* are divided by *raion,* and these *raiony* into parcels." See V. S., "A kto upravliaet lesom i rabotaet v nem?" 2.

39. VSNKh made its first attempt to gain control of all Russian forests as early as Aug. 1918, when it issued an audacious decree giving itself total authority over all forest-related matters. Although VSNKh argued plausibly that divided responsibility led to mayhem, the decree met resistance from TsULR and then Sovnarkom and never took effect. Many more attempts followed, however (RGAE f. 478, op. 9, d. 286, l. 11).

40. RGAE f. 478, op. 9, d. 1308, l. 34.

41. In the worst cases, federal commissariats lacked not only definite authority but any representatives in the provinces. Narkomzem, e.g., sent a number of directives to the Simbirsk *guberniia* commissariat of agriculture before learning late that year that no such office existed. See RGAE f. 478, op. 9, d. 285, l. 61.

42. RGAE f. 478, op. 9, d. 1536, l. 157.

43. P. Morozov, "Chto delat'?" 6.

44. RGAE f. 478, op. 9, d. 286, l. 10.

45. M. G. Zdorik claimed in 1923 that one hundred million *desiatiny* near the country's railroads had been stripped since the war had begun and converted into barrens. Zdorik's estimation may be an exaggeration—one hundred million *desiatiny* is roughly equal to 430,000 square miles, twice the size of Alaska—but the amount remains tremendous even if reduced by a factor of two, or ten. See Zdorik, "Ocherednye zadachi," 3. *Vestnik* published only one issue.

46. RGAE f. 478, op. 9, d. 1183, l. 36.

47. RGAE f. 478, op. 9, d. 1175, l. 87.

48. Instances of war interrupting forestry operations were not uncommon; the records of TsULR mention, e.g., a research committee sent to Tambov province in Sept. 1918, unable to "conduct its work as a consequence of the presence of Czechoslovak and White troops" (RGAE f. 478, op. 9, d. 200, l. 102).

49. RGAE f. 478, op. 9, d. 209, l. 25.

50. Kern, "Nasushchnye nuzhdy," 6. Kern's estimate did not include the forests lost in the Treaty of Brest-Litovsk. The first full census of forest workers taken by the Soviet government in 1924 counted in all 57,466 workers; only 5,460 of these were specialists. See Red'ko and Red'ko, *Istoriia,* 388.

51. Zdorik, "Lesnoe khoziaistvo," 28.

52. RGAE f. 478, op. 9, d. 201, l. 17. The *lesnichestva* were measured in *desiatiny;* Kostroma *lesnichestva* averaged 16,000 *desiatiny* in size, and one *desiatina* is equal to 2.75 acres. The staffing level suggested by Narkomzem placed 1.5 workers per ranger district, rejecting an appeal from the provincial level asking for 256 workers, or 3 per district. TsULR archives are filled with examples of insufficient staffing. To provide but one more example, "in the summer of 1918 it was proposed to form 120 forest organization parties numbering 1663 people," but by 1 Nov. 1919 only 597 had been hired (RGAE f. 478, op. 9, d. 1058, l. 5).

53. RGAE f. 478, op. 9, d. 1183, l. 34.

54. RGAE f. 478, op. 9, d. 2218, l. 26. Patrolmen suffered a smaller pay cut than more highly qualified workers, earning 8.33 rubles per month versus a prerevolutionary standard of 18, a drop of 54 percent; scientific foresters earned 30.9 rubles per month in 1924 but had earned between 120 and 150 in 1916, a 73 percent drop. Regional variation

meant that in some places the wages were lower still; in Samara province in 1923, for instance, patrolmen earned only 1.5 rubles per month. See P. G., "Zarabotnaia plata lesnykh rabotnikov," 14.

55. RGAE f. 478, op. 9, d. 286, l. 10.

56. Eitengen and Gainer, *Krest'ianskoe lesosnabzhenie posle revoliutsii*, 18.

57. In Apr. 1918, *Lesa respubliki*, betraying a naive misunderstanding of the task facing the country, announced the intention to catalog the nation's former private forests by 1 Oct. of that year, but as of Mar. 1923, only 25 percent of those forests had been surveyed (Zdorik, "Ocherednye zadachi," 3).

58. RGAE f. 478, op. 9, d. 1308, l. 33.

59. RGAE f. 478, op. 9, d. 87, l. 13. The peasants also displayed an awareness of legal norms in the forest, despite the frequent insinuation of the Bolsheviks that peasants could not understand the concept of property rights in the woods. The Smolensk provincial executive committee wrote a telegram to Moscow on 9 Apr. 1918 reporting that the rural population felt that the state's firewood committees were "employing forcible requisitioning of timber" that "the population did not consider to be authorized" (RGAE f. 478, op. 9, d. 87, l. 14).

60. RGAE f. 478, op. 9, d. 1175, ll. 72, 78. The All-Russian Union of Forest Workers met the same year and reached a similar conclusion: "At the present time, only an insignificant percentage of the annual allotments are cut according to proper standards. This is partially explained by the extended war that disturbed the economic life of the country. But of all the collapses, the collapse of the forest occupies far from last place, and is the cause of some of the other collapses." See RGAE f. 478, op. 9, d. 1308, l. 34.

61. RGAE f. 478, op. 9, d. 1540, l. 20.

62. RGAE f. 478, op. 9, d. 200, ll. 20–21.

63. RGAE f. 478, op. 9, d. 1099, l. 3.

64. RGAE f. 478, op. 9, d. 1535, l. 5.

65. Red'ko and Red'ko, *Lesnoe khoziaistvo*, 387.

66. The historical literature on the NEP era, which brought not only increased economic freedom but artistic and cultural liberalism, is extensive. Valuable overviews of the period include Ball, *Russia's Last Capitalists;* Fitzpatrick, *Russia in the Era of NEP;* Cohen, *Bukharin and the Bolshevik Revolution;* and Davies, *From Tsarism to the New Economic Policy.*

67. Red'ko and Red'ko, *Lesnoe khoziaistvo*, 198.

68. Quoted in ibid., 202.

69. Orlov, *Ob osnovakh*, 131.

70. Ibid., 131.

71. Ibid., 132.

72. Orlov had good reason to suspect that tyranny of the masses was the intention of the Bolsheviks, not least because their slogan "All Power to the Soviets" appeared to give total political power to a capricious and informal political unit and also because the Bolsheviks' proclaimed intention was to create a dictatorship of the proletariat. However, after a few years had passed, the organizers of the revolution began to speak out in favor of the value of expertise, such as when Lenin's wife, Nadezhda Krupskaia, insisted that "to throw out these achievements [of trained experts] would be laughable and barbaric" (quoted in Graham, *Science in Russia and the Soviet Union*, 90).

73. For a discussion of the return of the so-called bourgeois experts to positions of prominence in the 1920s, see ibid., 88–93.

74. Although Orlov began work in 1924, TsULR records contain the minutes of a 13 Nov. 1923 meeting at which Orlov was named as the author of the new instructions (RGAE f. 478, op. 9, d. 1988, l. 416).

75. LUK was described as the highest convened body in the article "V TsUL'e NKZ" (58).

76. For a statement of LUK's extensive responsibilities, see "V upravlenii lesami NKZ RSFSR," 70.

77. RGAE f. 478, op. 9, d. 1174, ll. 1–38.

78. RGAE f. 478, op. 9, d. 1883, l. 21.

79. RGAE f. 478, op. 9, d. 1536, ll. 158–59.

80. RGAE f. 478, op. 9, d. 1536, l. 121.

81. RGAE f. 478, op. 9, d. 1887, l. 10.

82. RGAE f. 478, op. 9, d. 1536, l. 297.

83. RGAE f. 478, op. 9, d. 1536, ll. 182, 65.

84. See RGAE f. 478, op. 9, d. 1540, ll. 31, 36.

85. RGAE f. 478, op. 9, d. 1988, l. 53. The terms *belomoshnik* and *zelenomoshnik* were recommended by Morozov.

86. RGAE f. 478, op. 9, d. 1988, l. 163.

87. The desire for more authority at the *guberniia* level was not, of course, universal; a conference of foresters from Novonikolaevsk argued that an "abundance of special agreements, rules, proposals, instructions, and so on . . . would only create confusion in the provinces, and therefore it is necessary for TsULR to produce one unified instructions for all." However, the large majority of provincial reports disagreed with this point of view (RGAE f. 478, op. 9, d. 1887, l. 111).

88. RGAE f. 478, op. 9, d. 2215, l. 53.

89. RGAE f. 478, op. 9, d. 1536, ll. 14–15.

90. RGAE f. 478, op. 9, d. 1536, ll. 120–21.

91. RGAE f. 478, op. 9, d. 1887, l. 12. Elsewhere TsULR recognized that "the population often must resort to unauthorized cuts . . . because of the restricted rights of the local foresters, the excessive centralization . . . and so on" (RGAE f. 478, op. 9, d. 2218, l. 66).

92. The law also created special concession zones to be leased to foreign companies, although the concession forests had only a small impact upon the shape of Soviet forest management, since they existed only for a few short years and were located in relatively remote locations. TsULR established administrations named Russangloles, Russgollan-dles, and Russnorvegoles to work with England, Holland, and Norway, respectively (RGAE f. 478, op. 9, d. 2307, l. 1). These entities were abolished by order of Sovnarkom, 1 Jan. 1929. See GARF f. 5446, op. 1, d. 44, l. 196.

93. RGAE f. 478, op. 9, d. 1629, l. 60.

94. RGAE f. 478, op.9, d. 2219, l. 3; RGAE f. 478, op. 9, d. 2546, l. 4.

95. RGAE f. 478, op. 9, d. 2215, ll. 41–42.

96. Savich, "Obsledovanie lesov na novykh nachalakh," 34.

97. Ibid., 35.

98. Sedletskii, "Zametki sovetskogo lesovoda," 21–22. Sedletskii wanted a new forest science that would "take the old crosses from the monastery buildings and ancient shrines and raise instead the red Soviet flag."

99. Predtechenskii, "Bol'shoi urok," 63. Predtechenskii indicated that the practice most likely to violate the life force of this forest society was clear-cutting (*grubie lesosechnye rubki*). These workers were later described as "hero ants" and "hero bees"

for their efforts to carry on with forest management after the highly qualified specialists vanished in the revolution. "Someday, historians, bards, and artists should explain to our descendants what these heroes did" (I. Morozov, "Vernites' k lesu," 45).

100. RGAE f. 478, op. 9, d. 2311, l. 23.

101. RGAE f. 478, op. 9, d. 2311, l. 4.

102. Shul'ts, "Problema lesnoi politiki," 29.

103. Maier, "Lesnaia promyshlennost' i lesoustroistvo," 6.

104. Iatsenko, "O novykh osnovaniiakh," 8.

105. "V Leningradskom lesnom obshchestve," 75; Iatsenko, "O novykh osnovaniiakh," 7.

106. Iatsenko, "O novykh osnovaniiakh," 6.

107. "V Leningradskom lesnom obshchestve," 75.

108. K. G., "Lesoustroitel'noe soveshchanie pri UL'e," 57.

109. Ibid, 57.

110. "V Leningradskom lesnom obshchestve," 112.

111. Orlov, "Tipy lesa," 3.

112. Workers employing the instructions on a trial basis near Leningrad found that the "instructions for determining forest types were lacking," but "nevertheless established nine different types for spruce, nine for pine, and two for mixed spruce-pine" (Liutovskii, "Lesnoi massif v raione," 12).

113. RGAE f. 478, op. 9, d. 2218, l. 13.

114. Zdorik, "Okhrana lesov," 23. Zdorik's essay also appeared in *Pravda*.

115. Kazakov, "Ledokhod nachalsia," 7.

116. Solov'ev, "Krest'ianstvo i lesnye rabotniki," 9–10.

117. RGAE f. 478, op. 9, d. 1958, l. 18. This arrangement often brought results rather worse than expected, due not to peasant obstreperousness, but to a lack of pine and spruce seeds. After three years of agricultural use, the leased forests tended to regenerate with white forest.

118. E. Ispolatov, "Vrednye sueveriia v lesnom khoziaistve," 51.

119. Aver'ianov, "Iz perspektivnogo i operatsionnogo plana," 138–39.

120. RGAE f. 478, op. 9, d. 2218, l. 14; "V Leningradskom gublesotdel," 64.

121. Selianin, "Uchastie 'vsekolesa,'" 9.

122. RGAE f. 478, op. 9, d. 1668, l. 43.

123. Nedzvetskii, "'Den lesa' v Veprinskom lesnichestve," 33.

124. M. Kalinin, "Beregite i vyrashchivaite lesa," 16.

125. Abramovich, "Sotsialen-li organizm lesa?" 57.

126. In his works for schoolchildren, Morozov urged students to see the forest as an almost sentient being: "The forest is not an agglomeration of woody vegetation, but a community of woody species in which individuals live not only an individual life but a communal one, exert various influences on one another, and create new social phenomena with which isolated trees are not acquainted" (G. F. Morozov, *Shkol'nye excursii v les,* 26).

127. "Ko vsem lesovodam SSSR," 63.

128. "Na mogile Prof. G. F. Morozova 9/V/1927 g.," 63. In Russian, the poem read: "Na mogile tvoiu, nash uchitel'-tvorets / My ne myshnye rechi, venki prinesli / No sobralis' sem'ei vo-edino / Ozarennye svetom liubvi. / Ves' tvoi pyl, vsia velikaia strastnost' tvoren'ia / Svetit iarkoi zvezdnoi, ukauiushchei put' / Po kotoromu dolg nash itti bez somnen'ia."

Chapter 4. Clear-cut: The Forest Felled by the Five-Year Plan

1. As a science, forestry remained mostly undisturbed by Marxism, as Yuri Slezkine argues in his book *Arctic Mirrors* was also true of ethnology. Slezkine indicates that the bolshevization of ethnology lagged behind other scientific disciplines because ethnology simply failed to attract the interest of young Communists, who saw other fields as more exciting. This explanation may apply to forest management as well, which possessed a decidedly humble reputation, although the difficulties in reinterpreting forest ecology through the critical lens of Marxism may have also played a part. See Slezkine, *Arctic Mirrors,* 247–63.

2. Arndt, "Lesoustroitel'noe soveshchanie," 67.

3. "Ocherednye zadachi," 3.

4. Bogoslovskii's name was sometimes spelled Boguslovskii, which is the name's more common spelling. However, his major works feature the name spelled with an *o* rather than a *u.*

5. As described in the first chapter, *bonitety* are classifications of site quality, used to categorize forests according to productivity. Measurements of the age and height of a forest's dominant trees are taken and compared to fixed charts. Stands are then assigned roman numerals (I to V) to denote their productivity. In Orlov's instructions, these designations were taken into account when making logging prescriptions; the best stands typically were prescribed long rotations (more than one hundred years) and the worst short.

6. Shvappakh, "Germanskoe lesnoe khoziaistvo," 66; RGAE f. 305, op. 1, d. 437.

7. Bogoslovskii, "K voprosu," 21.

8. RGAE f. 478, op. 9, d. 2218, l. 7. The time needed to reforest all the areas that had failed to regenerate as of 1926 was estimated at 120 years. See "Lesnoe khoziaistvo v 1927/28 godu," 239.

9. Bogoslovskii, "Printsip postoianstva," 31.

10. Quoted in Iatsenko, "Tsel' lesoustroistva," 24; Bogoslovskii, "Ideia gosudarstven-nogo," 31–32.

11. Bogoslovskii, *Novye techeniia,* 230, 17.

12. Iatsenko, "Tsel' lesoustroistva," 24.

13. "Lesnoe zakonodatel'stva RSFSR, BSSR i USSR," 101–3.

14. Iatsenko, "Ob oborote rubki," 12.

15. K. G., "Lesoustroitel'noe sovechchanie pri UL'e," 58.

16. Orlov wrote that "the principle of concentrated cutting possesses enormous significance for our country and should be expanded in our cutting plans . . . but only in well-defined conditions, so that its implementation does not violate the existing needs of management" (*Lesoustroistvo, t. III,* 146).

17. Orlov, "Novye techeniia v lesoustroistve," 18.

18. Bogoslovskii and Orlov, "O lesoustroitel'nykh nedorazumeniiakh," 65.

19. I. Morozov, "Lesokhoziaistvennye nozhnitsy," 11.

20. "Leningradskoe Lesnoe Obshchestvo za polgoda," 77.

21. Kliucharev, "U svezhikh mogil," 13.

22. Ivashkevich, "Po lesam sovremennoi Germanii," 51, 53–54. Ivashkevich noted that even Morozov's ideas were known to the experts he met with, since *The Theory of the Forest* had been published the summer before his visit. In 1929, the German forestry journal *Der deutsche Forstwirt* expressed surprise that Morozov, despite working on such

an interesting question, was basically unknown in Russia before the German publication of *The Theory of the Forest.*

23. Moshkov, "O nuzhdakh severnogo," 64. The original saying in Russian contains an element of ambiguity, since the Russian word for "German" (*nemets*) can also mean "foreigner." In Moshkov's usage, however, *nemets* was used explicitly to mean "German."

24. "Soveshchanie po lesoustroistvu," 56.

25. RGAE f. 342, op. 1, d. 191, ll. 35–36.

26. Morokhin, "Znachenie tipov," 56.

27. German soil fertility is indeed, on average, higher than in Russia, although local conditions vary greatly. According to data from 1929, Bavarian forests produced 4.5 m³ of wood per year, Prussian 5.4 m³, and Swabian 6.6 m³, whereas the average yield for the RSFSR was 1.3 m³. Prussian forests generated 30.00 rubles per hectare, Voronezh forests 11.28 rubles, and Siberian forests 3 kopecks. See Eitengen, "Lesnoe khoziaistvo," 64–65. However, the concept of forest-soil fertility is problematic, since the very issue that Russian foresters hoped to understand was whether soil fertility could be changed by well-adapted management techniques.

28. Graham, *Science in Russia,* 91–92.

29. This phenomenon is described in Erlich, *Soviet Industrialization Debate;* and Bailes, *Technology and Society under Lenin and Stalin.*

30. Schabel and Palmer, "Dauerwald," 21. In the nineteenth century, foresters as famous as von der Borch, Konig, and Gaier had expressed their displeasure with German high forestry.

31. Möller, "Kiefern-Dauerwaldwirtschaft," 4.

32. Troup, "Dauerwald," 80.

33. Orlov, "Khoziaistvennaia otsenka nepreryvno," 12; Gernits, "Nepreryvno proizvoditel'nyi les," 32.

34. Imort, "Eternal Forest—Eternal *Volk,*" 43. For a discussion of the xenophobic, if not militaristic, implications of ecological thinking, see also Groening and Wolschke-Bulmahn, "Some Notes on the Mania," 116–26.

35. Schabel and Palmer, "Dauerwald," 22. Deer thrive in disturbed sites, and *Dauerwald* strived toward the minimization of disturbance; accordingly, *Dauerwald* forests offered fewer deer for Göring to hunt than did the scientifically managed forests to which he was accustomed. *Dauerwald,* Schabel and Palmer assert, enjoyed something of a renaissance in the 1980s among foresters who found in it an environmentalist approach to forestry.

36. "V Leningradskom lesnom obshchestve" (Nov.–Dec. 1924), 78.

37. Damberg, "Ekskursiia v Pashe-Kapetskoe lesnichestvo," 58; Eitengen, "O plane rabot," 82.

38. Tiurin, "Professor M. M. Orlov," 7. Elsewhere, Orlov seemed quite skeptical about *Dauerwald,* basing his opinion on the findings of the 1925 All-Union German Forest Congress.

39. Narkomzem's journal *Lesnoe khoziaistvo* complained that "the instructions of 1926, for unknown reasons, retain the same mistakes present in the earlier instructions and in some aspects—especially related to forest regeneration—are even worse than the instructions of 1911 and 1914." See Tikhomorov, "Estestvennoe vozobnovlenie," 81.

40. Syromolotov, "Organizovat' lesnoe khoziaistvo," 4.

41. For examples of such debates, see Slezkine, *Arctic Mirrors;* Barber, *Soviet Historians in Crisis;* Bauer, *New Man in Soviet Psychology;* Brown, *Proletarian Episode*

in Russian Literature; Solomon, *Soviet Agrarian Debate;* Joravsky, *Soviet Marxism and Natural Sciences;* Graham, *Soviet Academy of Sciences.*

42. GARF f. 374, op. 9, d. 162, l. 4.

43. GARF f. 374, op. 9, d. 162, l. 7.

44. GARF f. 374, op. 9, d. 162, ll. 8, 12.

45. GARF f. 374, op. 9, d. 162, l. 65. Rabkrin's support of Narkomzem was steady and stretched back to 1923; see GARF f. 374, op. 9, d. 165.

46. GARF f. 374, op. 8, d. 1650, l. 17. According to VSNKh figures, in 1926 the Soviet Union exported 3.3 million m^3 of timber, while Finland exported 3.9 million and Sweden 5.0. VSNKh pointed out in its petition that "if America had been limited by the same constraints and had been forced to base its harvests on annual growth, it would have taken but a fraction of the timber that fueled its growth." Canada, too, VSNKh protested, benefited from harvesting wood according to its availability rather than its annual growth (GARF f. 374, op. 9, d. 1650, l. 61).

47. GARF 374, op. 8, d. 1650, l. 72.

48. Rees, *State Control in Soviet Russia,* 118, 227.

49. Fitzpatrick, *Politics of Soviet Industrialization,* 11.

50. Ibid., 24.

51. GARF f. 5466, op.2, d. 279, ll. 35, 38–39.

52. GARF f. 5466, op. 2, d. 279, l. 23.

53. GARF f. 5466, op. 2, d. 741, l. 1.

54. GARF f. 5466, op. 2, d. 741, ll. 23–24.

55. GARF f. 5466, op. 2, d. 740, ll. 60–61.

56. GARF f. 5466, op. 2, d. 740, ll. 72–73.

57. GARF f. 5466, op. 2, d. 740, l. 61.

58. GARF f. 5446, op. 1, d. 36, l. 230.

59. GARF f. 5446, op. 1, d. 36, l. 233.

60. Ibid.

61. "Postanovlenie Soiuznogo pravitel'stva," 6.

62. M. L., "Vazhneishii printsip," 9.

63. Ibid., 9.

64. Ibid., 10.

65. *Meropriiatiia po lesnomu,* 144.

66. Khoroshov, "O shtatakh lesnichestv," 28; Sviatkovskii, "O rekonstruktsii lesnogo khoziaistva," 49.

67. A. M., "Sverkhsmetnye otpuska," 71; N. D., "Kratkii obzor dekretov," 121.

68. Lapirov-Skoblo, "K voprosu o sozdanii," 8. According to the calculations of the Ural *oblast'* NK RKI, Narkomzem could deliver timber at 26 kopecks per cubic meter, whereas timber from the Volgo-Caspian trust cost 1.10 rubles.

69. RGAE f. 4372, op. 26, d. 1050, l. 61.

70. RGAE f. 4372, op. 26, d. 1050, l. 113.

71. RGAE f. 4372, op. 27, d. 453, l. 125.

72. RGAE f. 4372, op. 27, d. 453, ll. 66–67.

73. RGAE f. 4372, op. 26, d. 1050, l. 135.

74. Ibid.

75. RGAE f. 4372, op. 26, d. 1050, l. 134.

76. Ende, "Khod leszagotovok," 22.

77. "Krupnye industrializirovannye edinitsy," 8.

78. Ibid., 10.

79. "Nachinaetsia chistka," 1.

80. See "Mobilizuem les dlia industrializatsii!" 1.

81. "Voprosy lesnogo khoziaistva na II plenume TsK," 18.

82. Ibid., 20–21.

83. Ibid., 15.

84. Ibid., 32.

85. Indeed, as late as 16 Aug. 1929, Sovnarkom still drafted resolutions forwarding the concept that "forest management should be conducted on a basis providing for permanent and uninterrupted use of the forests, the improvement of their composition and quality, and the support and raising of productivity of forest soils." See GARF f. 3316, op. 33, d. 602, l. 8.

86. RGAE f. 5674, op. 1, d. 37, ll. 54–56.

87. RGAE f. 5674, op. 1, d. 37, l. 55.

88. "Po novomu puti," 37.

89. "Lesa peredany promyshlennosti," 1.

90. Bogoslovskii, "Printsip postoianstva," 17.

91. Bogoslovskii, "Nuzhen li peresmotr," 18.

92. Tiain and Drozdovskii, "'Lesoustroistvo' bez lesoustroistva," 68.

93. Zdorik, "Kakim byt' lesoustroistvo," 5.

94. Levin, "K voprosu o tom," 7.

95. Lavrov, "Piatletnii plan lesnogo khoziaistvo," 9; *Materialy po perspektivnomu planu,* 400–403.

96. RGAE f. 7758, op. 1, d. 2, l. 14.

97. GARF f. 3316, op. 23, d. 297, l. 8.

98. GARF f. 3316, op. 23, d. 297, ll. 29–30. The timber pricing rules of 16 Oct. 1924 provided Narkomzem with an especially useful tool to control forest exploitation throughout the 1920s; the rules forced VSNKh to maximize the output derived from each plot it logged rather than demand additional parcels, since VSNKh had to pay Narkomzem a fee for each parcel it logged.

99. Zdorik, "Pis'mo k redaktsiiu," 143.

100. Orlov, "Tekhnicheskie lesnye reformy," 7.

101. Ural, "O vliianii," 85.

102. Milovanovich, "Arkhaizmy lesnogo khoziaistva," 87.

103. M. Kalinin, "Sluzhenie russkomu lesu," 52.

104. In the summer of 1929, the Leningrad Forest Institute was renamed the Leningrad Forest-Technical Institute, reflecting forest management's new industrial orientation.

105. Orlov, *Lesoustroistvo, t. 1,* 69.

106. Zhurin, "O trude v lesnom khoziaistve," 4.

107. K. M., "Ocherednoe soprotivlenie," 2.

108. Red'ko and Red'ko, *Lesnoe khoziaistvo,* 199–200. Toward the end of his life, Malyshev expressed regret that he had taken part in Orlov's persecution.

109. Teplyakov et al., *History of Russian Forestry,* 70.

110. Alekseychik and Chagin, *Protiv reaktsionnykh teorii,* 27.

111. S. S. Lobov, e.g., the head of VSNKh's forest industry administration, argued in 1932 that "every worker in the forest industry should understand how harmful are the positions of the Orlovist-Morozovist school" (quoted in ibid., 10–11).

112. Naletov, "Metody," 9.

113. Ibid., 10.

114. Urmanskii, "Eshche o samovol'nykh," 68.

115. RGAE f. 396, op. 2, d. 76, l. 66.

116. Throughout the 1920s, e.g., peasants were offered the chance to gain usufruct of swamps they helped to drain and convert to forest. See RGAE f. 396, op. 2, d. 76, l. 37.

117. Velovich, "Den' lesa v 1929 godu," 6. Other slogans included "Cultured exploitation is a necessary condition for the maximization of forest resources for the industrialization of the country," and "All for the struggle with the backwardness of Soviet forest management!"

118. RGAE f. 7654, op. 1, d. 8, l. 89.

119. "Den' lesa v 1930 godu," 8–9.

Chapter 5. Regeneration: Forest Conservationism Returns to the Soviet Union

1. For a discussion of *Dauerwald* and the Nazi regime, see chapter 4.

2. Povari, "Fascist Government," 72–73. In its first years of existence, the fascist regime limited itself to legislative measures, but with the creation of the National Forest Militia in 1927, a more active approach was taken. The militia reforested 41,450 hectares between 1928 and 1933. In coordination with the Forest Militia, Benito Mussolini's brother Arnaldo founded the National Committee for Forestry, a body whose aim was "to send out to every citizen, and above all to the Fascist youth, the call for a rebirth of the nation's forests."

3. *China's Forestry*, 3–4. The Chinese program is, as of the year 2011, still ongoing.

4. *Environmentalism*, as used here, refers to the political and philosophical position that the health of the natural world should be an item of social concern, rather than psychological and educational theory. Environmentalism overlaps with, but is not coterminous with, conservationism (the belief that natural resources should be treated carefully so as to produce the greatest benefit) and preservationism (the belief that untrammeled nature has inherent value, whether ecological, economic, aesthetic, or spiritual, and therefore that some landscapes should be left undeveloped).

5. The tsar asked V. V. Dokuchaev, the founder of modern soil science, to lead a government expedition to determine the causes of the 1891 famine, and Dokuchaev concluded that the crop failures could be traced to climatic instability, a consequence of centuries of steady deforestation. For more about Dokuchaev, see Moon, "Environmental History of the Russian Steppes."

6. Roderick Nash describes a similar tactic taken by environmentalists seeking to protect the forests of the Adirondack Mountains in upstate New York, although those individuals sought state assistance in protecting the forests from industry, whereas the proponents of Soviet forest protection hoped to enact legislation to protect the forest from the state. See Nash, *Wilderness and the American Mind*, 116–21.

7. The campus newspaper of the Leningrad Forest-Technical Institute argued in Dec. 1931 that Bogoslovskii, "not understanding the role and significance of the [Five-Year] Plan, and not considering the transitional period, . . . carries forward the basic foundations of bourgeois forest economics . . . and ignores the theory of Soviet economics" (Kalinin, "Za chistotu," 3).

8. "Resoliutsiia po dokladu Soiuzlesproma," 52.

9. Nevesskii, "Eksploatatsiia," 21.

10. In July 1930, VSNKh's forestry organ held a conference that resolved that "in view of the necessity of satisfying the economy's demands for wood, the unevenness of

the distribution of the forests across the territory of the USSR, . . . and the presence of a large percentage of overmature stands in the forests of the north, Siberia, and Far East, it is necessary to reject management according to permanent, uninterrupted, and even use [*postoianstvo, nepreryvnosti i ravnomernosti*]. . . . The areas to be logged in the USSR should be established according to the economic demands of forest industry, based on the maximal supply of products" ("Soveshchanie [pri Lesprome]," 71).

11. "Kratkii obzor," 136. Management records of specific forests prove that promises of care went unfulfilled: "In general, the size of the main cut went far beyond the bounds of the estimate. The care for the forest stand in the enormous majority of cases remained forgotten. The plots are heaped with rubbish. The result has been strengthened swamping" (TsGAMO f. 7139, op. 1, d. 7, l. 7 obverse).

12. At the May 1932 All-Union Conference for the Reconstruction of Forest Industry, A. N. Sudarnikov admitted that "the forest exploitation during the first Five-Year Plan was not implemented uniformly" and that "the exploitation was in fact concentrated in areas comprising no more than 10 percent of the entire forest fund" (RGAE f. 7654, op. 1, d. 49, l. 33).

13. "Sostoianie lesnoi promyshlennosti," 77.

14. Tkachenko, "Zadachi lesnogo khoziaistva," 10.

15. RGAE f. 4372, op. 27, d. 453, l. 136.

16. Tkachenko, "Kontsentrirovannye rubki," 9.

17. Golubovich, "Za ratsionalizatsiiu," 30.

18. RGAE f. 9449, op. 1, d. 2069, l. 19.

19. Golubovich, "Za ratsionalizatsiiu," 30.

20. Ibid., 32–33.

21. RGASPI f. 17, op. 163, d. 790, l. 58.

22. RGAE f. 9465, op. 1, d. 1, l. 35; *Lesnoi spetsialist* 7–8 (July–Aug. 1931): 9–10, 11–12. The forests of the forest-industrial zone continued to be exploited as though planning for the future were inherently bourgeois; if in 1929–30, the timber harvested by VSNKh equaled 175 percent of the annual growth of the accessed forests, these numbers for 1932 through 1935 would be 248, 213, 193, and 180 percent (GARF f. 5467, op. 14, d. 44, l. 93).

23. GARF f. 5446, op. 1, d. 61, ll. 176–77.

24. Peter created both "protected" and "water-preserving" forests, although Peter Blandon, in *Soviet Forest Industries,* suggests that Peter's main goal was not to limit erosion or to control flooding, but rather to check the activity of the charcoal smelters who were rapidly stripping the riverside forests of timber that Peter wanted for his navy. Peter's belts were much larger than those of the Soviets: fifty *versts* (more than thirty-three miles) near major rivers and twenty *versts* (more than thirteen miles) near smaller ones. See Blandon, *Soviet Forest Industries,* 236.

25. RGAE f. 9465, op. 1, d. 1, ll. 3 (obverse), 38.

26. Pasynkov, "Perspektivy razvitiia," 3.

27. Belov, "Tragediia Sredne-Volzhskogo leskhoza," 66–67.

28. GARF f. 5466, op. 3. d. 695, l. 18.

29. TsGAMO f. 7139, op. 1, d. 7, ll. 2 obverse, 6 obverse.

30. TsGAMO f. 7139, op. 1, d. 10, l. 3.

31. TsGAMO f. 7139, op. 1, d. 10, l. 6.

32. RGAE f. 7654, op. 1, d. 45, ll. 2, 52.

33. RGAE f. 7654, op. 1, d. 49, ll. 96–97. Morozov's primary tenet was, "The cut and the regeneration are synonyms."

34. GARF f. 5446, op. 1, d. 70, l. 44.

35. GARF f. 5446, op. 1, d. 70, ll. 362–63.

36. GARF f. 5446, op. 1, d. 70b, l. 142.

37. TsGAMO f. 7139, op. 1, *predislovie*, l. iv. The decree expanding Moscow's protected forests, signed by Molotov, can be found in GARF f. 5446, op. 1, d. 70, l. 45.

38. RGAE f. 9465, op. 1, d. 21, l. 10 obverse.

39. RGAE f. 9465, op. 1, d. 66, l. 39.

40. TsGAMO f. 7139, op. 1, d. 12, l. 36.

41. GARF f. 9449, op. 1, d. 651, ll. 28, 37. A 28 percent failure rate was not bad, compared to some *leskhozy*; in Sumskii *leskhoz*, 93.3 percent of the pine forests, and 52 percent of the forests as a whole, failed to regenerate entirely.

42. GARF f. 5446, op. 17, d. 9, l. 141.

43. RGAE f. 9449, op. 1, *predislovie*, l. 1.

44. GARF f. 5446, op. 7, d. 10, l. 277.

45. GARF f. 5446, op. 17, d. 8, ll. 142–44.

46. RGAE f. 9449, op. 1, d. 654, ll. 23–24. In some places, protected forests greatly outnumbered unprotected; in the Belarussian republic, for instance, 3,032,000 hectares, out of a total of 3,662,000, were protected. See RGAE f. 9449, op. 2, d. 1, l. 13. The area of the water-protective zones was equal in size to 80 percent of all the forested area in Western Europe.

47. RGAE f. 9449, op. 1, d. 1984, l. 3. It is possible that Solov'ev was lying about Stalin's involvement, but given the political climate of the Soviet Union, this seems unlikely.

48. RGAE f. 9449, op. 2, d. 1, l. 5.

49. RGAE f. 9449, op. 1, d. 1984, l. 4.

50. RGAE f. 9449, op. 2, d. 1, l. 9.

51. RGAE f. 9449, op. 2, d. 1, ll. 20, 38.

52. RGAE f. 9449, op. 2, d. 1, l. 56.

53. RGAE f. 9449, op. 2, d. 1, l. 100. What took place in Perm does not fit the customary definition of an Italian strike, which usually refers to a protest wherein workers follow every workplace regulation to the letter, thereby making the ordinary functioning of a workplace impossible. In this instance, the loggers simply chose to act as though the laws of 1936 did not exist.

54. RGAE f. 9449, op. 2, d. 1, l. 127.

55. RGAE f. 9449, op. 1, d. 1983, l. 81.

56. RGAE f. 9449, op. 1, d. 1983, l. 88.

57. RGAE f. 9449, op. 2, d. 1, ll. 11, 46, 94.

58. RGAE f. 9449, op. 2, d. 1, l. 172.

59. RGAE f. 9449, op. 1, d. 1977a, l. 10.

60. RGAE f. 9449, op. 1, d. 651, ll. 12, 18.

61. RGAE f. 9449, op. 1, d. 659, ll. 3, 32.

62. RGAE f. 9449, op. 1, d. 659, ll. 34. Interestingly, the instructions also stipulated that "attention should be paid to the retention of the beauty of the forest landscape, especially near the major population and industrial centers and busy roads. . . . There should be left an untouched forest belt about fifty meters in width, if aesthetic considerations merit this." See RGAE f. 9449, op. 1, d. 661, l. 27.

63. TsGAMO f. 7139, op. 1, d. 57, ll. 98–103. Foresters in Taldomskii *leskhoz* used seven of Morozov's types: *sukhoi bor, kislyi bor, bor chernichnik, sosniak dolgomoshnik, el'nik brusichnik, el'nik kislichnik,* and *el'nik chernichnik.*

64. TsGAMO f. 7139, op. 1, d. 57, l. 65.

65. RGAE f. 9449, op. 1, d. 1977a, l. 61.

66. Morozov's *Uchenie o lese* (The Theory of the Forest) was indeed the kind of book that forest workers carried around with them into the field, both physically and mentally. One surveyor described his intellectual relationship with Morozov in this way: "Up ahead, we saw a valuable pine-oak stand. Looking closely at the composition, the age, and the *bonitet,* I look for some kind of undergrowth, but I cannot find any. What is the reason for this? Then I recall that Georgii Fedorovich willed to us that we should protect such parcels as monuments of nature. Back at camp, I am seized again by Morozov . . . to think again." See G. K., "Pervye shagi lesovoda-lesoustroitelia," 51.

67. The idea that nature preserves are prisons for nature is explored by Thomas Birch in his "Incarceration of Wilderness."

68. Red'ko and Redko, *Istoriia,* 395. After a drop in output because of the war, Soviet timber production boomed again: 1950, 238 million m³; 1955, 308 million m³; 1965, 355 million m³; 1970, 355 million m³; 1975, 372 million m³. The year 1975 marked the zenith of output, perhaps since annual yields had exceeded annual growth since 1960. See Red'ko and Red'ko, *Istoriia,* 401.

69. Melekhov, *Al'ma mater,* 11–12. Melekhov allowed that the forests of some tropical countries might have fared worse, if the 1980s and 1990s were taken into account.

70. Barr and Braden, *Disappearing Russian Forest,* 47. Peter Blandon estimates that the Soviet forest management apparatus was removing only one-half of 1 percent of the mature and overmature timber in its water-protective forests; like Barr and Braden, he suggests that the solution to a general slowdown in the Soviet timber industry in the 1980s was to increase exploitation of Group I forests, which the Soviets were very loath to do. See Blandon, *Soviet Forest Industries,* 235–39.

71. RGAE f. 9449, op. 1, d. 688, l. 1. GLO's 1941 booklet *Kratkoe rukovodstvo po tipam lesnykh kul'tur vodookhranoi zony i skhematicheskaia karta lesorastitel'nykh oblastei vodookhranoi zony* (A Short Guide to Forest Plantation Types in the Water-Protective Zones) underscored the importance of the complex structure that natural forests took, even when creating artificial ones: "The underestimation of the conditions of local growth and local ecology leads to the creation (such as those created under earlier, capitalist conditions) of unstable and short-lived stands. . . . These schemes of plantations [should be] differentiated . . . according to types of local growth." See RGAE f. 9449, op. 1, d. 2106, ll. 22, 45.

72. *Za zashchitu lesa* published under this provocative title for only nine months (from Sept. 1937 to June 1938), after which its name was changed to *Lesnoe khoziaistvo* (Forest Management).

73. "Vykorchevat' vragov naroda," 3.

74. Ibid., 3.

75. Iakimovich was rehabilitated after his death; see Koldanov's memoir *Gody moei zhizhni* (RGAE f. 538, op. 1, d. 16). At the time, Mikhail Tkachenko remarked with uncharacteristic bitterness and pessimism to his student Ivan Melekhov (later to become the Soviet Union's most illustrious forester) that "it is bad to be a forester now [*plokho byt' lesovodom*]." Although some defended Orlov's good name at meetings dedicated to the "struggle with bourgeois theories" at the Leningrad Forest-Technical Institute, most participated in the harassment of those who resisted. Others, such as Sukachev and Tkachenko, found it expedient to join the party. See Melekhov, *Al'ma mater,* 12.

76. Motovilov, "Po-bol'shevistski vskryt'," 2.

77. Bogoslovskii, "Systemy rubok," 6.

78. Bogoslovskii, "Ustroistvo lesov," 7–8.

79. Zdorik, "O vrednoi instruktsii," 3.

80. Zdorik, "Perspektivy razvitiia," 7. Much of the debate over protected forests touched on the proper interpretation of Lenin's assertion in *Materialism and Empirio-criticism:* "Until we know the law of nature, it exists and acts beyond our understanding, and makes us slaves of 'blind necessity'" (141).

81. Zdorik, "Perspektivy razvitiia," 7.

82. GLO fulfilled its national quotas for surveying and categorizing forests and for planting new ones in 1937, but individual regions such as the Lower Volga (32 percent) or Gork'ii (25 percent) offices fared far worse. See "Plan vesennikh lesokul'turnykh rabot," 5.

83. RGAE f. 9449, op. 1, d. 654, ll. 4–5, 20. In a letter from 9 July 1937, the Council of People's Commissars of the Udmurt Autonomous Republic complained that "the lack of a local office of forest protection hinders the oversight of the *leskhozy*" and asked for its own regional office. Though this appeal was rejected at first, by 1938 the Udmurt branch of GLO had opened. Likewise, the Chuvash Republic reported that without a local GLO outpost, its forests were disappearing at four times the rate of natural replenishment.

84. RGAE f. 9449, op. 1, d. 654, l. 27.

85. RGAE f. 9449, op. 1, d. 664, ll. 1–2.

86. RGAE f. 9449, op. 1, d. 669, l. 12.

87. RGAE f. 9449, op. 1, d. 2214, l. 3.

88. RGAE f. 9449, op. 1, d. 2199, l. 4.

89. In the summer of 1938, Gosplan submitted to Sovnarkom draft legislation (likely written by Zdorik) indicating that "the rules of logging the forest in the water-protective zones . . . are scientifically unfounded and composed according to formula . . . and should be fundamentally reworked," but Motovilov countered that "generally accepted scientific opinions about [our] practices are as of yet lacking" and therefore neither affirmed nor condemned GLO practices. A "fundamental reworking [was] not necessary." Sovnarkom sided with Motovilov. See RGAE f. 9449, op. 1, d. 2199, ll. 4, 7 obverse, 8. In addition, Sovnarkom received repeated requests to entrust protection measures to Narkomles, thereby obviating GLO. Sovnarkom always rejected them. See, e.g., RGAE f. 9449, op. 1, d. 11, l. 13.

90. GARF f. A-259, op. 2, d. 1093, l. 10.

91. GARF f. A-259, op. 2, d. 1093, l. 11.

92. GARF f. A-259, op. 4, d. 2867, ll. 35, 380.

93. The 1943 law also may have been a response to the extreme exploitation of the water-protective forests of the occupied zone by the Nazis, who leveled for firewood the forests of suburban Moscow and the Donbass in the first year of the war. See Red'ko and Red'ko, *Istoriia,* 396.

94. *Zapovedniki* were unique nature reserves, set aside by the Soviet state for the purposes of scientific study, rather than tourism or ecological functions per se. For detailed histories of the origin and development of the *zapovedniki,* see Douglas Weiner, *Models of Nature* and *Little Corner of Freedom.*

95. RGAE f. 9466, op. 5, d. 323, ll. 1–2.

96. RGAE f. 9466, op. 5, d. 207, ll. 25–35.

97. GARF f. A-259, op. 6, d. 3507, ll. 6, 10. In 1945, in keeping with the renaming of every branch of the government apparatus, the People's Commissariat of Forest Industry (Narkomlesprom) was redesignated the Ministry of Forest Industry (Minlesprom).

98. GARF f. A-259, op. 6, d. 3507, l. 76. A letter from the State Planning Commission to the deputy head of Sovnarkom RSFSR from 7 May 1946 reveals the exasperation that government officials felt when considering the industrialists' management of the forest;

it gave as the reasons for Minlesprom's failures its inability to "cope with the basic and urgent tasks for the fulfillment of the plan of logging, and its inability to create its own cadre of workers"—in other words, its basic incompetence.

99. RGAE f. 9466, op. 1, d. 22b, l. 2

100. RGAE f. 9449, op. 1, d. 228, ll. 2–5. Agencies that held their own forests and conducted their own logging included bureaus as diverse as the Ministry of Arms Production and the Ministry of Fishing.

101. RGAE f. 9466, op. 1, d. 22b, l. 1.

102. RGAE f. 9466, op. 1, d. 24a, l. 35. In 1949, Motovilov also commissioned a recalculation of the scope of allowable sanitary cuts in Group I forest; the new numbers called for a 63 percent reduction. See RGAE f. 9466, op. 5, d. 328, l. 41.

103. RGAE f. 9466, op. 1, d. 24a, ll. 36–37.

104. RGAE f. 9466, op. 1, d. 24a, l. 37.

105. GARF f. A-259, op. 6, d. 8640, ll. 16–18.

106. RGAE f. 9466, op. 5, d. 323, ll. 4–60.

107. RGAE f. 9466, op. 1, d. 252b, l. 3.

108. GARF f. A-337, op. 1, d. 7, l. 113.

109. GARF f. A-337, op. 1, d. 340, ll. 82–83.

110. GARF f. A-337, op. 1, d. 146, l. 208. The level of Minleskhoz's funding might provide an insight into its political influence; in 1948 it received 428 million rubles; in 1949, 510 million; in 1950, 798 million; in 1951, 519 million; in 1952, again 519 million, and in 1953 (the year of its elimination), 472 million. See GARF f. A-337, op. 1, dd. 1364, 1381, 1407, 1433, 1467, 1500.

111. RGAE f. 9466, op. 5, d. 328, l. 17. Unfortunately, the same booklet noted, "We still have people who do not scruple to spoil the forest."

112. RGAE f. 342, op. 1, d. 181, l. 43. This student of Morozov, himself named Morozov (Ivan Romanovich, no direct relation), wrote that the editor of the 1948 edition of *Uchenie o lese*, V. G. Nesterov, had "turned Morozov into a Lilliputian and himself into Gulliver, for in that novel, Gulliver often takes the Lilliputian by the collar and stands him where he likes" (RGAE f. 342, op. 1, d. 1885a, l. 84).

113. See Douglas Weiner, *Little Corner of Freedom*, 83–181; Shtil'mark and Geptner, "Tragediia sovetskikh zapovednikov"; Boreiko, *Belye piatna istorii prirodookhrany*.

114. The government's dedication to Minleskhoz had not wavered; at the same time that the *zapovedniki* were being legislated away, the Council of Ministers RSFSR took the republic's loggers to task (yet again) for improperly utilizing the forests allotted for their use. According to a decree from 3 Nov. 1951, seven million cubic meters of timber in distant Group III forests had gone untouched, as had four million in Group II, resulting in fines levied of five million rubles; logging firms were "obligated to determine those guilty for these violations . . . and to implement measures for the further development of Group III forests" (GARF A-259, op. 6, d. 8644, ll. 1–3).

115. RGAE f. 9466, op. 1, d. 252b, ll. 10–11.

116. RGAE f. 9466, op. 5, d. 337, l. 124.

117. RGAE f. 9466, op. 1, d. 171b, l. 32; RGAE f. 9466, op. 5, d. 343, ll. 77–78.

118. RGAE f. 9466, op. 1, d. 431, l. 142. Douglas Weiner gives a similar example in *Little Corner of Freedom*: in the Tul'skie zaseki zapovednik, the moose population had declined steeply as a consequence of the management regime there. Moose prefer open spaces, and when the forest was left untouched, it grew denser and provided no habitat for the moose (115).

119. Motovilov was removed unceremoniously in mid-1948, accused of "allowing excessive cuts, above the amount allowed by the government," and of allowing "nepotism and drunkenness" among the employees. See RGAE f. 9466, op. 1, d. 73, ll. 3–4. Another report charged that Motovilov tolerated "cohabitation with unauthorized [*postoronnye*] women" (RGAE f. 9466, op. 1, d. 76, l. 22). Whether the charges about ethical matters were founded in truth is impossible to know, but it is worth noting that a stated reason for firing Motovilov was not that he hindered industrial growth, but that he harbored an insufficiently protective attitude.

120. RGAE f. 9466, op. 5, d. 329, l. 96.

121. Lapirov-Skoblo, "Problema," 6. Lapirov-Skoblo's analysis used Narkomzem estimates of peasant demand that he considered "highly modest": the peasants may have in fact been getting less than 47 percent of their needed firewood and construction timber via legal means. Narkomzem was also less than pleased with the forests of local significance: its journal criticized the peasant forests for their "exceptionally primitive management." See Zanevskii, "Novye zadachi khoziaistva," 43.

122. Denisev, "Ob izvrashchenii klassovoi linii," 23. Denisev worried that "in many places the forests of local significance turn out to be owned by individuals; in Smolensk *guberniia,* the users of such forests are former landlords."

123. "Voprosy lesnoi promyshlennosti," 73.

124. Toropin, *Sbornik zakonov,* 3. Officially, the forests of local significance were left in the control of VSNKh after the 1931 law, then transferred to GLO's administration as water-protective forests in 1936. The collective-farm forests changed hands so often in the early 1930s that it was hard to know who was in control and nearly impossible to create coherent policies; instead, local control prevailed. See Pal'tsev, "Lesnoe khoziaistvo," 3–4.

125. GARF f. A-259, op. 6, d. 4731, l. 17.

126. GARF f. A-337, op. 1, d. 1232, l. 36.

127. GARF f. A-337, op. 1, d. 1236, l. 330.

128. GARF f. A-337, op. 1, d. 1236, l. 47.

129. GARF f. A-337, op. 1, d. 1263, l. 252.

130. GARF f. A-337, op. 1, d. 1232, ll. 68–69, 85.

131. GARF f. A-337, op. 1, d. 1263, l. 129.

132. GARF f. A-337, op. 1, d. 1275, l. 3.

133. Fitzpatrick, *Stalin's Peasants.*

134. GARF f. A-259, op. 7, d. 1847, ll. 1–3.

Chapter 6. Transformation: The Great Stalin Plan for the Transformation of Nature

1. Mark Bassin has described a similar conflict, although using the term *naturalism* rather than *technocracy,* and sees it operating not only in Soviet science but in Marxist philosophy as a whole. See Bassin, "Nature, Geopolitics and Marxism."

2. The Soviets embarked upon a "Great Retreat," according to Timasheff, because they "came to the conclusion that the pillars of society shaken by them in the course of the Communist experiment had to be reinforced. They reversed their policy relating to school in 1931, the family in 1934, and the Church in 1939. . . . When the necessity for reconstruction became clear to the Communists, they were unable to create new patterns, but directed society towards the revival of ore-Revolutionary institutions." See Timasheff, *Great Retreat,* 240. The concept of the Great Retreat, although influential, is venerable and has been called into question recently by a number of scholars. See

Hoffman, "Was There a 'Great Retreat' from Soviet Socialism?"; Dobrenko, "Socialism as Will and Representation"; Shearer, "Crime and Social Disorder in Stalin's Russia." To the degree that the Great Retreat paradigm applies to forest management, it does so according to the interpretation articulated by Terry Martin, the term referring to "the traditionalist turn in the social and cultural spheres after 1933." See Martin, *Affirmative Action Empire*, 415.

3. Pollock, *Stalin and the Soviet Science Wars*, 212–22.

4. Pollock claims that Lysenko could maintain his grip on power, despite the disapproval of Andrei Zhdanov and the Academy of Sciences, because Stalin personally liked Lysenko (ibid., 41). Valeri Soyfer claims that biology fell into a different category than did other sciences because "physics, chemistry, mathematics, and other natural sciences . . . were already far advanced, their laws and results were applied in practice everywhere," and hence the ability for ideology to gain dominance was greater (*Lysenko and the Tragedy of Soviet Science*, 2). Nikolai Krementsov stresses the importance of the Cold War in explaining the peculiar path that biology took: "It was the Cold War that gave Stalinist science its final form and enduring character. The pattern of interactions, structures, and styles 'frozen' in place by the Cold War from 1948 on defined the dynamics of the Lysenko controversy, Soviet science, and world science generally" (*Stalinist Science*, 289).

5. According to Loren Graham, the term *vernalization* eventually came to be used by Lysenko "for almost anything that he did to plants, seeds or tubers." For example, "when [Lysenko] planted potatoes he first allowed the sections of the potatoes to sprout before placing them in the ground. This is a practice known the world over and used by gardeners for centuries, but to Lysenko it was vernalization. He often soaked seeds before planting them, calling this vernalization, despite the fact that farmers and gardeners have also long done this to certain seeds." See Graham, *Science in Russia*, 124–25.

6. For a discussion of the triumph of Lysenkoism as a scientific movement, see Pollock, *Stalin and the Soviet Science Wars*; Roll-Hansen, *Lysenko Effect*; Lecourt, *Proletarian Science?*; Manevich, *Such Were the Times*.

7. James C. Scott discusses the phenomenon of high-modernist statecraft in *Seeing Like a State*.

8. Red'ko and Red'ko, *Istoriia*, 314.

9. Dokuchaev, *Izbrannye sochineniia*, t. 2. Diana Davis discusses a similar perceived ecological shift in *Resurrecting the Granary of Rome*.

10. Moon, "Environmental History of the Russian Steppes," 156. Moon suggests that Dokuchaev, at the very least, was aware of the intellectual trend of identifying Russia with the forest and Asia with the steppe, from his familiarity with (and admiration for) the works of Nikolai Gogol', suggesting that he was fully aware of the cultural implications of Russian geography.

11. For a discussion of the interaction of scientists and cultural voices in the growing awareness of forest destruction in late nineteenth-century Russia, see Jane Costlow's "Imaginations of Destruction" and "Who Holds the Axe?" Christopher Ely also develops this theme with reference to the visual arts in *This Meager Nature*.

12. "Les i step' v russkoi istorii," 676–77.

13. Moon provides an analysis of Dokuchaev's plans in action in the aforementioned "Environmental History of the Russian Steppes."

14. Kern, "Ekzoty i zasukha," 42.

15. According to the memoirs of a Soviet forestry minister, only 6,000 hectares of field-protective belts were established before 1917, but the plan was to establish more with every passing year after 1924. See RGAE f. 538, op. 1, d. 9, l. 340.

16. Aver'ianov, "Iz perspektivnogo i operatsionnogo plana," 138. Between 1918 and 1923, only 192 *desiatiny* of forest were planted with forest, in hopes of improving agricultural yields.

17. GARF f. 5446, op. 1, d. 61, l. 178.

18. "Postanovlenie Soveta," 9–10.

19. RGAE f. 9465, op. 1, d. 41, ll. 132–33.

20. RGAE f. 9465, op. 1, d. 61, l. 162. This *list* is the second in the *delo* numbered 162.

21. RGAE f. 9465, op. 1, d. 59, l. 6.

22. RGAE f. 9465, op. 1, d. 68, ll. 58–59.

23. RGAE f. 9449, op. 1, d. 1983, ll. 81–84.

24. "Velikaia godovshchina," 5.

25. Zdorik, "Perspektivy razvitiia," 8–9. Although the full name of the administration was the Glavnoe upravlenie lesookhrany i lesonasazhdenii, it was commonly called Glavlesookrana, or GLO for short.

26. RGAE f. 9449, op. 1, d. 8, l. 119.

27. RGAE f. 9449, op. 1, d. 8, l. 124.

28. RGAE f. 9449, op. 1, d. 8, l. 120.

29. Stepanov, "Tipy lesnykh kul'tur" (Oct. 1937), 7. Stepanov claimed that birch trees allow 77 percent of precipitation to reach the ground, while spruce allow only 50 and fir only 20 percent.

30. *Opodzolivanie,* or "podzolization," refers to the process whereby acidic organic materials in the soil decompose under wet conditions, leaching the organic material and soluble minerals (such as iron and aluminum) into layers far below the surface, where these nutrients are less available to young plants.

31. Gavrilov, "Spetsializirovannye khoziaistva," 24; Kozhevnikov, "Tipy lesnykh kul'tur USSR," 27.

32. GLO ratified and prescribed different planting patterns for each stand type. Damp pine forests (*vlazhnye bory*) were to be planted with pine, yellow acacia, and birch in the following pattern (P = pine, A = yellow acacia, B = birch): P P A P P A B A, plowed to a depth of 12–15 centimeters and in rows 0.7 meters apart. GLO established seventy-nine different planting patterns, although the details changed periodically. See RGAE f. 9449, op. 1, d. 2041.

33. RGAE f. 9449, op. 1, d. 2214, l. 5. GLO's quota for the fourth Five-Year Plan—the plan in effect when the war broke out—was to be 968,000 hectares, or 193,600 hectares per year. This compared quite favorably, GLO's leaders claimed, to achievements in countries like Switzerland, which afforested only 340 hectares per year. See RGAE f. 9449, op. 1, d. 2069, l. 4.

34. RGAE f. 9449, op. 1, d. 2214, ll. 77, 21.

35. RGAE f. 9449, op. 1, d. 2214, l. 65.

36. Only 38 percent of the 1940s total was planted in 1941, 5.7 percent in 1942, 6.1 percent in 1943, 13.2 percent in 1944, and 26.6 percent in 1945 (GARF A-259, op. 6, d. 3520, l. 20). It is noteworthy, and emblematic of the importance accorded to forestry matters in the Stalin era, that even during the darkest days of the war, afforestation never ceased completely and started up again before victory was fully guaranteed.

37. RGAE f. 538, op. 1, d. 16, l. 103. The decree instituting the Ministry of Forest Management explicitly specified as an objective of the new ministry "the afforestation of the steppe and of drought regions, especially in Povolzh'ia, the eastern parts of the Ukrainian republic, and the Kulundinskii and Baraninskii steppes of Central Asia." See RGAE f. 9466, op. 1, d. 22b, l. 2.

38. RGAE f. 243, op. 1, d. 1, ll. 1, 21.

39. RGAE f. 9466, op. 1, d. 23, l. 18.

40. Medvedev, *Soviet Agriculture*, 132–42.

41. RGAE f. 9466, op. 1, d. 73, l. 48.

42. RGAE f. 538, op. 1, d. 9, l. 244. Apparently, the question of who would carry out the bulk of the afforestation work on the collective farms was a prominent matter of dispute: "Some considered forest planting to be a task only of the state," Koldanov remembered, "and others, on the contrary, a task for the collective farmers. The review of the dispute from an economic, legal, and technical point of view allowed [the conference] to come to an agreement about the collective farm plantings." See RGAE f. 538, op. 1, d. 9, l. 243.

43. The formal name of the decree was "On the Plan for Field-Protective Afforestation, the Adoption of Grass-Field Crop Rotation, and the Construction of Ponds and Reservoirs to Ensure High and Stable Harvests in the Steppe and Forest-Steppe Regions of the European Part of the USSR."

44. "O plane polezashchitnykh lesonasazhdenii," 2–3.

45. *Zashchitnye lesnye nasazhdeniia*, 3.

46. Krementsov claims that "it was the Cold War that consolidated Soviet science, giving it its final form an enduring character" (*Stalinist Science*, 9).

47. For an example of an attempt to portray the Great Stalin Plan as a proxy fight in the developing Cold War, see Vasil'ev, "Razval teorii."

48. RGAE f. 9466, op. 1, d. 140, l. 5.

49. "O plane polezashchitnykh lesonasazhdenii," 2–3.

50. RGAE f. 337, op. 1, d. 7, l. 112.

51. According to a Minleskhoz report from 1952, collective farmers across the RSFSR had sown 439,000 hectares of field-protective belts between 1936 and 1948, but by 1952, only 180,000 hectares remained (RGAE f. 9466, op. 1, d. 417, ll. 93–94).

52. The quotas can be found in RGAE f. 9466, op. 1, d. 23, l. 19, while the numbers regarding achievements as of 11 Oct. 1948 are from GARF A-259, op. 6, d. 4730, ll. 2–40.

53. GARF f. A-259, op. 6, d. 4730, l. 66.

54. GARF f. A-259, op. 6, d. 4730, ll. 96, 123.

55. RGAE f. 243, op. 1, d. 1, l. 31.

56. RGAE f. 243, op. 1, d. 8, l. 189.

57. Sukachëv was the director of the USSR Academy of Sciences' Institute of Forests, while Pogrebniak was the director of the Ukraine's analogous institute. Many other well-regarded scholars of forestry, botany, and ecology took part in the council's work, including N. I. Sus, V. V. Ogievskii, and G. R. Eitingen, the expert who chose the species of spruce trees now found along the northern wall of the Kremlin (RGAE f. 243, op. 1, d. 8, ll. 241–42).

58. RGAE f. 243, op. 1, d. 8, l. 201.

59. Krementsov, *Stalinist Science*, 164.

60. Branched wheat was not engineered by Lysenko—it was known to ancient Egyptians—but of this Stalin was not aware. For a brief discussion of branched wheat, see Graham, *Science in Russia*, 133.

61. Numerous authors have described the Aug. meeting in considerable detail. See Medvedev, *Vzlet i padenie Lysenko*, 153–96; Soyfer, *Lysenko and the Tragedy of Soviet Science*, 183–204; Krementsov, *Stalinist Science*, 168–83.

62. RGAE f. 337, op. 1, d. 6, ll. 167–70.

63. Chekmenev gave a speech at the Aug. 1948 conference in which he dismissed intraspecfic competition as a "farfetched 'theory'" and claimed that, unlike himself, foresters such as Morozov had not been "in a position to change biological theory and to remove the reactionary position about intraspecfic competition" (RGAE f. 243, op. 1, d. 12, ll. 70–72).

64. Douglas Weiner, *Little Corner of Freedom,* 89. Most treatments of the Great Stalin Plan have provided Lysenko with a central role in its development. David Joravsky, e.g., saw Lysenko as "beyond any doubt . . . the top specialist responsible for the 'Great Stalin Plan for the Transformation of Nature'" (*Lysenko Affair,* 141–42).

65. Khanbekov, "Bor'ba," 45–49. Lysenko wrote in his main theoretical explication of the matter: "In the spring of 1949 on the fields of scientific research institutions in different regions of our country, and also in *leskhozy* and a few *sovkhozy* and *kolkhozy,* more than two thousand hectares of acorns were planted with the nest method." See Lysenko, *Posev,* 6.

66. Both Soyfer and Medvedev have commented upon the analogy between Lysenko's description of plant life and the relationships that would ostensibly prevail among humans under communism. For Lysenko's description, see *Posevm,* 23.

67. Ibid., 4.

68. Ibid., 7.

69. RGAE f. 243, op. 1, d. 12, l. 85.

70. Lysenko, *Posev,* 4, 9.

71. Khanbekov, "Bor'ba," 44.

72. *Zashchitnye lesnye nasazhdeniia,* 18.

73. RGAE f. 9466, op. 1, d. 285, ll. 401–6. All the quotations in this section are drawn from her speech at the 1951 conference.

74. Koldanov indicated that 52.9 percent of collective-farm belts had died by 1954, along with 36.5 percent of belts planted on gullies and 51.3 percent of state shelterbelts (RGAE f. 538, op. 1, d. 1, l. 20).

75. RGAE f. 538, op. 1, d. 9, l. 153. Other figures indicate that the numbers from Rostov *oblast'* may have been somewhat better, although still catastrophic; a letter sent to Minleskhoz from engineers working in the area claimed that "across Rostov *oblast'* 9650 ha of oaks were sown in 1950, but by the fall of 1952 80 percent had died" (RGAE f. 538, op. 1, d. 11, l. 452).

76. The Ministry of Forest Management planted 148,482 hectares of field-protective belts in the spring of 1949, equaling 114 percent of its quota. See GARF f. A-337, op. 1, d. 1190, l. 155. Minleskhoz workers, though, sometimes felt uncertain about what they were supposed to do; the supervisor of the Chapaevsk-Vladimirovka belt complained that "the majority of representatives from the scientific-research institutes have expressed the opinion that the belts should be built on the floodplain across from Vladimirovka, but our opinion is that the belt should be built along the banks of the Akhtuba. The problem needs to be decided quickly" ("Preniia po dokladam," 36).

77. The total area to be afforested under the Great Stalin Plan was calculated at 5,709,000 hectares. Of this, Minleskhoz was to plant 1,536,500 hectares, while the Ministry of Agriculture was to plant 3,529,500 hectares, albeit with Minleskhoz supervision. Sovkhozy were to make up the balance, 580,000 hectares (RGAE f. A-337, op. 1, d. 1183, l. 85).

78. According to a Minleskhoz report from 1952, collective farmers across the RSFSR sowed 439,000 hectares of field-protective belts between 1936 and 1948, but by 1952, only 180,000 hectares remained (RGAE f. 9466, op. 1, d. 417, ll. 93–94).

79. RGAE f. 243, op. 1, d. 42, l. 70.

80. RGAE f. 243, op. 1, d. 42, l. 193.

81. RGAE f. 243, op. 1, d. 42, ll. 206–7.

82. RGAE f. 243, op. 1, d. 11, l. 28.

83. RGAE f. 243, op. 1, d. 11, l. 114.

84. RGAE f. 243, op. 1, d. 133, ll. 19–24.

85. RGAE f. 9466, op. 1, d. 243, l. 53.

86. RGAE f. 9466, op. 1, d. 142, ll. 67–68.

87. RGAE f. 538, op. 1, d. 17, ll. 1–7. At 7 P.M. on 13 June 1947, Koldanov and Motovilov, plus two representatives from the Ministry of Forest Industry, met with Stalin, Mikoian, Beria, and Malenkov in Stalin's Kremlin office. Most of the meeting concerned timber mills in the Russian Far East, but when the deputy minister of the Ministry of Forest Industry indicated that he was interested in logging some rare birch stands that Koldanov thought should remain protected, Stalin said, "I know that place well; I swam there in my time . . . back in 1913 I ran around there." And with that remark, the group moved on to another subject.

88. RGAE f. 538, op. 1, d. 1, ll. 239–40.

89. RGAE f. 538, op. 1, d. 1, ll. 228–31.

90. RGAE f. 538, op. 1, d. 1, l. 298.

91. Sukachëv intensely disliked Lysenko and what he stood for, but his response to Lysenkoism was a calm faith that this too shall pass. When one of Sukachëv's students, in the dangerous and depressing days following the Aug. 1948 VASKhNIL meeting, urged him to confront Lysenko directly, Sukachëv answered (more than once), "It is important to protect scientific cadres, to decrease as much as possible the damage of these decisions, to impede pseudoscientific research. . . . There will come a time, it *can't* not come, when our science will again develop unmolested" (Rabotov, "O Vladimire Nikolaeviche Sukacheve," 148).

92. Douglas Weiner, *Little Corner of Freedom,* 90. It was not easy to convince serious scientists to take part in the expedition. One geobotanist recalled in a memorial volume published after Sukachëv's death that she initially turned down Sukachëv's offer to join the expedition, uninterested in Lysenko's "pseudoscience," but Sukachëv insisted and the scientist relented. See Grudzinskaia, "Vospominaniia o Vladimire Nikolaeviche Sukachëve," 50.

93. Zonn, *Otchet,* 3.

94. Ibid., 9.

95. "Komsomol'sko-molodezhnaia," 10.

96. RGAE f. 9466, op. 1, d. 216, l. 16.

97. RGAE f. 9466, op. 1, d. 218, l. 7.

98. RGAE f. 9466, op. 1, d. 218, ll. 5–6.

99. The report from Stalingrad came from a conference held in Feb. 1951 (RGAE f. 9466, op. 1, d. 285, ll. 314, 316).

100. RGAE f. 548, op. 1, d. 1, l. 444.

101. As of early 1951, belts in the forest-steppe zone died 12.2 percent of the time; in the steppe zone, 18.3 percent; in the dry steppe, 37.5 percent, and in the semidesert, 45.5 percent. These numbers grew worse with time (RGAE f. 9466, op. 1, d. 327, l. 14).

102. GARF f. 259, op. 6, d. 8648, ll. 52–58. Results for various *oblasti* were sometimes much worse; Kursk *oblast'* fulfilled 45 percent of the 1951 plan, Stalingrad 41, Krasnodar 59 (GARF f. A-259, op. 7, d. 83, l. 57). The failure to perform sufficient follow-up work ensured a low survival rate for the forests.

103. GARF f. A-259, op. 6, d. 8648, ll. 11–12.

104. RGAE f. A-337, op. 1, d. 206, l. 115.

105. GARF f. A-259, op. 6, d. 8648, l. 21.

106. RGAE f. A-337, op. 1, d. 206, ll. 165, 170.

107. RGAE f. 9466, op. 1, d. 216, l. 107.

108. On 7 Aug. 1951, Minleskhoz issued a decree calling the nest method into question by indicating that "in 1951 there were 992 hectares of nested oak under the cover of agricultural crops in the Kamyshin-Stalingrad belt; but with the onset of high temperatures and dry winds, these died completely by 15 July 1951." On 27 July 1951, Minleskhoz upbraided the Ministry of Agriculture for "not implementing the needed guidance for the care for forest plantings" and for allowing the forest to be "trampled by cattle, destroyed by fire, and harmed by sowing with crops." See RGAE f. 538, op. 1, d. 9, ll. 206, 208–9.

109. According to Ethan Pollack, Stalin had been complaining about Lysenko before his Arakcheev speech, telling the Georgian linguist Arnold Chikobava that "Lysenko is making life impossible for everyone," but if Stalin did indeed intend to target Lysenko with his criticism of Arakcheevism, the blows missed their mark (Pollock, "Politics of Knowledge," 184).

110. Reporters did seem to feel free to make cutting statements; the director of the Voronezh forest management institute stated quite bluntly, "It seems to me that an indisputable proposition should be that the universality of no matter what method in different natural conditions is undoubtedly mistaken" (RGAE f. 243, op. 1, d. 327, l. 156). Lysenko's influence likely evinced itself most not so much in any hostile treatment that dissenters received, but in their tendency to edit out inconvenient information. At a Nov. 1951 meeting about the nest method held in the Tatar republic, one reporter noted, "Early sowing, under the cover of grain crops, did not give good results. Therefore I wrote nothing about it in my report" (RGAE f. 243, op. 1, d. 329, l. 28).

111. RGAE f. 243, op. 1, d. 328, l. 9.

112. Blaming the collective farmers for failing to understand the essence of the nest method was perhaps the most commonly proffered explanation for the poor results. A representative from the Ministry of Agriculture, e.g., claimed that "in those collective farms where we receive very unfavorable results, we also see the gross violation of agronomic technique" (RGAE f. 243, op. 1, d. 327, l. 190).

113. RGAE f. 243, op. 1, d. 328, ll. 234–46.

114. RGAE f. 538, op. 1, d. 9, l. 180.

115. RGAE f. 538, op. 1, d. 9, l. 179.

116. RGAE f. 538, op. 1, d. 9, ll. 57–58.

117. RGAE f. 9466, op. 1, d. 264, ll. 381–84.

118. In contrast, forests planted with the traditional row method featured 5,000 or more seedlings per hectare 42.5 percent of the time; between 2,500 and 5,000 seedlings 27.7 percent of the time; and fewer than 2,500 seedlings 26.9 percent of the time—demonstrably better figures; in 1951 these figures improved to 51 percent, 27 percent, and 19 percent, respectively (RGAE f. 243, op. 1, d. 481, l. 8).

119. In a 1952 letter from Bovin to Chekmenev, Bovin indicates that all densities under 2,500 seedlings per hectare should be considered dead (RGAE f. 538, op. 1, d. 11, l. 512).

120. RGAE f. 243, op. 1, d. 919, l. 4; RGAE f. 243, op. 1, d. 528, l. 92.

121. The Kursk regional office of GUPL claimed that collective farmers performed 100 percent of the first round of follow-up care, 69 percent of the second round, and 15

percent of the third round, when in fact these numbers should have been 62.6 percent, 14.3 percent, and 4 percent (RGAE f. 243, op. 1, d. 528, l. 128).

122. RGAE f. 9466, op. 1, d. 373, ll. 40, 51.

123. RGAE f. 243, op. 1, d. 481, ll. 42, 48–49.

124. RGAE f. 243, op. 1, d. 481, l. 42. The cost of rehabilitating an oak forest, Koldanov reported, could reach a thousand rubles per hectare.

125. RGAE f. 243, op. 1, d. 481, l. 44.

126. RGAE f. 538, op. 1, d. 11, l. 449.

127. RGAE f. 438, op. 1, d. 11, l. 452.

128. RGAE f. 9466, op. 1, d. 471, l. 107.

129. RGAE f. 9466, predislovie, l. 2.

130. RGAE f. 538, op. 1, d. 1, l. 212; RGAE f. 538, op. 1, d. 2, l. 14; RGAE f. 538, op. 1, d. 2, l. 260.

131. GARF f. A-259, op. 7, d. 80, l. 2; RGAE f. 538, op. 1, d. 75.

132. RGAE f. 538, op. 1, d. 1, l. 124.

133. RGAE f. 538, op. 1, d. 1, l. 150.

134. RGAE f. 538, op. 1, d. 16, l. 104.

135. RGAE f. 538, op. 1, d. 5, l. 5.

136. Koldanov indicated that 52.9 percent of collective-farm belts had died by 1954, along with 36.5 percent of belts planted on gullies and 51.3 percent of state shelterbelts (RGAE f. 538, op. 1, d. 1, l. 20).

137. Rostankowski, "Transformation of Nature," 389.

138. In 1949, the Ministry of Agriculture planted 152,000 hectares of forest, in 1950 368.2, in 1951 260, and in 1952 257.2 (RGAE f. 538, op. 1, d. 1, l. 355; RGAE f. 538, op. 1, d. 9, l. 340). The total number of field-protective belts, including those planted on collective-farm lands by Minleskhoz, equaled 1.295 million hectares; 48 percent of these had died by 1 Jan. 1954, and more than 200,000 hectares died over the next three years (RGAE f. 538, op. 1, d. 1, l. 130).

139. RGAE f. 538, op. 1, d. 11, l. 109. Similar findings came from a nearby collective farm, where winter wheat yields within one hundred meters of the forest were 33.5 centners per hectare, but only 25.7 centners per hectare more than three hundred meters from the belt.

140. Koldanov, "Oblesenie stepei nashei rodiny," 59.

Conclusion

1. While it might be noted here that Stalin himself was Georgian rather than Russian, authors such as David Brandenberger have shown that Stalin was capable of being as Russocentric as any Muscovite. See Brandenburger, National Bolshevism.

2. Kotkin, Magnetic Mountain.

3. Katerina Clark, Petersburg, 25.

BIBLIOGRAPHY

Archives

All citations to archives conform to the pattern *fond, delo, opis', and list.*

GARF	**Gosudarstvennyi Arkhiv Rossisskoi Federatsii**
Fond A-259	Sovet Narodnykh Kommissarov RSFSR
Fond A-337	Ministerstvo Lesnogo Khoziaistva RSFSR
Fond 374	Narodnyi Kommissariat Raboche-Krest'ianskoi Inspektsii
Fond 3316	Tsentral'nyi Ispolnitel'nyi Komitet
Fond 5446	Sovet Narodnykh Kommissarov
Fond 5466	Tsentral'nyi Komitet Profsoiuza Sel'skokhoziaistvennykh Rabochikh
Fond 5467	Tsentral'nyi Komitet Lesnykh Rabochikh
Fond 5674	Sovet Truda i Oborony
Fond 6757	Ekomicheskoe Soveshchanie
RGAE	**Russkii Gosudarstvennyi Arkhiv Ekonomiki**
Fond 243	Glavnyi Upravlenie Polezashchitnogo Lesorazvedeniia v Sovet Ministrov
Fond 342	Lichnyi Fond Ivana Romanovicha Morozova
Fond 396	Pis'ma Gazete "Krest'ianskaia Gazeta"
Fond 478	Narodnyi Kommissariat Zemledeliia
Fond 538	Lichnyi Fond Vasiliia Iakovlevicha Koldanova
Fond 4372	Gosplan
Fond 7654	Glavnoe Lesnoe Upravlenie Narodnogo Kommissariata Zemledeliia

Fond 9449   Glavnoe Upravlenie Lesnoi Okhrany i Lesorazvedeniia v Sovet Narodnykh Kommissarov

Fond 9465   Glavnoe Upravlenie Lesnogo Khoziaistva i Polezashchitnogo Lesoraz-
vedniia Narodnogo Kommissariata Zemledeliia

Fond 9466   Ministerstvo Lesnogo Khoziaistva SSSR

RGASPI   Russkii Gosudarstvennyi Arkhiv Sotsial'no-Politicheskoi Istorii
Fond 17   Protokoly Politbiuro

TsGAMO   Tsentralnyi Gosudarstvennyi Arkhiv Moskovskoi Oblasti
Fond 7139   Moskovskoe Oblastnoe Upravlenie Lesnogo Khoziaistva

Journals

Biulleten' lesnoe khoziaistvo i okhota

Lesnaia kooperatsiia

Lesnaia pravda

Lesnaia zhizn' i khoziaistvo

Lesnoe delo

Lesnoe khoziaistvo

Lesnoe khoziaistvo i lesnaia promyshlennost'

Lesnoe khoziaistvo i okhota

Lesnoe khoziaistvo, lesopromyshlennost' i toplivo

Lesnoi nabat

Lesnoi rabochii

Lesnoi spetsialist

Lesnoi zhurnal

Lesopromyshlennoe delo

Lesopromyshlennyi vestnik

Lesovedenie i lesovodstvo

Lesovod

Lesovodstvo, lesnye kultury i pochvovedenie

Rabotnik zemli i lesa

Vestnik lesnogo khoziaistva

Za zashchitu lesa

Books and Articles

Abramovich, K. "Sotsialen-li organizm lesa?" *Lesnoe khoziaistvo* 1 (1929): 49–58.

Åhlander, Ann-Mari Satre. *Environmental Problems in the Shortage Economy: The Legacy of Soviet Environmental Policy.* Aldershot, UK: E. Elgar Publishers, 1994.

Aleksandrov, V. A. *Stalinskii plan preobrazovaniia prirody v deistvii.* Moscow: Moskovskii Obshchestva Ispytatelei Prirody, 1952.

Alekseychik, N., and B. Chagin. *Protiv reaktsionnykh teorii na lesnom fronte.* Moscow: Gosudarstvennoe lesnoe tekhnicheskoe izdatel'stvo, 1932.

Algvere, Karl V. *Forest Economy in the USSR.* Stockholm: Royal College of Forestry, 1966.

Andreev, I. "O bor'be s maiskim zhukom." *Lesnoi zhurnal* 6–7 (1915): 1032–39.

Anonymous. "Neskol'ko slov k voprosu o tipakh lesonasazhdenii." *Lesopromyshlennyi vestnik* 18 (29 April 1904): 273–75.

Arkhangel'skii, D. "Istoricheskii ocherk deiatel'nosti Romanovskoi lesnoi shkoli za dvadtsatipiatiletnee eia sushchestvovanie." *Lesnaia zhizn' i khoziaistvo* 2 (September 1913): 1–8.

Arkhipov, S. S. *Razlichie v ucheniiakh o tipakh lesa.* Moscow: Goslestekhizdat, 1933.

Arndt, P. "Lesoustroitel'noe soveshchanie v TsUL'e (Novoe napravlenie v organizatsii lesoustroistva i lesnaia politika TsUL'a)." *Lesnoe khoziaistvo, lesopromyshlennost' i toplivo* 12–18 (March–April 1924): 66–67.

Arnol'd, F. K. *Istoriia lesovodstva.* Moscow: Izdatel'stvo Moskovskogo gosudarstvennogo universitet lesa, 2004.

Astanin, L. P., and K. N. Blagosklonov. *Conservation of Nature.* Moscow: Progress Publishers, 1983.

Aver'ianov, F. A. "Iz perspektivnogo i operatsionnogo plana lesomeliorativnykh rabot v otnoshenii borb'y s peskami i ovragami v RSFSR." *Lesovedenie i lesovodstvo* 1 (March 1926): 135–50.

Backman, Charles, and Thomas Waggener. *Soviet Timber Resources and Utilization: An Interpretation of the 1988 National Inventory.* Seattle: Center for International Trade in Forest Products, 1991.

Bagrinovskii, "Ocherk po bor'be s vrednymi nasekomyi v Kulikovskom lesnichestve Tambovskago guberniia za 1912 god." *Lesnaia zhizn' i khoziaistvo* 5 (January 1913): 31–35.

Bailes, Kendall. *Technology and Society under Lenin and Stalin.* Princeton: Princeton University Press, 1978.

Ball, A. M. *Russia's Last Capitalists: The Nepmen, 1921–1929.* Berkeley: University of California Press, 1987.

Baranovskii, S. "K voprosu ob osnovykh ekonomicheskikh zadachakh sovremennogo lesoustroistva v sviazi s zemleustroistvom." *Lesovod* 4–5 (October–November 1924): 34–38.

———. "Lesoustroistvo i zemleustroitel'naia politika." *Lesovod* 4 (April 1925): 28–31.

Barber, John. *Soviet Historians in Crisis, 1928–1932.* London: Macmillan Press, 1981.

Barr, Brenton M., and Kathleen E. Braden. *The Disappearing Russian Forest: A Dilemma in Soviet Resource Management.* Totowa, NJ: Rowman and Littlefield, 1988.

Bassin, Mark. "Nature, Geopolitics and Marxism: Ecological Contestations in Weimar Germany." *Transactions of the Institute of British Geographers,* new series, 21, no. 2 (1996): 315–41.

Bater, James A., and R. A. French, eds. *Studies in Russian Historical Geography.* London: Academic Press, 1983.

Bauer, Raymond. *The New Man in Soviet Psychology.* Cambridge: Harvard University Press, 1952.

Beilin, I. G. *Georgii Fedorovich Morozov—vydaiushchiisia lesovod i geograf.* Moscow: Izdatel'stvo Akademii Nauk SSSR, 1954.

———. *Ocherki po istorii lesnykh obshchestv dorevoliutsionnoi Rossii.* Moscow: Goslesbumizdat, 1962.

Belaenko, A. P., et al. *Dvokhsotletie uchrezhdeniia lesnogo departmenta 1798–1998.* Moscow: BVIITslesresurs, 1998.

Belov, Lesovod. "Tragediia Sredne-Volzhskogo leskhoza." *Lesnoe khoziaistvo i lesnaia promyshlennost'* 82–83 (July–August 1930): 66–67.

Billington, James. *The Icon and the Axe: An Interpretive History of Russian Culture.* New York: Vintage Books, 1966.

Birch, Thomas. "The Incarceration of Wilderness: Wilderness Areas as Prisons." *Environmental Ethics* 12 (1990): 3–26.

Blandon, Peter. *Soviet Forest Industries.* Boulder: Westview Press, 1983.

Bobrov, R. V. *Dom u zolotogo pruda.* St. Petersburg: Sankt-Peterburgskii nauchno-issledovatel'skii institute lesnogo khoziaistva, 2001.

Bogarevich, K. "O sokhranenii pamiatnikov prirody." *Lesnaia zhizn' i khoziaistvo* 8 (June 1913): 26–33.

Bogoslovskii, S. A. "Finliandskii metod ucheta lesnykh resursov." *Lesnoe khoziaistvo* 2–3 (1929): 3–27.

———. "Ideia gosudarstvennogo lesnogo khoziaistva i lesoustroistva." *Lesovod* 2–3 (August–September 1924): 29–35.

———. "K voprosu o gosudarstvennom lesnom khoziaistve." *Lesnoe khoziaistvo i okhota* 3 (February 1923): 1–23.

———. *Novye techeniia v lesoustroistve.* Leningrad: Izdatel'stvo leningradskogo lesnogo instituta, 1925.

———. "Nuzhen li peresmotr ekonomicheskikh osnovanii sovremennogo lesoustroistva?" *Lesnoe khoziaistvo* 10–11 (1929): 11–18.

———. "Printsip postoianstva pol'zovaniia v lesnom khoziaistve." *Lesnoe khoziaistvo* 4 (1929): 17–36.

———. "Systemy rubok glavnogo pol'zovaniia v lesakh SSSR." *Za zashchitu lesa* 1 (September 1937): 6–14.

———. "Ustroistvo lesov vodookhranoi zony." *Za zashchitu lesa* 3 (November 1937): 7–14.

Bogoslovskii, S., and M. Orlov, "O lesoustroitel'nykh nedorazumeniiakh i raz"iadneniiakh." *Lesnoe khoziaistvo, lesopromyshlennost' i toplivo* 21–22 (June–July 1925): 64–65.

Bonhomme, Brian. *Forests, Peasants, and Revolutionaries: Forest Conservation and Organization in Soviet Russia, 1917–1929.* Boulder: East European Monographs, 2005.

Boreiko, V. E. *Belye piatna istorii prirodookhrany: SSSR, Rossiia, Ukraina.* Kiev: Kievskii ekologo-kul'turnyi tsentr, 1996.

Botsianovskii, A. "O ratsional'nom i udobnom sposobe obrabotki taksatsionnykh dannykh, dobytykh pri lesoustroistve." *Lesnoi zhurnal* 10 (1915): 1496–1502.

Bramwell, Anna. *Ecology in the Twentieth Century: A History.* New Haven: Yale University Press, 1989.

Brandenburger, David. *National Bolshevism.* Cambridge: Harvard University Press, 2002.

Brown, Edward J. *The Proletarian Episode in Russian Literature, 1928–1932.* New York: Octagon Press, 1953.

Brüggemeier, Franz-Josef, Mark Cioc, and Thomas Zeller, eds. *How Green Were the Nazis?* Athens: Ohio University Press, 2005.

Chekhov, Anton. *Uncle Vanya.* Trans. Curt Columbus. Chicago: Ivan R. Dee, 2002.

Chernogubov. "Iz zapisok taksatora." *Lesovod* 7 (July 1927): 11–22.

China's Forestry. Beijing: China Forestry Publishing House, 2000.

Clark, Katerina. *Peterburg, Crucible of Revolution.* Cambridge: Harvard University Press, 1995.

Cohen, Stephen F. *Bukharin and the Bolshevik Revolution.* Oxford: Oxford University Press, 1980.

Costlow, Jane. "Dmitrii Kaigorodov and the Ethics of Attentiveness: Knowledge, Love and Care for *Rodnaia Priroda.*" In *Shirokaja Russkaja Natura—Transformations in Russian Nature,* ed. Arja Rosenholm and Sari Autio-Sarasmo. Helsinki: Kikimora Publications, 2005.

———. "Imaginations of Destruction: The 'Forest Question' in Nineteenth-Century Russian Culture." *Russian Review* 62 (January 2003): 91–118.

———. "Who Holds the Axe? Violence and Peasants in Nineteenth-Century Russian Depictions of the Forest." *Slavic Review* 68, no. 1 (2009): 10–30.

D., N. "Kratkii obzor dekretov i postanovlenii." *Lesnoe khoziaistvo i lesnaiapromyshlennost'* 62 (November 1928): 121–22.

Damberg, E. F. "Ekskursiia v Pashe-Kapetskoe lesnichestvo." *Lesovod* 11 (November 1925): 58–59.

———. "O lesnoi tekushchei statistike." *Lesnoi zhurnal* 5 (May 1911): 866–69.

———. "Tipy kak osnovanie klassifikatsii lesov pri ikh zemskom otsenochno-statisticheskom izsledovanii." *Lesnoi zhurnal* 8 (1914): 1210–14.

Danilov, L. V., and A. K. Sokolov, eds. *Traditsionnyi opyt prirodopol'zovaniia v Rossii.* Moscow: "Nauka," 1998.

Davies, R. W. *From Tsarism to the New Economic Policy: Continuity and Change in the Economy of the USSR.* Ithaca: Cornell University Press, 1991.

Davis, Diana. *Resurrecting the Granary of Rome.* Athens: Ohio University Press, 2007.

DeBardeleben, Joan. *The Environment and Marxism-Leninism: The Soviet and East German Experience.* Boulder: Westview Press, 1985.

"Den' lesa v 1930 godu." *Lesnoi spetsialist* 7–8 (April 1930): 8–10.

Denisev. "Ob izvrashchenii klassovoi linii v lesnom khoziaistve." *Lesovod* 12 (December 1929): 19–24.

Deutscher, Isaac. *Stalin: A Political Biography.* New York: Vintage Books, 1960.

Dmitriev, V. S. *Stalinskii plan preobrazovaniia prirody pretvoriaetsia v zhizn'.* Moscow: Izdatel'stvo "Pravda," 1950.

Dobrenko, E. A. "Socialism as Will and Representation; or, What Legacy Are We Rejecting?" *Kritika* 5, no. 4 (2004): 675–708.

Dokuchaev, V. V. *Gorizontal'nye i vertikal'nye pochvennye zony.* St. Petersburg, 1898.

———. *Izbrannye sochineniia.* Moscow: Gosudarstvennoe izdatel'stvo sel'skokhoziastvennoi literatury, 1948.

Donskov. "O smene porod v lesnom khoziaistve." *Les* 3 (July 1916): 29–34.

Egorov, Lesnik. "O budushchnosti lesov Arkhangel'skoi guberniia v sviazi s sushchest-vuiushchimi priemami lesnogo khoziaistva." *Lesnoi zhurnal* 6–7 (1915): 1008–25.

Egorov, M. "Iskusstvo na pomoshch' lesnomu khoziaistvo." *Lesovod* 8 (August 1927): 22–24.

Eitengen, G. P. "Lesnoe khoziaistvo zapadnoi evropy." *Lesnoe khoziaistvo* 1 (1929): 59–91.

———. "O plane rabot tsentral'noi lesnoi opytnoi stantsii NKZ RSFSR na 1929/30 operatsionnyi god." *Lesnoe khoziaistvo* 7 (1929): 82–87.

Eitengen, G. P., and I. L. Gainer. *Krest'ianskoe lesosnabzhenie posle revoliutsii*. Moscow: Izdatel'stvo NKRKI SSSR, 1927.

Ely, Christopher. *This Meager Nature*. DeKalb: Northern Illinois University Press, 2002.

Ende, B. "Khod leszagotovok." *Lesovod* 3 (March 1929): 21–24.

Epshtein, Mikhail. *Priroda, mir, tainik vselennoi . . . : Sistema peizazhnykh obrazov v russkoi poezii*. Moscow: Vysshaia shkola, 1990.

Erlich, Alexander. *The Soviet Industrialization Debate, 1924–1928*. Cambridge: Harvard University Press, 1960.

Fernow, Bernard. *A Brief History of Forestry in Europe, the United States and Other Countries*. Washington, DC: American Forestry Association, 1913.

Feshbach, Murray. *Ecological Disaster: Cleaning Up the Hidden Legacy of the Soviet Regime*. New York: Twentieth Century Fund Press, 1995.

Feshbach, Murray, and Alfred Friendly Jr. *Ecocide in the USSR: Health and Nature under Siege*. New York: Basic Books, 1992.

Figes, Orlando. *Natasha's Dance: A Cultural History of Russia*. New York: Picador Press, 2003.

Fitzpatrick, Sheila. *Politics of Soviet Industrialization: Vesenkha and Its Relationship with Rabkrin, 1929–30*. Washington, DC: Kennan Institute for Advanced Russian Studies, 1983.

———, ed. *Russia in the Era of NEP*. Bloomington: Indiana University Press, 1991.

Frängsmyr, T., J. L. Heilbron, and R. E. Rider, eds. *The Quantifying Spirit in the Eighteenth Century*. Berkeley: University of California Press, 1990.

French, R. A. "Russians and the Forest." In *Studies in Russian Historical Geography*, ed. James H. Bater and R. A French. London: Academic Press, 1983.

G., K. "Lesoustroitel'noe soveshchanie pri UL'e." *Lesnoe khoziaistvo, lesopromyshlennost' i toplivo* 19 (April 1925): 57–58.

G., P. "Zarabotnaia plata lesnykh rabotnikov." *Rabotnik zemli i lesa* 1 (May–June 1923): 14–16.

Gasparov, Boris, Robert Hughes, and Irina Paperno, eds. *Cultural Mythologies of Russian Modernism: From the Golden Age to the Silver Age*. Berkeley: University of California Press, 1992.

Gavrilov, B. I. "Spetsializirovannye khoziaistva v sosnovykh lesakh vodookrannoi zony." *Za zashchitu lesa* 1 (January 1938): 24–29.

Gernits, A. "Nepreryvno proizvoditel'nyi les." *Lesnoe khoziaistvo, lesopromyshlennost' i toplivo* 13 (October 1924): 31–35.

Gershman, I. "Ocherk istorii lesovladeniia, lesnoi sobstvennosti i lesnoi politiki v Rossii." *Lesnoi zhurnal* 4 (April 1911): 493–519.

———. "Ocherk istorii lesovladeniia, lesnoi sobstvennosti i lesnoi politiki v Rossii." *Lesnoi zhurnal* 5 (May 1911): 794–816.

Gladilin, A. "Maiskii zhuk v Fashchevskom lesnichestve Tambovskoi guberniia." *Lesnoi zhurnal* 4–5 (April–May 1909): 569–81.

Goldman, Marshall. *The Spoils of Progress*. Cambridge: MIT Press, 1972.

Golubovich, I. D. "Za ratsionalizatsiiu sposobov rubki." *Lesnoi spetsialist* 15–18 (August–September 1930): 30–33.

Grachev, A. *Lesopolosa Kamyshin-Stalingrad*. Stalingrad: Stalingradskoe knizhnoe izdatel'stvo, 1957.

Graham, Loren. *Science in Russia and the Soviet Union: A Short History*. Cambridge: Cambridge University Press, 1993.

———. *The Soviet Academy of Sciences and the Communist Party, 1927–1932*. Princeton: Princeton University Press, 1967.

Grebenshchikov, O. S. *Geobotanicheskii slovar'*. Moscow: Izdatel'stvo "Nauka," 1965.

Grekov, P. "Neskol'ko slov k vypusku instruktsii dlia ustroistva, revizii lesoustroistva i izsledovaniia kazennykh lesov 1911 goda." *Lesnoi zhurnal* 9–10 (November–December 1911): 1487–95.

Groening, Gert, and Joachim Wolschke-Bulmahn. "Some Notes on the Mania for Native Plants in Germany." *Landscape Journal* 11, no. 2 (1992): 116–26.

Grudzinskaia, I.A. "Vospominaniia o Vladimire Nikolaeviche Sukachëve." In *Vladimir Nikolaevich Sukachev: Ocherki, vospominaniia sovremennikov*, ed. A. L. Ianshin. Leningrad: Izdatel'stvo "Nauka," 1986.

Guman, V. V. *Rubki poslednogo desiatiletiia (1914–1924) i vozobnovlenie vyrobok i garei*. Leningrad: Izdanie leningradskogo sel'sko-khoziaistvennogo instituta, 1926.

Hays, Samuel P. *Conservation and the Gospel of Efficiency*. Pittsburgh: University of Pittsburgh Press, 1959.

Hoffman, David. "Was There a 'Great Retreat' from Soviet Socialism?" *Kritika* 5, no. 4 (2004): 651–74.

Husband, William. "'Correcting Nature's Mistakes': Transforming the Environment and Soviet Children's Literature, 1928–1941." *Environmental History* 11, no. 2 (2006): 300–318.

Hutchings, Stephen. *Russian Modernism: The Transfiguration of the Everyday*. Cambridge: Cambridge University Press, 1998.

Iakovlev, S. "G. F. Morozov, kak pedagog." *Lesnoe khoziaistvo* 2 (1928): 78–82.

Iannovskii, L. "Udovletvorenie mestnykh nuzhd, kak osnovnaia zadacha narodnogo lesnogo khoziaistva, v sviazi s voprosom o khoziaistvennykh zagotovkakh." *Lesnoi zhurnal* 4–6 (April–June 1917): 221–27.

Ianshin, A. L., ed. *Vladimir Nikolaevich Sukachev: Ocherki, vospominaniia sovremennikov*. Leningrad: Izdatel'stvo "Nauka," 1986.

Iashnov, K. "Lesnye tipy i lesnoe khoziaistvo." *Lesovedenie i lesovodstvo* 5 (June 1928): 163–69.

Iashnov, L. "Beregite lesa!" *Lesnoi zhurnal* 4–6 (April–June 1917): 342–46.

Iatsenko, I. I. "Esteticheskaia okhrana lesov i lesoustroistvo: Doklad Petrogradskomu Lesnomu Obshchestvu, zaslushannyi 21 Ianvaria 1917 goda." *Lesnoi zhurnal* 7–8 (July–August 1917): 369–86.

———. "O novykh osnovaniiakh lesoustroistva." *Lesnoe khoziaistvo, lesopromyshlennost' i toplivo* 13 (October 1924): 5–13.

———. "Ob oborote rubki." *Lesnoe khoziaistvo, lesopromyshlennost' i toplivo* 19 (May 1925): 12–17.

———. "Tsel' lesoustroistva i ego osnovye zadachi." *Lesnoe khoziaistvo, lesopromyshlennost' i toplivo* 17–18 (February–March 1925): 23–28.

Imort, Michael. "Eternal Forest—Eternal *Volk*." In *How Green Were the Nazis?* ed. Franz-Josef Brüggemeier, Mark Cioc, and Thomas Zeller. Athens: Ohio University Press, 2005.

"Instruktsiia dlia ustroistva lesov mestnogo znacheniia." *Lesnoe khoziaistvo, lesopromyshlennost' i toplivo* 12 (September 1924): 116–19.

Instruktsiia dlia ustroistva, revizii lesoustroistva i izsledovaniia kazennykh lesov. St. Petersburg: Glavnoupravleniia zemleustroistvo i zemledeliia, 1908.

Instruktsiia dlia ustroistva, revizii lesoustroistva i izsledovaniia kazennykh lesov. St. Petersburg: Glavnoupravleniia zemleustroistvo i zemledeliia, 1911.

Instruktsiia dlia ustroistva, revisii lesoustroistva i izsledovaniia kazennykh lesov. St. Petersburg: Glavnoupravleniia zemleustroistvo i zemledeliia, 1914.

Instruktsiia dlia ustroistva, revizii ustroistva i lesoekonomicheskogo obsledovaniia obshchegosudarstvennykh lesov RSFSR. Moscow: Izdatel'stvo "Novaia derevnia," 1927.

Ispolatov. "Samovol'nye porubki." *Les* 1 (May 1916): 39–48.

Ispolatov, E. "Vrednye sueveriia v lesnom khoziaistve." *Lesnoe khoziaistvo i okhota* 2 (January 1923): 50–52.

Iunitskii, A. "Neskol'ko slov k voprosu o tipakh nasazhdenii." *Lesopromyshlennyi vestnik* 2 (13 January 1905): 13–15.

Iurin, N. "Lesnoe khoziaistvo SSSR i zakon o merakh k ego uporiadocheniiu ot fevraliia 1928 g." *Lesnoe khoziaistvo* 4 (1928): 20–29.

Ivanits, Linda. *Russian Folk Belief.* Armonk, NY: M. E. Sharpe, 1989.

Ivanov, P., ed. *Stalinskii plan preobrazovaniia prirody: Velikie stroiki kommunizma. Sbornik dokumentov.* Moscow. Gosudarstvennoe izdatel'stvo politicheskoi literatury, 1952.

Ivashkevich, B. A. "Po lesam sovremennoi Germanii." *Lesovod* 2 (February 1929): 46–54.

Jancar, Barbara. *Environmental Management in the Soviet Union and Yugoslavia.* Durham: Duke University Press, 1987.

Joravsky, David. *The Lysenko Affair.* Cambridge: Harvard University Press, 1970.

———. *Soviet Marxism and Natural Sciences.* New York: Columbia University Press, 1961.

Josephson, Paul R. *Industrialized Nature: Brute Force Technology and the Transformation of the Natural World.* Washington, DC: Island Press, 2002.

———. *Resources under Regimes: Technology, Environment and the State.* Cambridge: Harvard University Press, 2004.

———. *Totalitarian Science and Technology.* Amherst: Humanity Books, 2005.

K., G. "Pervye shagi lesovoda-lesoustroitelia." *Lesovod* 8 (August 1925): 51–52.

"K prestoiashchemu XXV-letiiu nizshikh lesnykh shkol—Okrytoe pis'mo." *Lesnoi zhurnal* 10 (December 1912): 1359–62.

Kalinin, B. "Za chistotu marksistko-leninskoi teorii!" *Lesnaia pravda* 59 (31 December 1931): 3.

Kalinin, M. "Beregite i vyrashchivaite lesa." *Rabotnik zemli i lesa* 2 (July 1923): 16.

———. "Sluzhenie russkomu lesu." *Lesnoi vestnik* 16–17 (8 August–13 September 2001): 50–55.

Kaluzhnyi, Grigorii. *Zhizn' G. F. Morozova.* Moscow: Entsiklopediia sel i dereven', 2004.

Kazakov, A. "Ledokhod nachalsia." *Lesovod* 1 (1924): 6–8.

Kazantsev, N. K. "Poslovitsy o lese u lesnykh promyslakh." *Lesovod* 3 (March 1928): 12–16.

Kern, E. E. "Ekzoty i zasukha." *Lesovod* 8 (August 1925): 42–44.

———. "Nasushchnye nuzhdy russkago lesnogo khoziaistva." *Lesnoe delo* 1 (1 November 1918): 6–10.

Khanbekov, I. I. "Bor'ba za razvedenie lesov v stepi." *Lesnoe khoziaistvo* 1 (October 1948): 45–49.

Khoroshov, V. A. "O shtatakh lesnichestv, veduiushchikh 100% khozzagotovki." *Lesnoe khoziaistvo i lesnaia promyshlennost'* 53–54 (February–March 1928): 28–33.

Kirpakh, A. "Lesokhoziaistvennye zametki." *Lesnaia zhizn' i khoziaistvo* 2 (July 1912): 37–38.

Kliucharev, N. N. "U svezhikh mogil." *Lesovod* 12 (December 1926): 11–16.

Kliuchnikov, V. F. "Instruktsiia dlia lesoustroistva, revizii lesoustroistva i izsledovaniia kazennykh lesov, izdanie 1911 goda." *Lesnoi zhurnal* 4–5 (April–May 1912): 559–73.

———. "Lesoustroistvo ili lesnoe khoziaistvo?" *Lesopromyshlennyi vestnik* 19 (13 May 1910): 209–12.

———. "Znachenie tipov v lesoustroistve." *Lesnoi zhurnal* 3 (1914): 406–26.

Kniazev, V. P. *Polezashchitnye lesnye polosy: Vernoe sredstvo bor'by s zasukhoi i leuro-zhiami.* Moscow: Izdatel'stvo Akademii Nauk SSSR, 1951.

"Ko vsem lesovodam SSSR." *Lesovod* 6 (June 1926): 63.

Koldanov, Vasil'ii. "Oblesenie stepei nashei rodiny." *Priroda* (May 1958): 50–63.

Komarov, Boris [Ze'ev Wol'fson, pseud.]. *The Destruction of Nature in the Soviet Union.* London: Pluto Press, 1980.

"Komsomol'sko-molodezhnaia gosudarstvennaia lesnaia polosa." *Lesnoe khoziaistvo* 2 (July 1949): 8–12.

Korsh, V. "Neskol'ko slov o vydele nasazhdenii." *Lesnoi zhurnal* 4–6 (April–June 1917): 232–34.

Kotkin, Stephen. *Magnetic Mountain.* Berkeley: University of California Press, 1995.

Kozhevnikov, P. P. "Tipy lesnykh kul'tur USSR." *Za zashchitu lesa* 2 (February 1938): 27–37.

Kozhurin, S. I., V. V. Shutov, M V. Yermushin, and V. I. Metel'nikov. *Istorii lesnogo dela v Rossii.* Kostroma: Kostroma gosudarstvennyi tekhnologicheskii universitet, 2004.

"Kratkii obzor zakonodatel'stva po lesnoi promyshlennost ii lesnomu khoziaistvo." *Lesnoe khoziaistivo i lesnaia promyshlennost'* 6 (June 1930): 136–38.

Kravchinskii, D. M. "Po povodu khoziaistvennago zhacheniia tipov nasazhdenii." *Lesnoi zhurnal* 2 (February 1904): 310–30.

———. "Po povodu khoziaistvennago zhacheniia tipov lesonasazhdenii." *Lesopromyshlennyi vestnik* 21 (20 May 1904): 313–14.

Krementsov, Nikolai. *Stalinist Science.* Princeton: Princeton University Press, 1997.

"Krest'ianskaia lesnaia sobstvennost' v Nerekhtskom uezde." *Lesopromyshlennyi vestnik* 16 (15 April 1904): 256–57.

Kriudener, A. A. *Beskrainie prostory: Vospominaniia o Tsarskoi imperii.* Moscow: Izdatel'stvo Moskovskogo Gosudarstvennogo Universita Lesa, 2001.

———. *Osnovy klassifikatsii tipov nasazhdenii.* Moscow: Izdatel'stvo Moskovskogo gosudarstvennogo universiteta lesa, 2003.

"Krupnye industrializirovannye edinitsy lesnogo khoziaistva (Resheniie II plenuma TsK soiuza)." *Lesovod* 5–6 (May–June 1929): 8–11.

Kuznetsov, N. "Gosudarstvennye lesa i pol'zovanie imi pri zemel'noi reforme." *Lesnoi zhurnal* 9–10 (1917): 649–78.

———. "Instruktsiia 1908 g. dlia ustroistva kazennykh lesov." *Lesnoi zhurnal* 4–5 (April–May 1910): 445–69.

Kviatkovskii, S. I. "S"ezdu g.g. lesnykh chinov 4 raiona Tambovskoi gub." *Lesnaia zhizn' i khoziaistvo* 6 (November 1915): 13–16.

L., M. "Vazhneishii printsip." *Lesovod* 6 (June 1928): 9–10.

Lagarinskii. "Iz byta lesnykh konduktorov." *Lesnaia zhizn' i khoziaistvo* 7 (May 1914): 26–29.

Lapirov-Skoblo, S. "K voprosu o sozdanii lesosyr'evoi bazy narodnogo khoziaistva." *Lesnoe khoziaistvo* 4 (1929): 3–16.

———. "Problema lesosnabzheniia krest'ianstva." *Lesnoe khoziaistvo* 4 (1928): 3–14.

Lavrov, I. S. "Piatletnii plan lesnogo khoziaistvo i lesnoi promyshlennosti SSSR." *Lesnoe khoziaistvo i lesnaia promyshlennost'* 73 (October 1929): 9–12.

Lecourt, Dominique. *Proletarian Science?* London: NLB, 1977.

Lemeshev, Mikhail. *Bureaucrats in Power—Ecological Collapse.* Moscow: Progress Publishers, 1990.

Lenin, Vladimir. *Materialism i empiriokrititsizm.* Moscow: Izdaniie "Zveno", 1909.

"Leningradskoe Lesnoe Obshchestvo za polgoda." *Lesnoe khoziaistvo, lesopromyshlennost' i toplivo* 21–22 (June–July 1925): 76–78.

Leonov, Leonid. *The Russian Forest.* Trans. Bernard Isaacs. Moscow: Progress Publishers, 1966.

———. *Russkii les.* Moscow: Izdatel'stvo TsK VLKSM "Molodaia gvardiia," 1955.

"Les i step' v russkoi istorii po V. Kliuchevskomu." *Lesnoi zhurnal* 3 (March 1905): 676–81.

"Lesa peredany promyshlennosti." *Lesnoi rabochii* 19 (21 July 1929): 1.

Lesnik. "Neskol'ko slov o tipakh nasazhdenii." *Lesnoi zhurnal* 3 (March 1905): 633–41.

Lesnik, Egorov. "O budushchnosti lesov Arkhangel'skoi guberniia v sviazi s sushchestvuiushchimi priemami lesnogo khoziaistva." *Lesnoi zhurnal* 6–7 (1915): 1008–25.

Lesnoe khoziaistvo SSSR. Moscow: Izdatel'stvo "Lesnaia promyshlennost'," 1977.

"Lesnoe khoziaistvo v 1927/28 godu." *Lesovedenie i lesovodstvo* 5 (June 1928): 237–39.

"Lesnoe zakonodatel'stva RSFSR, BSSR i USSR." *Lesnoe khoziaistvo, lesopromyshlennost' i toplivo* 18 (April 1925): 101–4.

"Lesoustroistvo v krest'ianskikh lesakh." *Lesopromyshlennyi vestnik* 13 (1 April 1910): 145.

Lesovodstvo, lesnye kultury i pochvovedenie. St. Petersburg: Lesotekhnicheskaia Akademiia, 1998.

Levin, M. "K voprosu o tom, kakim dolzhno byt' lesoustroistvo." *Lesnoe khoziaistvo* 8 (1929): 5–15.

"Literatura po tipam nasazhdenii za 1913–1914 gg." *Lesnoi zhurnal* 4 (1915): 701–6.

Liutovskii, N. "Lesnoi massif v raione Leningrad-Rybinskoi zhel. dorogi." *Lesnoe khoziaistvo, lesopromyshlennost' i toplivo* 46–47 (July–August 1927): 8–17.

Lowood, H. E. "The Calculating Forester: Quantification, Cameral Science, and the Emergence of Scientific Forest Management in Germany." In *The Quantifying Spirit in the Eighteenth Century,* ed. T. Frängsmyr, J. L. Heilbron, and R. E. Rider. Berkeley: University of California Press, 1990.

Lysenko, T. D. *Posev polezashchitnykh lesnykh polos gnezdovym sposobom.* Moscow: Izdatel'stvo Akademii Nauk SSSR, 1950.

M., A. "Sverkhsmetnye otpuska lesa po Leningradskoi Oblasti na 1927–1928 gg." *Lesnoe khoziaistvo i lesnaia promyshlennost'* 54–55 (February–March 1928): 71–73.

M., K. "Ocherednoe soprotivlenie." *Lesnaia pravda* 25 (7 November 1930): 2.

Maes, Francis. *A History of Russian Music: From* Kamarinskaya *to* Babi Yar. Berkeley: University of California Press, 2002.

Maier, V. "Lesnaia promyshlennost' i lesoustroistvo." *Lesnoe khoziaistvo, lesopromyshlennost' i toplivo* 1 (October 1923): 6–7.

Manevich, Eleanor. *Such Were the Times: A Personal View of the Lysenko Era in the USSR.* Northampton, MA: Pittenbruach Press, 1990.

Martin, Terry. *The Affirmative Action Empire: Nations and Nationalism in the Soviet Union, 1923–1939.* Ithaca: Cornell University Press, 2001.

Massey-Stewart, John, ed. *The Soviet Environment: Problems, Policies and Politics.* Cambridge: Cambridge University Press, 1992.

Materialy po perspektivnomu planu razvitiia sel'skogo i lesnogo khoziaistva. Chast' II-ia. Lesnoe khoziaistvo. Moscow: Izdatel'stvo "Novaia Derevnia," 1929.

Matreninskii, V. V. "Vospominaniia o G. F. Morozove." *Lesovedenie i lesovodstvo* 1 (March 1926): 32–41.

Medvedev, Zhores. *Soviet Agriculture.* New York: W. W. Norton and Company, 1987.

———. *Vzlet i padenie Lysenko.* Moscow: Izdatel'stvo "Kniga," 1993.

Melekhov, I. S. *Al'ma mater: Vospominaniia o lesotekhnicheskoi akademii.* St. Petersburg: Gosudarstvennyi komitet RSFSR po delam nauki v vysshei shkoly, 1992.

———. *Lesovodstvo.* Moscow: Izdatel'stvo Moskovskogo gosudarstvennogo universiteta lesa, 2002.

———. *Ocherk rasvitiia nauki o lese v Rossii.* Moscow: Izdatel'stvo Moskovskogo gosudarstvennogo universiteta lesa, 2004.

Meropriiatiia po lesnomu khoziaistvu RSFSR. Leningrad: Narodnyi Kommissariat Zemledeliia upravlenie lesami, 1927.

Migunova, E. S. "Lesovodstvo i pochvovedenie." *Ekologiia* (1994): 134–50.

Mikul'skii, S. "O maiskom zhuke." *Lesnaia zhizn' i khoziaistvo* 5 (January 1912): 1–14.

———. "Zhizn' maiskago zhuka, prichiniaemyi im vred lesu i bor'ba s nim." *Lesnaia zhizn' i khoziaistvo* 8 (June 1911): 1–32.

Milovanovich, D. "Arkhaizmy lesnogo khoziaistva." *Lesovod* 7–8 (July–August 1929): 87–89.

"Mobilizuem les dlia industrializatsii! Lesorazrabotki otstaiut ot rosta potrebnosti v lese. Nuzhno izgnat' iz lesa lishnykh zagotovitelei." *Lesnoi rabochii* 7 (19 April 1929): 1.

Möller, Alfred. "Kiefern-Dauerwaldwirtschaft." *Zeitschrift für Forst- und Jagdweisen* (January 1920): 1–23.

Moon, David. "Agriculture and the Environment on the Steppes in the Nineteenth Century." In *Peopling the Russian Periphery: Borderland Colonization in Eurasian History,* ed. Nicholas Breyfogle. New York: Routledge Press, 2007.

———. "The Environmental History of the Russian Steppes: Vasilii Dokuchaev and the Harvest Failure of 1891." *Public Transactions of the Royal Historical Society,* no. 1 (2005): 149–74.

Moran, Dominique. "*Lesniki* and *Leskhozy:* Life and Work in Russia's Northern Forests." *Environment and History* 10 (2004): 83–105.

Morokhin, D. "Znachenie tipov i bonitetov v lesoustroistve." *Lesnoe khoziaistvo* 7–8 (1928): 50–58.

Morozov, G. F. "Doklad vserossiiskomu s"ezdu soiuza lesovodov." *Lesa respubliki* 9–10 (1917): 612.

———. *Izbrannye trudy.* Moscow: Izdatel'stvo Moskovskogo gosudarstvennogo universitet lesa, 2001.

———. *Izbrannye trudy v trekh tomakh.* Moscow: Pochvennyi institut imeni V. V. Dokuchaeva, 1994.

———. "K voprosu o tipakh nasazhdeniia." *Lesopromyshlennyi vestnik* 22 (29 May 1903): 389–407.

———. "K voprosu o Vserossisskom s"ezde lesovodov." *Lesnoi zhurnal* 1–3 (January–March 1917): i–vi.

———. "Neskol'ko slov priveta Petrovskoi akademii." *Lesnoi zhurnal* 8–9 (August–September 1915): 1–3.

———. "O biogeograficheskikh osnovaniiakh lesovodstva." *Lesnoi zhurnal* 1 (January 1914): 12–27.

———. *Ocherki po lesokul'turnomu delu.* Moscow: Sel'khozgiz, 1930.

———. "Pamiati Alekseia Nikolaevicha Soboleva." *Lesopromyshlennyi vestnik* 51 (1911): 35.

———. "Pis'mo po povodu izbraniia v pochetnye chleny pochvennogo komiteta pri Moskovskom o-ve sel'skogo khoziaistva." *Pochvoved* 1–4 (1 March 1916): 1–3.

———. *Shkol'nye excursii v les.* Moscow: Gosudarstvennoe izdatel'stvo, 1928.

———. *Uchenie o tipakh nasazhdenii.* Moscow: Gosudarstvennoe sel'sko khoziaistvennoe izdatel'stvo "Sel'khozgiz," 1930.

———. "Zamechaniia na proekt lesoustroistel'noi instruktsii dlia Ukrainy." *Lesovedenie i lesovodstvo* 2 (May 1926): 119–36.

Morozov, I. "Lesokhoziaistvennye nozhnitsy." *Lesovod* 3–4 (March–April 1926): 11–14.

———. "Vernites' k lesu." *Lesnoe khoziaistvo, lesopromyshlennost' i toplivo* 43 (April 1927): 45–48.

Morozov, P. "Chto delat'?" *Lesnoe khoziaistvo, lesopromshlennost' i toplivo* 21–22 (June–July 1925): 4–13.

Moshkov, P. S. "O nuzhdakh severnogo lesnogo khoziaistva." *Lesovod* 8 (August 1926): 62–64.

Motovilov, G. P. "Po-bol'shevistski vskryt' i izzhit' nedostatiki v rabote Glavlesookhrany." *Za zashchitu lesa* 4 (April 1938): 2–8.

Murzaev, E., and B. Murzaev. *Slovar' mestnykh geograficheskikh terminov.* Moscow: Gosudarstvennoe izdatel'stvo geograficheskoi literatury, 1959.

"Na mogile Prof. G. F. Morozova 9/V/1927 g." *Lesovod* 8 (August 1927): 63.

"Nachinaetsia chistka." *Lesnoi rabochii* 11 (26 May 1929): 1.

Naletov, A. "Metody i soderzhanie lesoobshchestvennoi raboty v derevne." *Lesovod* 3 (March 1925): 6–15.

Narodnyi Komissariat Zemledeliia RSFSR. *Materialy po perspektivnomu planu razvitiia sel'skogo i lesnogo khoziaistva (1928/29–1932/33 gg.) chast' 11-ia: Lesnoe khoziaistvo.* Moscow: Izdatel'stvo "Novaia Derevnaia," 1929.

Nash, Roderick Frazier. *Wilderness and the American Mind.* New Haven: Yale University Press, 1967.

"Natsionalizatsiia lesov i provedenie eia v Tambovskoi gub." *Lesnaia zhizn' i khoziaistvo* 4–6 (December 1917): 1–38.

Naumov. "Melkaia-razdrobitel'naia prodazha lesa krest'ianam v Raevskom lesnichestve, eia obstanovka i nuzhdy." *Lesnaia zhizn' i khoziaistvo* 7 (May 1912): 14–38.

———. "Znachenie melkago kredita v lesnom khoziaistve." *Lesnaia zhizn' i khoziaistvo* 6 (March 1914): 1–5.

Nedzvetskii. "'Den lesa' v Veprinskom lesnichestve, Gomel'skaia guberniia." *Rabotnik zemli i lesa* 6 (November 1923): 33.

Nekhoroshev, T. "Lesnoe delo pri A. V. Krivoshein." *Lesnoi zhurnal* 5 (1916): 1–68.

Nesmianov, P. "Po povodu unichtozheniia khrushcha i ego lichniki." *Lesnoi zhurnal* 4–5 (April–May 1912): 646–47.

Nevesskii, N. M. "Eksploatatsiia lesnykh massifov v sviazi s rekonstruktsiei lesnogo khoziaistva." *Lesnoi spetsialist* 1–2 (January 1930): 20–25.

Nikulin, "K voprosu o roli lipy v lesu i khoziaistvo." *Lesnoi zhurnal* 6 (June 1916): 708–20.

Nilsson, Sten, Ola Sallnäs, Mårten Hugosson, and Anatoly Shvidenko. *The Forest Resources of the Former European USSR.* Pearl River, NY: Parthenon Publishing Group, 1992.

"O plane polezashchitnykh lesonasazhdenii, vnedreniia travopol'nykh sevooborotov, stroitel'stva prudov i vodoemov dlia obespecheniia vysokikh i ustoichivykh urozhaev v stepnykh i lesostepnykh raionakh evropeiskoi chasti SSSR." *Lesnoe khoziaistvo* 1 (October 1948): 2–3.

"O polozhenii lesnykh konduktorov (Pis'mo v redaktsiiu)." *Lesnoi zhurnal* 4–5 (April–May 1912): 630–32.

"O pol'zovanii v krest'ianskikh lesakh." *Lesopromyshlennyi vestnik* 37 (16 September 1910): 404.

O vserossiiskom s"ezde lesovodov i lesnykh tekhnikov byvshem v g. Petrograd s 28-go aprelia po 2-oe maia 1917. St. Petersburg: Tipografiia "Sel'skii Vestnik," 1917.

"Ocherednye zadachi lesnoi sektsii v oblasti proizvodstvenno-ekonomicheskoi raboty." *Lesovod* 12 (December 1926): 3–5.

"Okhrana lesa v Rossii i zakon" 4 aprelia 1888 g." *Lesnaia zhizn' i khoziaistvo* 6 (March 1914): 38.

Oldfield, Jonathan. *Russian Nature: Exploring the Environmental Consequences of Societal Change.* Aldershot, UK: Ashgate Publishing Limited, 2005.

Orlov, M. M. "Khoziaistvennaia otsenka nepreryvno proizvoditel'nogo lesa." *Lesnoe khoziaistvo, lesopromyshlennost' i toplivo* 26–27 (November–December 1925): 11–16.

———. *Lesoustroistvo, t. 1.* Leningrad: Izdanie zhurnala "Lesnoe khoziaistvo, lesopromyshlennost' i toplivo," 1927.

———. *Lesoustroistvo, t. 2.* Leningrad: Izdanie zhurnala "Lesnoe khoziaistvo i lesnaia promyshlennost'," 1928.

———. *Lesoustroistvo, t. 3.* Leningrad: Izdanie zhurnala "Lesnoe khoziaistvo i lesnaia promyshlennost'," 1929.

———. "Napravleniie sovremennago lesoustroistva." *Lesnaia zhizn' i khoziaistvo* 1 (July 1912): 30–32.

———. "Novye techeniia v lesoustroistve." *Lesnoe khoziaistvo, lesopromyshlennost' i toplivo* 17–18 (February–March 1925): 17–23.

———. *Ob osnovakh russkago gosudarstvennago lesnogo khoziaistva.* St. Petersburg: Petrogradskii Lesnogo Instituta, 1918.

———. "Sud'ba poniatia 'tip nasazhdeniia' v russkoi lesnoi literature." *Lesopromyshlennyi vestnik* 50 (15 December 1911): 553–55.

———. "Tekhnicheskie lesnye reformy." *Lesnoe khoziaistvo i lesnaia promyshlennost'* 71–72 (August–September 1929): 7–14.

———. "Tipy lesa v nashei sovremennoi lesoustroitel'noi praktike." *Lesnoe khoziaistvo, lesopromyshlennost' i toplivo* 48 (September 1927): 1–4.

P., A. "Na raznykh temakh." *Lesopromyshlennyi vestnik* 2 (8 January 1905): 2–5.

Palimpsestov, I. "Vstupitel'naia beseda o sel'skom khoziaistve Novorossiisskogo kraia." *Zhurnal Ministerstva Gosudarstvennikh Imushchestv* 48 (1853): 89–128.

Pallot, Judith. "Forced Labour for Forestry: The Twentieth Century History of Colonisation and Settlement in the North of Perm' *Oblast'*." *Europe-Asia Studies* 54, no. 7 (2002): 1055–83.

Pasynkov, E. F. "Perspektivy razvitiia lesnoi promyshlennosti." *Lesnaia pravda* 69 (25 April 1932): 3.

Pavlovskii, E. S., ed. *Polezashchitnoe lesorazvedenie v SSSR.* Moscow: Agropromizdat, 1987.

Pedanov, G. "K voprosu o tipakh lesonasazhdenii v sviazi s nekotorymi nabliudeniiami, kasaiushchimsia vozobnovleniia Kavkazskoi eli v lesakh Zakavkaz'ia." *Lesnoi zhurnal* 2–3 (February 1909): 317–26.

Perekhod, V. I. *Modernizm v lesovodstve i demokratizatsiia tipologicheskago ucheniia: Popytka novoi klassifkatsii tipov nasazhdenii.* St. Petersburg: Izdatel'stvo zhurnala Les, 1913.

———. "Staryia i novyia idei v lesovodstve." *Les* 1 (May 1916): 27–38.

Peterson, D. J. *Troubled Lands: The Legacy of Soviet Environmental Destruction*. Boulder: Westview Press, 1993.

Pisarenko, A. I., and V. V. Strakhov. *Lesnoe khoziaistvo Rossii ot pol'zovaniia—k upravleniiu*. Moscow: Iurisprudentsiia, 2004.

"Pis'mo v redaktsiiu." *Lesnoi zhurnal* 7 (July 1905): 1210–19.

"Plan vesennikh lesokul'turnykh rabot i zadachi stakhanovskogo dvizheniia." *Za zashchitu lesa* 2 (February 1938): 5–10.

"Po novomu puti." *Lesovod* 7–8 (July–August 1929): 37–42.

Pokaliuka, K. I. "K voprosu o reorganizatsii upravleniia kazennymi lesnichestvami." *Lesopromyshlennyi vestnik* 7 (19 February 1909): 73–75.

Pollock, Ethan. "The Politics of Knowledge." PhD dissertation, University of California–Berkeley, 2000.

———. *Stalin and the Soviet Science Wars*. Princeton: Princeton University Press, 2006.

"Postanovlenie Soiuznogo pravitel'stva o lesnom khoziaistve." *Lesovod* 4 (April 1928): 5–8.

"Postanovlenie Soveta narodnykh komissarov Soiuza SSSR ob organizatsii lesnogo khoziaistva." *Lesnoi spetsialist* 7–8 (July–August 1931): 9–10.

Postanovleniia, priniatyia XII Vserossisskim S"ezdom lesovladel'tsev i lesokhoziaev, s uchastiem lesozavodchikov i lesopromyshlennikov, sostoiavshimsia v g. Arkhangel'ske 15–25 iiulia 1912 goda. Archangel: Arkhangel'sk" tipo-lit. t. d. V. Cherapanova N-ki.

Predtechenskii, E. "Bol'shoi urok." *Lesovod* 8 (August 1925): 63–64.

"Preniia po dokladam." *Lesnoe khoziaistvo* 2 (April 1949): 36–47.

Protokoly vneocherednogo vserossiiskago s"ezda lesovladel'tsev i lesokhoziaev v SPB. 23—27 ianvaria 1911 g. St. Petersburg: Tipographiia S.-Peterburgskago Gradnonach, 1911.

Protokoly XI vserossiiskago s"ezda lesovladel'tsev i lesokhoziaiev v g. Tule. St. Petersburg: Tipografiia Spb. Gradonachal'stva, 1910.

"Protokoly zasedanii S-Peterburgskago Lesnogo Obshchestva." *Lesnoi zhurnal* 6 (August 1908): 811–21.

Pryde, Philip R. *Conservation in the Soviet Union*. Cambridge: Cambridge University Press, 1972.

———. *Environmental Management in the Soviet Union*. Cambridge: Cambridge University Press, 1991.

Rabotov, T. A. "O Vladimire Nikolaeviche Sukacheve." In *Vladimir Nikolaevich Sukachev: Ocherki, vospominaniia sovremennikov*, ed. A. L. Ianshin. Leningrad: Izdatel'stvo "Nauka", 1986.

Red'ko, G. I., and N. G. Red'ko. *Istoriia lesnogo khoziaistva Rossii*. Moscow: Izdatel'stvo Moskovskogo gosudarstvennogo universiteta lesa, 2002.

———. *Lesnoe khoziaistvo Rossii v zhizneopisanii ego vydaiushchikhsia deiatelei*. Moscow: Izdatel'stvo MGUL, 2003.

Rees, E. A. *State Control in Soviet Russia: The Rise and Fall of the Workers' and Peasants' Inspectorate, 1920–34*. Houndsmills, UK: Macmillan Press, 1987.

"Resoliutsiia po dokladu Soiuzlesproma i sotsialisticheskoi rekonstruktsii i ratsionalizatsii lesnoi i derevoobrabatyvaiushchei promyshlennosti." *Lesnoi spetsialist* 1 (January 1931): 49–54.

Robinson, Geroid Tanquary Robinson. *Rural Russia under the Old Regime.* Berkeley: University of California Press, 1960.

Rodd, E. G. "Uchenie o tipakh nasazhdenii." *Lesnoi zhurnal* 1–2 (January–February 1911): 94–118.

Roll-Hansen, Nils. *The Lysenko Effect.* Amherst, NY: Humanity Books, 2005.

Rostankowski, Peter. "Transformation of Nature in the Soviet Union: Proposals, Plans and Reality." *Soviet Geography* 23, no. 6 (June 1982): 380–89.

Rudzskii, Aleksandr Felitsianovich. *Lesnye besedy dlia russkikh lesovladel'tsev i lesnichikh.* 1881.

S., M. "Bol'she peshitel'nosti." *Lesovod* 1 (January 1929): 27.

S., V. "A kto upravliaet lesom i rabotaet v nem?" *Lesnoi nabat* (15 September 1920): 2.

Savich, V. "Obsledovanie lesov na novykh nachalakh." *Lesovod* 1 (July 1924): 34–36.

Sazhen, D. K. "Lesoustroistvo i smety otpuskam lesa v kazennykh lesakh." *Lesnoi zhurnal* 4–5 (April–May 1910): 565–73.

———. "O kazennoi prodazha lesa krest'ianam bez torgov." *Lesnoi zhurnal* 1 (January 1905): 91–102.

———. "Prodazha lesa bez torgov v ekonomicheskom otnoshenii." *Lesnoi zhurnal* 7 (July 1905): 1450–67.

———. "Vol'nye i nevol'nye samovol'nye porubki." *Lesnoi zhurnal* 9–10 (November–December 1911): 1455–64.

Schabel, Hans G., and Siegfried L. Palmer. "The Dauerwald: Its Role in the Restoration of Natural Forests." *Journal of Forestry* 97 (1999): 20–25.

Schroeder, W. R., and J. Kort. "Shelterbelts in the Soviet Union." *Journal of Soil and Water Conservation* 44 (February 1989): 130–34.

Scott, James C. *Seeing like a State.* New Haven: Yale University Press, 1998.

Sedletskii, Sergei. "Zametki sovetskogo lesovoda." *Lesovod* 2–3 (August–September 1924): 21–23.

Selianin, N. "Uchastie 'vsekolesa' v organizatsii 'dnia lesa' v 1924 godu." *Lesnaia kooperatsiia* 9–10 (September–October 1924): 8–10.

Shabak, E. "Tipy i bonitety." *Lesnoi zhurnal* 9–10 (1914): 1406–20.

Shakhmamet'ev. "Posadka sosny v Pri-usmanskom lesnichestve." *Lesnaia zhizn' i khoziaistvo* 9 (August 1914): 13–21.

Shal'vinskii. "Otpusk lesa po ruchatel'stvam." *Lesnaia zhizn' i khoziaistvo* 1 (July 1913): 9–14.

Shearer, David. "Crime and Social Disorder in Stalin's Russia." *Cahiers du Monde Russe* 39, nos. 1–2 (1998): 119–48.

Shelgunov, N. V. *Istoriia russkago lesnogo zakonodatel'stva.* St. Petersburg: Tip. Ministerstva gosudarstvennykh imushchestv, 1857.

Shostakovich, Dmitri. *Pesn' o lesakh.* Moscow: State Music Publishers, 1950.

Shtil'mark, Feliks. *History of the Russian Zapovedniks, 1895–1995.* Trans. G. H. Harper. Edinburgh: Russian Nature Press, 2003.

Shtil'mark, F. R., and M. V. Geptner, "Tragediia sovetskikh zapovednikov (k 40-letiiu 'reorganizatsii' zapovednoi sistemy v SSSR)." *Biulleten' MOIP* 98, no. 2 (1993): 97–113.

Shturm, V. I. "Les i zemleustroistvo." *Lesnoi zhurnal* 1 (January 1906): 1–16.

Shul'ts, A. I. "Problema lesnoi politiki." *Lesovod* 1 (1924): 29–31.

———. "Verit' li obeshchaniiam VSNKh?" *Lesnoi rabochii* 14–15 (15 June 1929): 3.

Shvappakh. "Germanskoe lesnoe khoziaistvo i leskhoziaistvennaia vystavka i lesotekhnicheskaia iarmarka v Kenigsberge. Otdel za granitsei." *Lesovod* 2–3 (August–September 1924): 66–67.

Singleton, F., ed. *Environmental Problems in the Soviet Union and Eastern Europe.* Boulder: Lynne Rienner, 1987.

Skliadnev. "K kharakteristike sbyta lesnykh materialov iz Sokol'nikovskago lesnichestva Morshanskago uezda." *Lesnaia zhizn' i khoziaistvo* 3 (November 1911): 12–26.

Slezkine, Yuri. *Arctic Mirrors.* Ithaca: Cornell University Press, 1995.

Smith, Alison. *Recipes for Russia: Food and Nationhood under the Tsars.* DeKalb: Northern Illinois University Press, 2008.

Solomon, Susan Gross. *The Soviet Agrarian Debate: A Controversy in Social Science.* Boulder: Westview Press, 1977.

Solovëv. "Krasota v prirode." *Voprosy filosofii i psikhologii* 1 (1889): 1–24.

Solov'ev, V. "Krest'ianstvo i lesnye rabotniki." *Lesovod* 4–5 (October–November 1924): 9–11.

Solovëv, Vladimir. *Opravdanie dobra: Nravstvennaia filosofiia.* 1897.

"Sostoianie lesnoi promyshlennosti." *Lesnoe khoziaistvo i lesnaia promyshlennost'* 84–85 (September–October 1930): 77–79.

"Soveshchanie po lesoustroistvu." *Lesovod* 4 (April 1925): 55–56.

"Soveshchanie (pri Lesprome) po voprosam organizatsii lesnogo khoziaistva, mekhanizatsii i ratsionalizatsii rubki, vozki i splava 6–12 July 1930 g." *Lesnoe khoziaistvo i lesnaia promyshlennost'* 82–83 (July–August 1930): 71–87.

Soyfer, Valeri. *Lysenko and the Tragedy of Soviet Science.* New Brunswick: Rutgers University Press, 1994.

Speranskii, V. "Iz literatury po lesnoi politike za 1905 i 1906 gody." *Lesnoi zhurnal* 8 (September 1908): 1076–90.

Sperber, Jonathan. *The European Revolutions, 1848–1851.* Cambridge: Cambridge University Press.

Stepanov, N. N. "Tipy lesnykh kul'tur." *Za zashchitu lesa* 2 (October 1937): 7–17.

———. "Tipy lesnykh kul'tur." *Za zashchitu lesa* 3 (November 1937): 28–32.

Sukachëv, V. N. *Kratkoe rukovodstvo k issledovaniiu tipov lesov.* Moscow: Izdatel'stvo "Novaia derevnia," 1927.

———. *Stalinskii plan preobrazovaniia prirody.* Moscow: Izdatel'stvo Akademii Nauk SSSR, 1950.

———. "Tipy lesa i ikh znachenie dlia lesnogo khoziaistva vodookhrannoi zony." *V zashchitu lesa* 4 (December 1937): 2–9.

Suny, Ronald. *The Soviet Experiment.* New York: Oxford University Press, 1998.

Sviatkovskii, Orest. "O rekonstruktsii lesnogo khoziaistva v Siberi." *Lesovod* 11 (November 1928): 49–51.

Syromolotov, F. "Organizovat' lesnoe khoziaistvo vokrug promyshlennosti." *Torgovaia-promyshlennaia gazeta* 266 (1928): 4.

T., K. "Vrediteli i bor'ba s nimi v lesnichestvakh Tamb. guberniia. v 1912 g." *Lesnaia zhizn' i khozaiastvo* 7 (May 1913): 25–28.

Taranovich, V. "Obzor periodicheskii pechati po voprosam lesnogo khoziaistva i lesnoi promyshlennosti za revoliutsionnyi period." *Lesnoe khoziaistvo, lesopromyshlennost' i toplivo* 11 (July–August 1924): 120–21.

Tarasenko, V. P., and V. K. Tepliakov. *Russkii les v antropogene.* Moscow: Stagarit, 2003.

Teplyakov, V. K. *Les v istorii dopetrovskoi Rusi.* Moscow: Moskovskii lesotekhnicheskii institut, 1992.

Teplyakov, Viktor, et al. *A History of Russian Forestry and Its Leaders.* Pullman: Washington State University Press, 1998.

Tiain, A., and E. Drozdovskii, "'Lesoustroistvo' bez lesoustroistva." *Lesnoe khoziaistvo i lesnaia promyshlennost'* 65–66 (February–March 1929): 68–69.

Tikhomorov, V. "Estestvennoe vozobnovlenie v lesoustroitel'noi instruktsii 1926 goda." *Lesnoe khoziaistvo* 7–8 (1928): 81–83.

Timasheff, Nicholas. *The Great Retreat.* New York: E. F. Dutton and Company, 1946.

Tisenhausen, N. "Lesnye porubki i okrestnye krest'iane." *Lesopromyshlennyi vestnik* 18 (5 May 1911): 206.

Tiurin, A. V. "Professor M. M. Orlov (K priznaniiu ego zasluzhennym deiatelem nauki i tekhniki)." *Lesovedenie i lesovodstvo* 7 (August–September 1929): 5–12.

Tkachenko, M. E. *D. N. Kaigorodov.* Leningrad: Leningradskii Gublit, 1925.

———. "Kontsentrirovannye rubki i letnie zagotovki lesa." *Lesnoi spetsialist* 14 (July 1930): 10–14.

———. "Zadachi lesnogo khoziaistva i 'Den' Lesa' v 1930 godu." *Lesnoi spetsialist* 7–8 (April 1930): 10–13.

Tol'skii, A. "Iz praktiki zapadno-evropeiskogo lesovodstva." *Lesnoe khoziaistvo, lesopromyshlennost' i toplivo* 8 (May 1925): 23–27.

Toropin, G. M., ed. *Sbornik zakonov, rasporiazhenii i instruktsii po lesam mestnogo znacheniia.* Leningrad: Izdanie leningradskogo oblastnogo upravleniia lesami mestnogo znacheniia, 1933.

Troup, R. S. "Dauerwald." *Forestry* 1 (1927): 78–92.

Trudy soveshchaniia po lesnoi tipologii, 3–5 fevralia 1950 g. Moscow: Izadatel'stvo akademii nauk SSSR, 1951.

Ts., I. "Ocherk lesokhoziaistvennykh uslovii Vilenskoi guberniia." *Lesopromyshlennyi vestnik* 7 (17 February 1911): 78.

Tucker, Robert C. *The Soviet Political Mind.* New York: W. W. Norton, 1971.

Turnbull, M. *Soviet Environmental Policies and Practices: The Most Critical Investment.* Aldershot, UK: Dartmouth Publishing Company, 1991.

Turskii, Mitrofan Kuz'mich. *Lesovodstvo.* St. Petersburg, 1892.

Uglitskikh, A. N. "Printsipy klassifikatskii sosnovykh nasazhdenii po bonitetam i dobrotnostiam." *Lesnoi zhurnal* 7–8 (September 1911): 1157–85.

Ural, V. P. "O vliianii ekonomicheskikh uchenii na teoriiu lesnogo khoziaistvo." *Lesnoe khoziaistvo* 10–11 (1929): 81–86.

Urmanskii. "Eshche o samovol'nykh porubkakh i bor'be s nimi." *Lesovod* 10 (October 1926): 68–69.

Vasil'ev, P. V. "Razval teorii i praktiki burzhuaznogo lesnogo khoziaistva v kapitalis-ticheskikh stranakh." *Lesnoe khoziaistvo* 2 (December 1949): 11–17.

"Velikaia godovshchina." *Za zashchitu lesa* 3 (November 1937): 2–6.

Velovich, A. "Den' lesa v 1929 godu." *Lesovod* 3 (March 1929): 3–6.

"V Leningradskom gublesotdel." *Lesnoe khoziaistvo, lesopromyshlennost' i toplivo* 9 (June 1924): 64.

"V Leningradskom lesnom obshchestve." *Lesnoe khoziaistvo, lesopromyshlennost' i toplivo* 9 (June 1924): 74–75.

"V Leningradskom lesnom obshchestve." *Lesnoe khoziaistvo, lesopromyshlennost' i toplivo* 14–15 (November–December 1924): 77–78.

"V Leningr. lesnom obshchestve." *Lesnoe khoziaistvo, lesopromyshlennost' i toplivo* 7 (April 1927): 112.

"V TsUL'e NKZ." *Lesnoe khoziaistvo, lesopromyshlennost' i toplivo* 4 (January 1924): 58–59.

"V upravlenii lesami NKZ RSFSR." *Lesovod* 3–4 (March–April 1926): 69–74.

Vitkovskii, Iosif. "XXV let zavedovaniia Vyshenskim lesnichestvom Spasskago uezda Tambovskoi gubernii 1888–1913 g.g." *Lesnaia zhizn' i khoziaistvo* 2 (December 1913): 9–13.

Voit, K. "O sud'be Lesnogo zhurnala." *Lesnoe delo* 1–2 (February 1919): 11–12.

Volygin, Ivan, ed. *Environmental Deterioration in the Soviet Union and Eastern Europe.* New York: Praeger Publishers, 1974.

"Voprosy lesnogo khoziaistva na II plenume TsK." *Lesovod* 7–8 (July–August 1929): 12–36.

"Voprosy lesnogo khoziaistva na IV soveshchanii zemorganov RSFSR." *Lesovod* 1 (January 1929): 65–66.

"Voprosy lesnoi promyshlennosti i lesnogo khoziaistva na 2-y sessii VTsIK 14-go sozyva." *Lesnoe khoziaistvo i lesnaia promyshlennost'* 75 (December 1929): 73–90.

Vorontsov-Dashkov, I. I. "Dva dnia v lesakh pri s. Novo-Tomnikove." *Lesnaia zhizn' i khoziaistvo* 1 (June 1911): 3–18.

"Vserossiskii s"ezd lesovodov i lesnykh tekhnikov." *Lesnoi zhurnal* 4–6 (1917): 145–68.

"Vserossisskii Soiuz Lesovodov i Lesnykh Tekhnikov (Konduktorov)." *Lesnoi zhurnal* 1–3 (1917): 128–30.

"Vykorchevat' vragov naroda iz lesnogo khoziaistva." *Za zashchitu lesa* 1 (September 1937): 3–5.

Vysotskii, G. N. "O putevodnoi ideinosti v nashei agrarnoi politike i v rossiskom lesovladenii." *Lesnoi zhurnal* 2–3 (February–March 1906): 22–35.

Weiner, Douglas. "Demythologizing Environmentalism." *Journal of the History of Biology* 25, no. 3 (1992): 385–411.

———. *A Little Corner of Freedom.* Berkeley: University of California Press, 1999.

———. *Models of Nature: Ecology, Conservation, and Cultural Revolution in Soviet Russia.* Bloomington: Indiana University Press, 1988.

Weiner, Jack. "The Destalinization of Dmitri Shostakovich's 'The Song of the Forests,' Op. 81 (1949)." *Rocky Mountain Review of Language and Literature* 38, no. 4 (1984): 214–22.

Yanitsky, Oleg. *Russian Environmentalism: Leading Figures, Facts, Opinions.* Moscow: Mezhdunarodnyje Otnoshenija Publishing House, 1993.

"Za sotsialisticheskuiu teoriiu lesnogo khoziaistva." *Lesnaia pravda* 60 (15 January 1932): 1.

Zanevskii, A. "Novye zadachi khoziaistva v lesakh mestnogo znacheniia." *Lesnoe khoziaistvo* 4 (1929): 37–45.

Zashchitnye lesnye nasazhdeniia v bor'be s zasukhoi i navolneniiami. New York: East European Fund, 1952.

Zdorik, M. G. "Kakim byt' lesoustroistvo." *Lesnoe khoziaistvo* 5–6 (1929): 3–17.

———. "Lesnoe khoziaistvo." *Lesnoe khoziaistvo i okhota* 2 (January 1923): 27–32.

———. "O vrednoi instruktsii po organizatsii lesnogo khoziaistva v vodookhranoi zone." *Za zashchitu lesa* 2 (October 1937): 2–7.

———. "Ocherednye zadachi lesnogo khoziaistva." *Vestnik lesnogo khoziaistva* 1–2 (March 1923): 3–6.

———. "Okhrana lesov." *Biulleten' lesnoe khoziaistvo i okhota* 1 (December 1922): 23–25.

———. "Perspektivy razvitiia lesnogo khoziaistva vodookhrannoi zony v tret'em piatletii." *Za zashchitu lesa* 5 (May 1938): 4–10.

———. "Pis'mo k redaktsiiu (Otvet Prof. M. M. Orlovu)." *Lesnoe khoziaistvo i lesnaia promyshlennost'* 74 (November 1929): 142–44.

Zhitkov, G. R. "O sokhrashchenii sroka operatsii po sosnovym deliankam v Fashchevs-kom lesnichestve." *Lesnaia zhizn' i khoziaistvo* 1 (July 1912): 18–21.

Zhurin, V. "O trude v lesnom khoziaistve." *Lesnaia pravda* 6 (15 January 1930): 4.

"Zhurnal 10-go ocherednogo zasedaniia Lesnogo Obshchestva v S-Peterburge." *Lesnoi zhurnal* 4–5 (April–May 1910): 608–37.

Ziegler, Charles. *Environmental Policy in the USSR.* London: Frances Pinter Publishers, 1987.

Zonn, S. V. *Otchet o deiatel'nosti kompleksnoi nauchnoi ekspeditsii po voprosam polezashchitnogo lesorazvedeniia za 1949–1952 gg.* Moscow: Izdatel'stvo Akademii Nauk SSSR, 1955.

INDEX

Note: page numbers in italics refer to figures.